THE POSTAGE STAMP GARDEN BOOK

THE POSTAGE STAMP GARDEN BOOK

Grow tons of vegetables in small spaces

by
DUANE and KAREN NEWCOMB

Adams Media Corporation
Holbrook, Massachusetts

Published by
Adams Media Corporation
260 Center Street, Holbrook, MA 02343

ISBN: 1-58062-123-6

Printed in the United States of America

J I H G F E D C B

Library of Congress Cataloging-in-Publication Data
Newcomb, Duane G.
The postage stamp garden book / Duane and Karen Newcomb.—
2nd ed., revised and updated.
p.   cm.
Includes index.
ISBN 1-58062-123-6
1. Vegetable gardening. 2. Organic gardening. I. Newcomb, Karen. II. Title.
SB321.N45   1999
635—dc21   98-31918
CIP

Interior illustrations by Barry Littmann.
Cover illustration by Irena Roman and Roberta Collier-Morales.

This book is available at quantity discounts for bulk purchases.
For information, call 1-800-872-5627 (in Massachusetts, 781-767-8100).

Visit our home page at http://www.adamsmedia.com

Contents

Preface . . . . *vii*

Chapter One: Planning Your Postage Stamp Garden 1

Chapter Two: What Goes into Your Soil? 33

Chapter Three: Getting Your Soil Ready 43

Chapter Four: When and How to Plant 53

Chapter Five: Basic Vegetables and Herbs You'll Love to Grow 69

Chapter Six: Plants That Like Each Other 143

Chapter Seven: The All-Inclusive Salad Garden 153

Chapter Eight: Controlling Pests and Diseases 169

Chapter Nine: Bringing Vegetables and Herbs to the Table 181

Chapter Ten: Watering the Garden 203

Appendix A: How to Compost 210

Appendix B: Seed Catalog Sources 219

Glossary 223

Index 229

Preface

In the 1890s, outside Paris, a few enterprising Frenchmen began raising crops using a new method they discovered. Over their land they spread an 18-inch layer of manure (plentiful in the day of the horse and buggy) and planted their vegetables so close together in this rich material that the leaves touched one another as the plants grew. Under this carpet of leaves, the ground remained moist, warm, and vigorous. During periods of frost, they set glass jars over the tiny plants to give them an early start. So good were the Frenchmen in devising fresh ways of growing things that they were able to produce nine crops a year. Such was the birth of the French Intensive method of gardening, an early form of what we now call intensive, or wide-row, gardening.

In the following two decades, another organic gardening movement developed. In Switzerland, a remarkable philosopher from Austria, Rudolf Steiner, and his followers invented a gardening method called biodynamic. They emphasized the exclusive and balanced use of organic fertilizers—composted leaves, grass, manure, and so on. They investigated what is now called companion planting and found that certain plants when grown together (like beans and cabbages) do better than others (like beans and onions). They also sought new ways of arranging crops. These biodynamic gardeners hit upon the idea of planting in mounded beds that permitted adequate drainage and that were narrow enough so that a person didn't have to walk over them.

Between the 1930s and the 1960s, an Englishman, Alan Chadwick, set out to combine the French Intensive and biodynamic methods and to add to them various ideas of his own, such as planting by the phases of the moon. In the 1960s he brought his meld of techniques to America, to the 4-acre Garden Project at the University of California at Santa Cruz. The acreage that he was given had "impossible" soil, in which even weeds failed to grow. In one season, using simple hand tilling and organic materials, Chadwick and his students brought the acreage to fertility. In a few seasons they had the richest, most beautiful gardens around.

The intensive method that Chadwick and his students used produced four times as many vegetables as a conventional garden using standard rows. It also used half the water and took less time to maintain. And the vegetables were wonderfully plump, tasty, and nutritious.

Chadwick's method, which came to be known as French Intensive Biodynamic Gardening, has proved to be perfectly adapted to small space gardening. Using intensive methods, you can, for instance, grow as many carrots in 1 square foot as you can in a 12-foot row in a conventional garden. Properly handled, a 25-square-foot bed (5 by 5 feet) will produce a minimum of 200 pounds of vegetables.

To accommodate today's lifestyles, a garden needs to fit easily into a very small plot, take as little time as possible to work, require a minimum amount of water, and still produce prolifically. That's exactly what a postage stamp garden does.

Postage stamp gardens are small. The smallest beds we recommend are 4 by 4 feet, the largest, 10 by 10 feet. Regardless of which size you choose, your garden will produce a tremendous amount of vegetables and, after the initial preparation, require little extra work, even less if you let an automatic drip system do the watering.

Over the last twenty-two years, our experience growing vegetables the intensive way has been happy, one filled with surprising results. We continue to try new ideas and methods, especially when it comes to growing vine crops (winter squash, cucumbers, and melons) in the space above the bed.

This book offers simple, easy methods that work. We hope you will try the intensive methods using postage stamp size beds, and then experiment on your own. We are sure you will be surprised and extremely happy with the results.

CHAPTER ONE

Planning Your Postage Stamp Garden

For some of us, there are few things more fun than planning the garden for next season. The best wintertime garden dreamers draw up dozens of illustrations of what their next garden is going to look like. We suggest that you do it too. After all, things always go better with a plan. A good plan keeps your mistakes to a minimum by giving you some idea in advance of where to put your garden, what to plant in it, how much space to allocate, and what shape it should have.

Where to Put Your Garden

The first thing to do in planning your garden, of course, is to decide where to put it. Your plants don't really care where they grow so long as you give them a lot of tender loving care—that is, good fertile soil, enough water, and whatever heat and daylight they need. In most cases, vegetables need direct sunlight, a requirement you can satisfy practically anywhere. We have a friend who lives in one room behind a drugstore and grows a productive little garden in a sunny 5-by-9-foot space between the back door and a brick wall.

By following a few rules, you can certainly do as well in your own backyard. The main rule to consider is this: Most vegetables need minimally about six hours of direct sunlight. So long as they receive this minimum amount of direct sunlight every day, you can put your garden almost anywhere. Consider, though, that you can never give your warm-weather vegetables (tomatoes, squash, peppers) too much sun. Cool-weather vegetables (lettuce, greens, cabbage) will tolerate a little shade.

In addition, there are a few other placement considerations. Keep your garden bed at least 20 feet away from shallow-rooted trees like elms, maples, and poplars. Not only will the foliage of these trees block out the sun, but also their roots will compete for water and nutrients. Generally, tree roots take food from the soil in a circle as wide as the tree's farthest reaching branches, and plants usually do poorly within this circle.

Don't put your garden in a low area that will collect standing water or near a downspout, where the force from a sudden rain can wash out some of your plants. Yet do try to place your garden near a water outlet. By so doing, you will eliminate having to drag a hose long distances. Also, try to place your garden as near the tool storage area as possible.

What Do You Eat?

Before you rush out and plant a garden, spend a little time thinking about how you cook and how your family eats. Do you like salads, low-calorie cooking, pasta, or hearty chowders and stews? We don't care much for turnips, yet we love tomatoes and use them in almost everything. Our son hates turnips, rutabagas, Brussels sprouts, and spinach, so in our planning stage we often eliminate all of these vegetables, even if they are easy to grow.

After you make your choices, you can then select the number of plants you need by checking Table 1-1. Try new recipes that call for unfamiliar vegetables, and use a notebook to keep track of the vegetable varieties you've enjoyed.

To decide which herbs you'll need, look at the jars of dried herbs you already have in your kitchen. These are probably the ones you'll eventually want in your garden. We do not recommend that you plant everything the first year. Start with two or three herbs in your first garden, and add to them as you go along. You will also need to decide whether you want to plant herbs in with the vegetables or to have separate beds for them.

As you cook, you can also look at this the other way around. When Karen is making a hearty chicken soup, for instance, she frequently goes out into the garden with a basket to see what she can come up with to put into the pot. Often she comes back with rosemary, oregano, parsley, onions, celery, garlic, and carrots. Her soups and stews are always a tasty vegetable surprise.

What you find to eat in your garden also depends on the season. In some areas of the country, you can grow lettuce, broccoli, cabbage, tomatoes, cucumbers, and peppers all together during the summer. In the warmer areas, lettuce and other greens are grown in the spring and fall; tomatoes, cucumbers, squash, and similar vegetables are grown in the summer. Where we live in California, we can grow all types of stir-fry greens and snow peas all winter long. Karen loves this bonus growing season because it gives her the chance to try recipes that are different from our favorite summer ones.

TABLE 1-1 NUMBER OF PLANTS PER PERSON

VEGETABLE	PLANTS PER PERSON	VEGETABLE	PLANTS PER PERSON
Bean, snap	2–3	Melon	2
Bean, snap (pole)	1–2	Mustard	4–6
Bean (shell)	3–4	Okra	1–2
Beet	10–20	Onion	10–30
Brussels sprouts	1	Parsnip	10
Cabbage	2	Pea, snap	3–4
Cabbage, Chinese	2–3	Pepper	1–2
Carrot	30–50	Potato	1–2
Cauliflower	6–10	Pumpkin	1
Celeriac	1	Radish	20–60
Celery	1–2	Rutabaga	3–6
Collards	2–5	Salsify	2–10
Corn, sweet	5–6	Shallot	4–10
Cucumber	1–2	Spinach	3–7
Eggplant	1	Spinach, New Zealand	5
Garlic	4	Squash, summer	1
Horseradish	1–2	Squash, winter	2
Kale	2–3	Sweet potato	2
Kohlrabi	4–6	Swiss chard	1
Leek	6–10	Tomato	2
Lettuce, head	3–4	Tomato, paste	3
Lettuce, leaf	2–4	Turnip	8–15
		Watermelon, bush	1

What Else Would You Like?

Consider also what else you want out of a garden. We often plant flowers among the vegetables, partially because some of them repel insects and nematodes, or they have beneficial effects for the other vegetables. Edible flowers add color and taste to salads, and some flowers have such sweet scents they attract bees and hummingbirds to the garden.

Favorite Edible Flowers

Many cooks say that nasturtiums are an essential part of their garden. Nasturtiums are often used in salads to add a peppery taste and color. They are also used as a garnish on many other dishes. Fastidious cooks like them because of the variety of colors they can add. *Creamsicle* has petals with a swirled pastel that highlights a deep red throat, *Peach Melba* has yellow petals accented with raspberry,

Moonlight has pale yellow blossoms, and *Sungold* has deep butter yellow petals.

You can select from 1-foot compact types to 6-foot climbing/trailing varieties. Plant after all danger of frost is past. Nasturtiums thrive when their roots are cool and moist. Plants that get too much water have large leaves but few flowers.

The edible flower petals of calendula are used in ales and for food coloring. These plants also make a colorful ornamental that brightens the corner of any garden. In warm areas, they will bloom and be available all winter long.

Plants that Attract Butterflies

Some gardens are planted to attract butterflies, birds, and beneficial insects. Butterflies seem to add magic to the garden, especially when a swallowtail or a painted lady lights on a nearby flower. Butterfly gardens need plenty of flowers for nectar and food plants for caterpillars. Most caterpillars confine themselves to one plant family or one specific plant. Some butterfly plants are bee balm, coreopsis, morning glory, verbena, and zinnia. Shrubs such as the butterfly bush, fruit trees, mock orange, and spirea also attract butterflies.

W. Atlee Burpee offers a butterfly bird garden in their catalog. Here is what they suggest:

Silvia coccinea	Cosmos
Snapdragon	Zinnia
Blue boy	Lady in red
Sensation white	Red rocket
Cornflower	Marigold

Plants that Attract Hummingbirds

Birds also make a garden come alive, but at certain times of the year, they can also eat everything as soon as it pops out of the ground. As a result, when we plant early in the spring—when birds seem to be the hungriest—we have to plant most crops under row covers. If you are a bird lover, concentrate on hummingbirds: they make for good natural insect control since they regularly pick off insects. They also gather nectar from flowers with their needlelike bills and long tongues. To attract them you might want to set out one or two hummingbird feeders or add their favorite plants to your garden. Some suggestions are columbine, coral bells, sage, fuchsia, monkey flower, gilia, honeysuckle, or butterfly bush.

Orchard Mason Bees

With the present pollination crisis caused by infestations of honey bees, Orchard Mason bees help fill the void. The Orchard Mason bees are small black bees that do not harm humans or pets. These native bees do not dwell in hives. When the weather warms up in early spring, the bees emerge from their holes.

After they mate, the females begin to make their nests and gather pollen and nectar from the spring blossoms. Gardeners can make their own nesting blocks out of 1- or 2-foot-long ponderosa pine or Douglas fir pieces. Simply drill a number of holes in the block and hang it around the garden.

Attracting Bugs to Your Garden

It is possible to lure insects that prey on vegetables pests, pollinate plants, and build soil. Start with a 10-gallon plastic tub, which you can find at hardware stores. Drill holes in the tub's bottom to provide drainage. Fill the tub with a mixture of planting soil and compost.

Now, include six to eight of these plants, which are rich in pollen: nicotonia, autumn sage, lemon queen, catmint, blue daze, verbena, silver thyme, lavender, cosmos, nasturtium, and trailing rosemary. Water several times a week, and feed with fish emulsion on a weekly basis. Ask at your local nursery where to purchase them.

Seed Shopping by Catalog

Garden catalogs are essential tools for planning your garden. There are probably several hundred vegetable, flower, and herb catalogs. Many of them have unique personalities and a seed selection you'll never find on the seed racks.

Horticultural Enterprises caters to pepper afficionados; it offers dozens of varieties. Tomato Growers Supply is entirely devoted to tomatoes. Shepherd's Garden Seeds and The Cook's Garden give priority to gourmet and specialty varieties. Many catalogs offer planting tips. Some even offer recipes.

Before you start your garden, we suggest you send for some of the catalogs listed in the Appendix. This is one of our favorite preplanning chores every year. It gives us a chance to select new and different varieties that we really want to try.

Other Considerations

Your garden will need to be defined by the number of hours you're willing to spend each week in your garden, how much money you can afford to put into your garden, the space you have available, how your garden fits into your yard, and what site makes the most sense. You'll also have to decide whether you're going to garden at ground level or in raised beds and whether you want to include a special garden for the kids. Here's a checklist:

1. What do I really want to grow?
2. Do I want a combination in-ground and container garden?
3. How big should I make my garden?
4. How much time do I have to spend each week?
5. Can I integrate my garden into my landscaping?
6. Do I want raised beds?
7. Do I need to grow my garden against a fence to support my vine plants?
8. Do I want to garden vertically?
9. Does pocket gardening make sense in my yard?
10. Do I want to grow enough vegetables to freeze or can?

Time and Money

Unless they're retired, most people are short on time. If you have a job and small children, you may only have an hour or two a week to spend in the garden. If you don't have to weed or water as much, you'll have more time for other activities, which is a consideration for a busy family or a couple. The less time you have to spend gardening, the smaller you need to make your garden. Everyone knows that the couple who rushes out and plants the entire backyard in plants winds up spending every spare moment just keeping up with it.

Gardening can be extremely expensive, or it can cost practically nothing. You can, for instance, buy garden compost or make your own. You can buy $42 pruners or $6 ones, pay $46 for pliant pants or garden in a pair of old jeans. You may want to splurge on kneeling pads, garden vests, and other gardening accessories—the choice belongs to you.

We feel that it pays to start small, spend a modest amount the first year, and then decide how much you can afford and want to spend on your garden as you go along.

How to Design Your Garden

By proper placement of individual vegetables in your intensive postage stamp garden, you can produce extremely large quantities of vegetables in an extremely small space. The following are IPS (intensive postage stamp) planning rules that will help you obtain maximum results:

1. Plant tall vegetables on the north end of your garden to avoid shading the smaller crops, and plant the other vegetables in descending order of size down toward the south end of the garden.

2. Forget about planting in rows. In an IPS garden you scatter the seeds, to use all the space in your garden, and then thin out the seedlings (the small plants) as they come up. If you set out seedlings rather than seeds, space them without concern for straight rows. The mature plants should just touch one another on all sides. (In Chapter 4 we discuss seeds and seedlings, as well as the best spacing for various plants.)

3. If your plot is large—say 10 by 10 feet or even 8 by 8 feet—you can plant different types of vegetables in separate squares or rectangles. In plots more than 5 or 6 feet wide, you'll need pathways in order to reach all your plants. However, if the plot is narrow or small, simply block out irregular groups of vegetables and fill in the spaces any way you wish.

4. For root vegetables (such as carrots and beets), leafy vegetables (such as lettuce and spinach), and corn you need a special plan. The areas chosen for each of these vegetables should be subdivided into thirds or fourths, and each subsection should be seeded or planted a week to ten days apart. In this way you get continual harvests—as one subsection stops bearing mature vegetables, another begins. This is not so with, for example, tomatoes and cucumbers, which bear from the same plant over a long period of time. After you've harvested a subsection of leafy or root vegetables, you can replant that subsection. That way your garden will produce everywhere all the time.

5. Use the air space above your garden as much as possible. That is, train tomatoes, cucumbers, and other vines and trailing plants to grow up trellises, fences, or poles, so that they won't run all over your garden bed, crowding out the other plants. The better you get at vertical growing, the more things you'll be able to pack into your IPS garden. (In Chapter 5 several methods of vertical growing are discussed in the detailed sections on each vegetable.)

6. Don't limit yourself necessarily to vegetables. We always include marigolds and some herbs in our garden. You'll love the fragrance and color of a vegetable garden grown this way. And, equally important, many veteran gardeners feel that herbs and some flowers have a tremendous beneficial effect on garden health (see Chapter 6).

Garden Plans You Can Use

In the next few pages, various plans are given for some intensive postage stamp gardens. The plans are intended as guidelines or possibilities only and should be modified by your own experience to fit your needs. For one thing, you needn't limit yourself to conventional rectangles. Choose almost any shape for your garden that you wish—square, rectangular, triangular, circular, kidney-shaped—you name it. Give vegetables water, sun, the right amount of heat, and good soil, and away they grow. The shape of the garden generally doesn't mean a thing to them.

Putting Your Garden on Paper

Begin by putting your garden plan on paper, even if it is a small garden. Some gardeners draw this plan to scale (for example, making $1/4$ inch equal 1 foot), which allows them to allocate space accurately. Others simply draw a rough sketch and go from there. I like to use graph paper because it enables me to see at a glance how much space I have. With a 5-foot bed, I let each square equal 2 inches, and with a 10-foot bed, 4 inches. Graphing allows you to easily plant in small groups. You can count the number of plants, or even seeds, that you are going to use.

Here are a few tips:

- Major vegetables such as tomatoes, peppers, and eggplants should be surrounded by secondary vegetables or herbs: green onions, bush beans, celery. Plant vegetables that mature quickly between those that mature more slowly. For instance, plant radishes in the same space in which you have transplanted tomatoes. Harvest the radishes four to five weeks before the tomato vines take over the space. You can also use this same space underneath the grown tomatoes as a microclimate for radishes in warm weather to ensure a continuous supply of radishes long after they stop growing in the regular garden.

- Plant vines (cucumbers, melons, peas, squash) against a fence or support at the north end of your garden. This ensures that the smaller plants get enough sun each day and keeps them from being shaded out by the taller plants. Use smaller vertical supports within the interior of the garden. These can be planted with bush varieties of cucumbers and winter squash.

- Include herbs and flowers in every garden. Certain plants can repel or attract insects. Borage, for instance, can attract bees, while marigolds are said to keep bean beetles away from snap beans and to repel nematodes. Garlic and chives may repel aphids. We urge you to put herbs and flowers among the vegetables when you have the space.

- Plan successive plantings of such vegetables as bush beans, lettuce, and radishes. This ensures a continued supply of these vegetables throughout the growing season.

- Make sure you space all major plants properly on your plan. Winter squash, for instance, requires at least 12 inches between plant centers (if grown up a fence). This means that if you have a 5-by-5-foot garden, you can plant six squash across the north end to grow up the vertical support frame.

Twelve Garden Plans

We offer twelve postage stamp garden plans that you can use to design your own garden. Just adjust them to fit your own needs. See Figures 1-1 to 1-12.

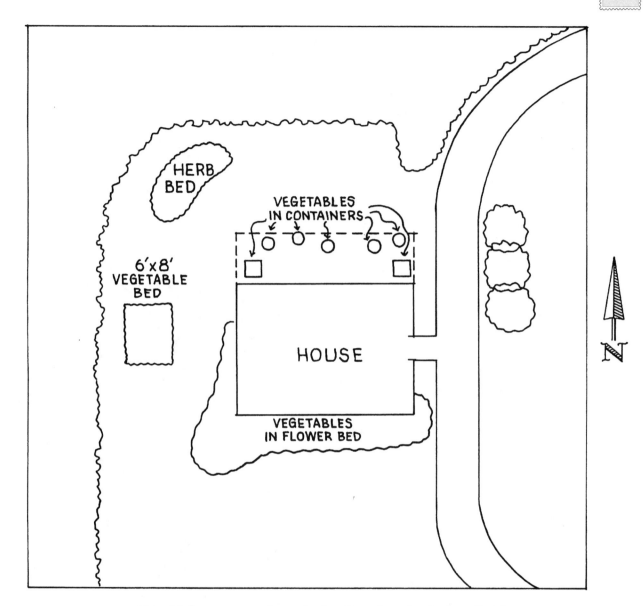

Figure 1-1. Postage stamp gardens can be planted in sections rather than in one big bed.

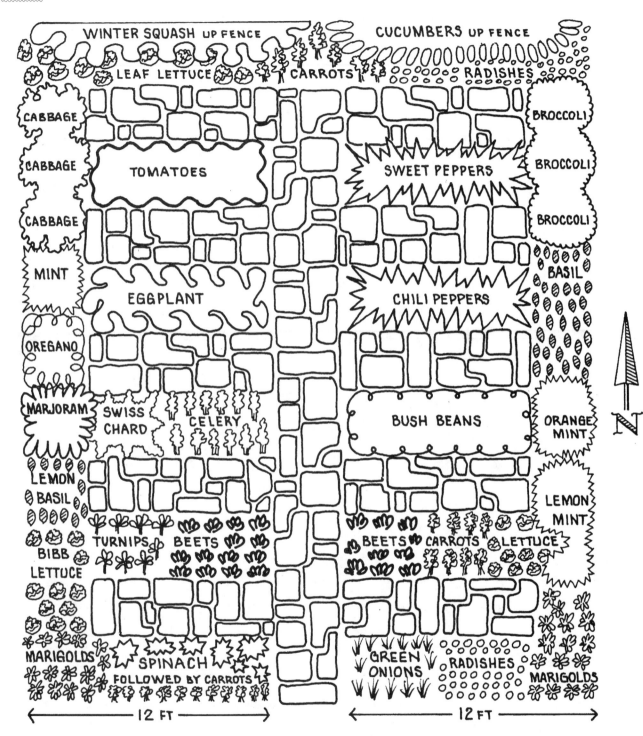

Figure 1-2. Large postage stamp garden. Select varieties from text.

Figure 1-3. Summer postage stamp garden. 10' x 4' bed.

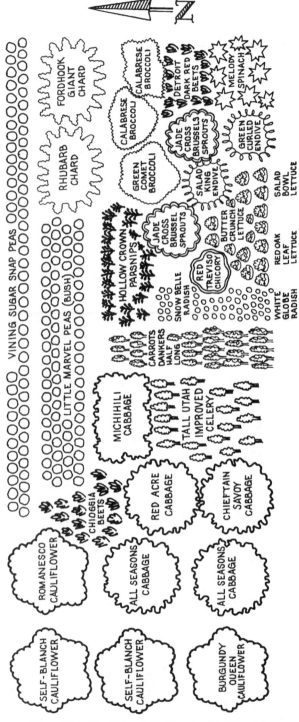

Figure 1-4. Fall/spring postage stamp garden. 10' x 4' bed.

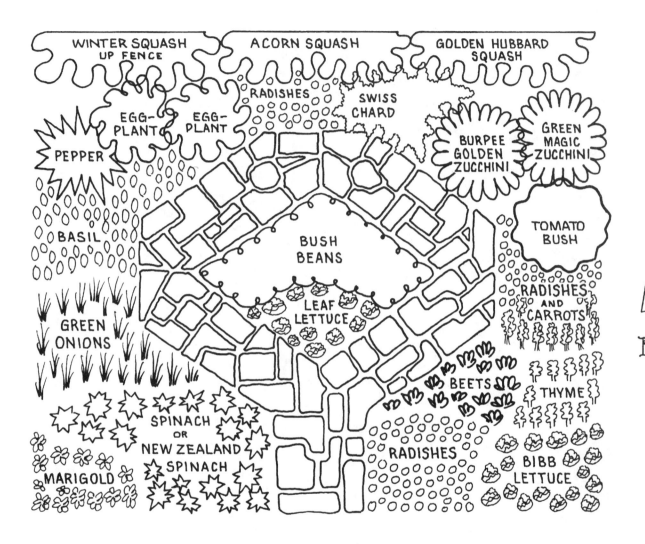

Figure 1-5. Select varieties from text. 10' x 7' bed.

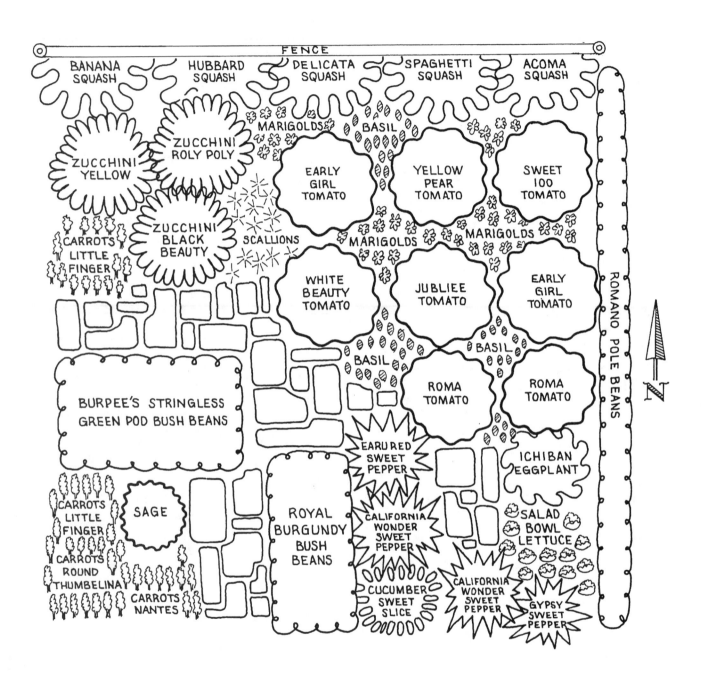

Figure 1-6. Large postage stamp garden possibilities. 9' x 9' bed.

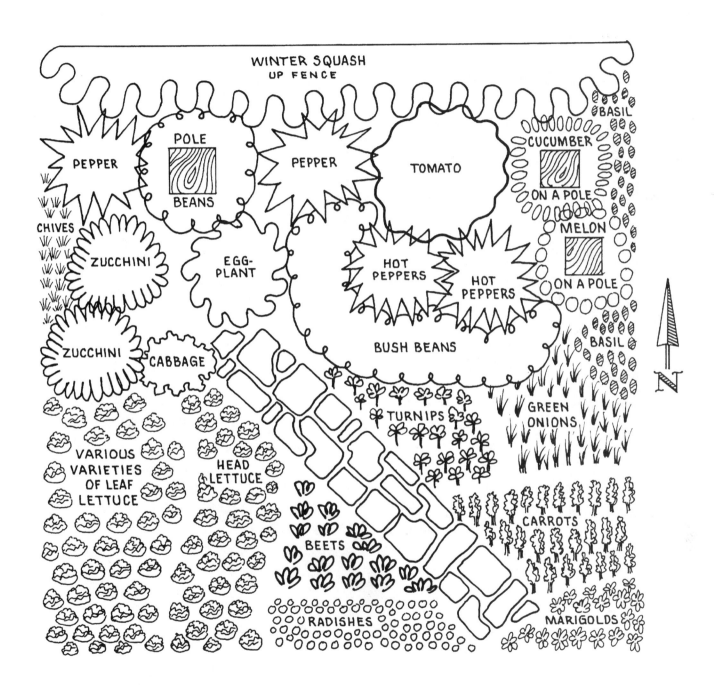

Figure 1-7. General postage stamp garden. Select varieties from text. Plant and harvest peas before planting winter squash. Plant radishes at 2-week intervals. Intercrop radishes, leaf lettuce, and green onion with larger plants, and harvest before they take over the space. 5' x 5' bed.

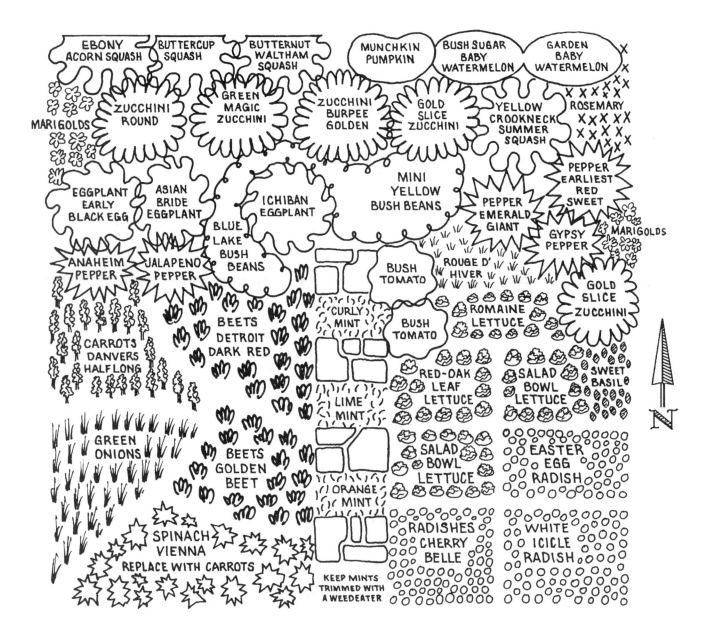

Figure 1-8. Postage stamp garden stressing winter and summer varieties. 6' x 6' bed.

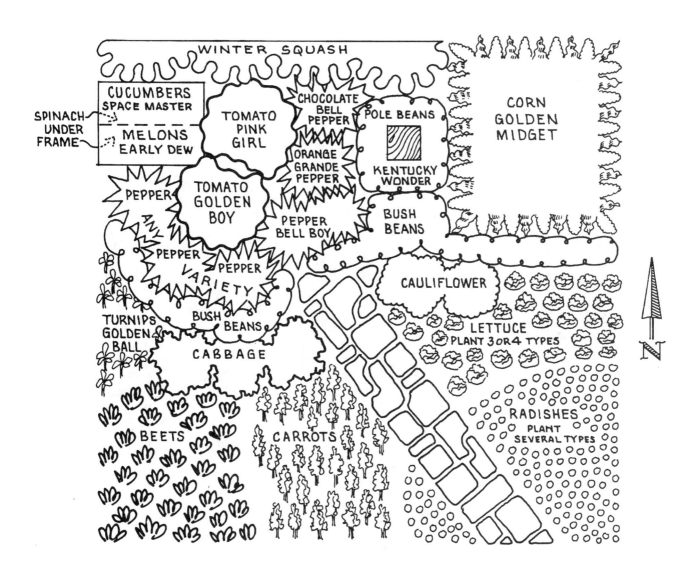

Figure 1-9. Postage stamp garden. Plant peas before winter squash. Intercrop radishes, leaf lettuce, and green onion with larger plants. 4' x 4' bed.

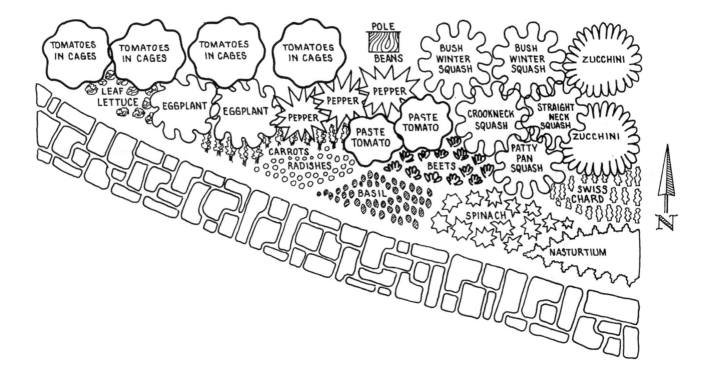

Figure 1-10. Flower bed postage stamp garden.

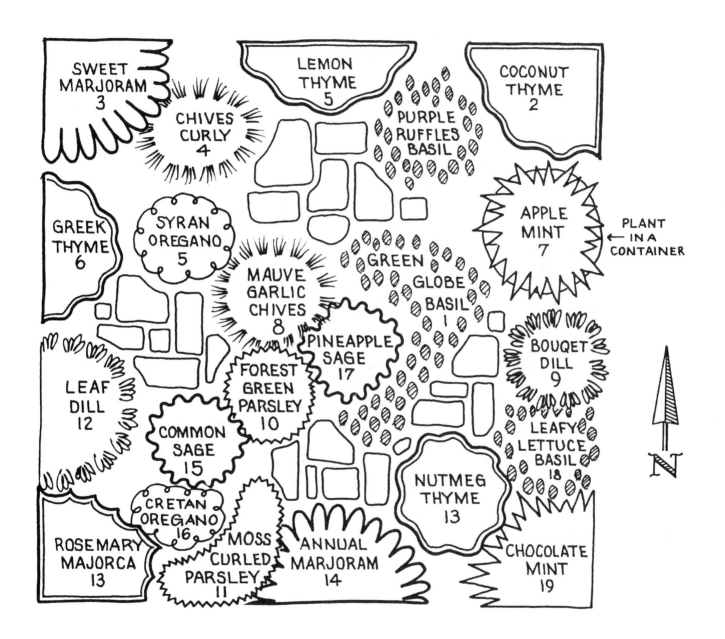

SWEET MARJORAM 3

LEMON THYME 5

COCONUT THYME 2

CHIVES CURLY 4

PURPLE RUFFLES BASIL

GREEK THYME 6

SYRAN OREGANO 5

APPLE MINT 7

PLANT ← IN A CONTAINER

MAUVE GARLIC CHIVES 8

GREEN GLOBE BASIL 1

PINEAPPLE SAGE 17

BOUQET DILL 9

LEAF DILL 12

FOREST GREEN PARSLEY 10

COMMON SAGE 15

LEAFY LETTUCE BASIL 18

CRETAN OREGANO 16

NUTMEG THYME 13

N

ROSEMARY MAJORCA 13

MOSS CURLED PARSLEY 11

ANNUAL MARJORAM 14

CHOCOLATE MINT 19

Figure 1-11. Gourmet herb garden. 4' x 4' bed.

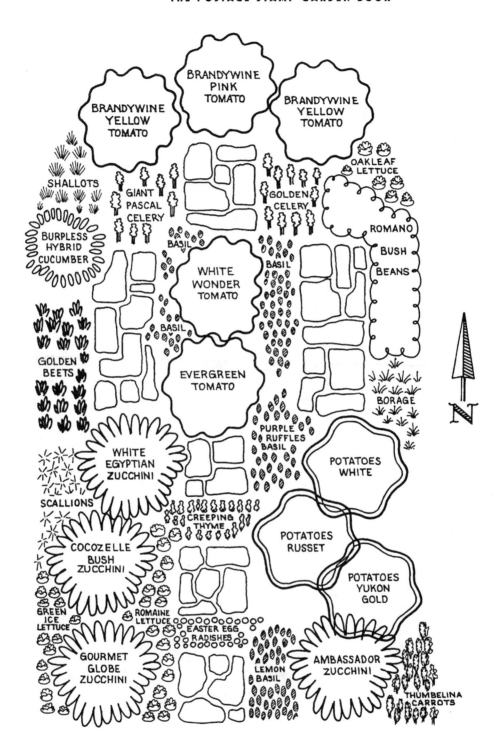

Figure 1-12. Experimental postage stamp garden. 5' x 10' bed.

The Regular Flower Bed Garden

Who says that you have to grow a formal vegetable garden? Nobody, right? Not only can you mix vegetables with flowers in any flower bed, but a lot of gardeners will tell you that flower beds are really the natural place to grow vegetables. A friend of ours who follows this theory produces great quantities of vegetables. Her showy cabbage grows by itself, in a conspicuous spot. A number of vegetables make up the flower bed borders. Corn grows in the corner in one big bunch. Vine plants grow up the back fences. It's all very attractive and amusing.

Here are some rules she gave us that you'll find helpful in "vegetablizing" your flower beds:

1. Plant vines such as cucumbers and small melons against walls. Plant beanstalks against a wall or stake them. Plantings like this give your garden an especially lush look.
2. Use leaf lettuce and Swiss chard as a flower bed edging. Grow head lettuce just behind the edging.
3. Plant root crops in small sections.
4. Plant cabbage where you're looking for a show-off.
5. Plant corn in a sunny corner. A 4-by-6-foot plot with plants 10 inches apart will produce a good crop.
6. Use peppers as an ornamental to complement other plants.

4-by-4-Foot Boxed Gardens

For some reason, 4-by-4-foot boxed gardens spark the imagination of a lot of people, and we see more of such gardens around every year. They're neat, clean, and easy to handle. You can walk all the way around them, you can thin the plants without getting dirty, and you can have as many as you want in any arrangement you like—one or two or a bunch.

Actually a boxed garden is not really a "box" with a bottom. It's more of a frame. To make one, all you have to do is measure out a 4-by-4-

Wood frame boxes

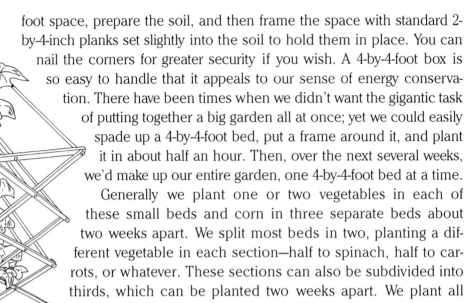

A drying rack can be the perfect frame for vertical gardening.

foot space, prepare the soil, and then frame the space with standard 2-by-4-inch planks set slightly into the soil to hold them in place. You can nail the corners for greater security if you wish. A 4-by-4-foot box is so easy to handle that it appeals to our sense of energy conservation. There have been times when we didn't want the gigantic task of putting together a big garden all at once; yet we could easily spade up a 4-by-4-foot bed, put a frame around it, and plant it in about half an hour. Then, over the next several weeks, we'd make up our entire garden, one 4-by-4-foot bed at a time.

Generally we plant one or two vegetables in each of these small beds and corn in three separate beds about two weeks apart. We split most beds in two, planting a different vegetable in each section—half to spinach, half to carrots, or whatever. These sections can also be subdivided into thirds, which can be planted two weeks apart. We plant all root and leafy vegetables this way. We train cucumbers, cantaloupe, beans, and other vines and trailers to grow up stakes, trellises, or cages.

Container Gardening

By planting vegetables in containers, you can grow your garden almost anywhere, indoors or out. Start by looking for places you might squeeze in a container or two.

For patios and balcony gardens, measure your space. A 9-by-15-foot balcony, for instance, contains 135 square feet. Estimate how much space you'll need for general living, lounging, barbecuing, and so on. Then subtract this amount from the total space available. If you feel you need about half the total space for general living, you still have more than 65 square feet left in which to cultivate your garden.

Now walk through your house looking for unused space where you might grow vegetables, either in a window space or under lights. Consider bedrooms, living rooms, closets, bathrooms, and any additional interior space. You can grow many vegetables under lights—the only limit is your imagination.

You can plant in standard containers that you buy from a garden center, or you can turn almost anything into a vegetable container—the sources are endless (see Figure 1-13).

We like to shop the import stores looking for unusual baskets, which Karen turns into attractive vegetable planters. The secret is to coat the inside of the basket or box with polyester resin and strips of newspaper. First, buy clear polyester resin, hardener, and a paint brush from any craft store. Next, tear the newspaper into long strips, 5 inches wide. Brush the polyester resin on the inside of the basket's bottom and sides, and then cover the resin with newspaper strips. Continue the resin/paper process until you've lined the basket with six coats of paper. When you are finished, add an additional coat of resin.

Figure 1-13. Extraordinary ideas for vegetable containers.

As a general rule, the larger and deeper the container, the better the yields. While you can grow small bush-type tomatoes in smaller containers, the larger varieties require up to 20 gallons (3 cubic feet) of soil to produce a good crop.

Windowsill and Window Box Gardens

With 12 feet of sunny windowsill, you can raise enough salad to feed a family of four for a year. You can "farm" twenty-five 4-inch pots in which you can grow:

- 5 or 6 kinds of herbs
- 20 to 30 carrots
- 30 to 35 beets

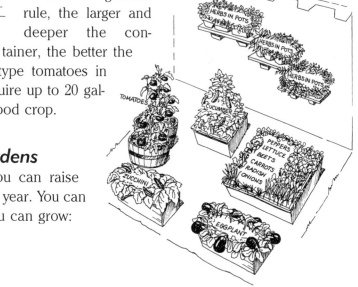

Figure 1-14. A variety of window box containers.

➴ All the radishes you can eat

➴ Even a few tomatoes

That windowsill space is a potential green mine. You can grow anything on a windowsill that requires a 1- or 2-inch spacing between plants, or single plants that keep producing an edible crop. This gives you a choice of four categories:

Sprouts: radish seeds, alfalfa seeds, mung beans, soybeans, wheat, buckwheat, and cress

Root vegetables: carrots, beets, green onions, and garlic

Herbs: chives, parsley, basil, dill, rosemary, sage, summer savory, tarragon, and sweet marjoram

Tomatoes: Tiny Tim is the most popular.

In an outside window box, you can grow almost anything. In window boxes, it's easiest to plant in pots and simply set the pots in the box. Most gardeners like to mix vegetables, herbs, and flowers in this setting (Figures 1-14 and 1-15).

**Figure 1-15.
Large plant containers.**

Planting Your Patio

Whiskey barrel halves make great patio planters. They are 22 inches across, so they hold enough soil to support good vegetable growth. A single barrel will hold seven to eight corn plants, two or three zucchini plants, and two or three tomatoes. You can place them on wheels and roll them around the patio. Wheels can be purchased at any hardware store. A wheelbarrow also works well (Figure 1-16).

Wooden boxes are also excellent for standard patio planting. Wood has a high insulation value

**Figure 1-16. A wheelbarrow
makes a great container.**

and keeps the hot summer sun of most patio areas from drying the soil out rapidly and damaging the roots. You can buy these boxes from a garden center or make them. Boxes come in many sizes. Terra cotta pots also come in many shapes and sizes (Figure 1-17a-b).

Some gardeners like the paper pulp pots. They are easy to lift and fill with potting soil. We recommend using pots with either a 12-inch or an 18-inch inside diameter, depending on what you want to plant. You can plant carrots and lettuce in 12-inch pots and eggplant, tomatoes, peppers, and other larger plants in 18-inch pots. Hanging wire baskets and containers also enhance any patio garden.

Figure 1-17a.
Terra cotta pots.

Eight Easy Steps

Follow these steps for planting your container vegetables:

1. Select an attractive container with drainage holes. If the container you select doesn't have holes, drill them.
2. Add commercial potting soil to within an inch of the top of the container. Use a planting mix with sphagnum peat moss.
3. Moisten the soil before planting.
4. You can plant both herbs and vegetables in the same container. When you plant them together, you can crowd them a little bit. An 18-inch pot, for instance, will easily hold as many as ten herbs.
5. If you are planting several vegetables and herbs together in the same container, set the taller varieties in the center.
6. Water to settle the soil around the roots.
7. Add more soil if it's needed after watering.
8. Keep the container moist and fertilized.

Figure 1-17b.
Hanging planters.

Container Soil Mixes

Container soil is a combination of organic materials (bark, compost, peat moss) and minerals. Any container mix must also provide the right nutrients for vegetable growth and enough air space (despite compacting) to allow good air and water movement. You can also grow vegetables in the commercial soilless mixes (such as Supersoil) since many of them contain all the ingredients necessary for good plant growth.

No-Mess Mixing

We hate the mess that sometimes occurs when you are gardening indoors or on a patio. If this is your problem, we have an answer. You'll need a 5-gallon plastic pail and a 1-quart kitchen measuring cup, along with a large wooden spoon and a plastic sheet to put over your work area to catch any spillage.

Mix your ingredients in the kitchen or work area sink. Moisten the contents with hot water to cut down on the dust. Stir slowly with the wooden spoon until everything is mixed.

Planting Seeds and Seedlings in Containers

When planting seeds in a container, you don't have to space them any particular distance apart. Simply scatter the seeds across the entire container. Later, however, you will have to thin the seedlings. Carrots, for instance, are thinned first to $^3/_4$ of an inch apart, then to 1 to 2 inches apart. You can throw the small carrots you're thinning into a soup or a stew, and you won't feel as if you're wasting anything. The 8-inch containers of carrots planted on a 1-inch spacing will produce the equivalent of a 5-foot row grown in an outdoor garden.

If you plant young seedlings in outdoor containers, you should get them used to outdoor conditions by taking them out in the morning and back inside at night. Gradually expose the seedlings to low temperatures and more sunlight for about two weeks or until you can leave them out without damage from frost.

No-Mess Watering Techniques

Watering your indoor containers shouldn't be any problem. Pots less than 8 inches in diameter should be watered from above with a 1-quart kitchen measuring cup. Another technique is to submerge the bottom half of the pot in a pail of water (or fill a kitchen sink). When the air bubbles stop coming up from the soil, take the pot out and let it drain. Large containers should be watered from above with a plastic pail, or a gentle stream from a hose, until the soil is completely saturated.

Don't water again until the soil is dry to a depth of 1 inch. To find out how dry the soil is, poke a finger into the soil, or take some soil from this depth and rub it between your thumb and index finger. If it's dry, water. If the soil is mud-coated or feels wet, it won't need water for at least twenty-four hours.

You should not let your containers dry out since vegetables must grow rapidly to maturity. If the plant is overwatered, the soil becomes waterlogged, forcing air from the soil and suffocating the plant. If at all possible, we suggest that you connect your containers with a drip system, put the whole thing on an automatic timer, and water each container with an emitter.

You can also buy large self-watering pots. They come in a number of shapes and sizes. These contain a built-in reservoir that gets filled through a slot in the side of the pot. During warm, dry weather, you need to refill these reservoirs once or twice a week. You can also fertilize these pots by adding fish emulsion directly to the water. Dump the water when it turn brackish.

Midget Fruits and Vegetables

If we didn't know better, we'd say that plant breeders developed the whole range of midget vegetables just for container gardeners. Over the last few years, a number of vegetables have been developed that are only half, even a fifth, the size of regular ones. The ones listed below have both generic descriptions as well as information on varieties. The seed source codes listed throughout this book correspond with the codes in the Appendix.

Baby Gourmet Beets

To grow baby gourmet beets, scatter the seeds across an entire container. Cover with about $1/4$ inch of planter mix. Thin to stand 1 to 2 inches apart.

GLADIATOR   Crimson, gold ball-sized beet. Seed source: GUR
LITTLE BALL   Smooth 1-inch ball. Seed source: BURP HIG ORN PAR PIN SEE SHE STO TER TIL TWI WILL

Baby Cabbage

Start the midget cabbages from seeds indoors in aluminum pans or peat pots about six to eight weeks before you intend to plant them in containers. For outdoor containers, plant midget cabbage about 4 inches apart. For windowsills or under lights, plant in 6-inch pots. Keep the temperature between 60° to 70°F.

BABY EARLY   A 2-pound, red, tight-headed cabbage. Seed source: COM

BADGER BABYHEAD   2- to 3-pound baby cabbage. Great flavor. Seed source: HEN

Baby Carrots

Plant baby carrots in the spring, and continue the planting throughout the summer. Plant 6 to 10 per each 4-inch pot. You can grow carrots in windowsill pots, under lights, or in larger containers outdoors.

LITTLE FINGER   Extra sweet, 3 to 4 inches long. A gourmet Nantes-type carrot. Seed source: BOU COM GUR JLH JUN ORN PIN VER

SHORT 'N' SWEET   A bright orange, 3-inch long carrot. Seed source: FAR LED

Baby Cauliflower

Start from seed indoors about six to eight weeks before you intend to plant in containers. For outdoor containers, plant midget cauliflower about 5 inches apart.

GARNAT   White, 2- to 4-inch head. Seed source: THO

Baby Corn

Plant midget corn 5 inches apart in 12-inch or larger pots. Midget corn grows especially well in 5-gallon cans. Plant in the spring after your patio has warmed up. Make additional plantings every few weeks for a continuous harvest. You can also grow 5-gallon containers of midget corn behind a south-facing window.

GOLDEN MIDGET   Yellow, 4-inch ears, 10 rows of kernels. Seed source: ABU GAR SEED VER

Baby Cucumbers

Plant these midget cucumbers in 6- to 8-inch pots, and cover with 1 inch of soil. You can plant in larger containers with 4-inch spacing between the plants. Place the containers out on the balcony or patio after the weather has warmed up in the spring.

BUSH PICKLE   20- to 24-inch vine, dark green cucumber for pickling. Seed source: BURP GUR HEN JUN LED LIB MEY PAR STO

PATIO PIC	6½-inch cucumbers. Seed source: GLE

Baby Eggplant

Plant seed ⅓-inch deep in compressed peat pots. Plant pot and all in a 12-inch or larger container. Place in full sun, and don't move outdoors until the weather warms up in the spring.

BABY WHITE TIGER	This is a tiny eggplant, 1 to 2 inches long. Seed source: SEE
BAMBINO	This eggplant is only 12 inches tall with small fruit. Seed source: BURP GUR LIB SHE STO TER
EARLY BLACK EGG	Shiny black fruit, 4-by-2-inch egg-shaped fruit. Seed source: GAR GLE SOU

Baby Lettuce

Plant baby lettuce directly in a container 4 to 5 inches apart. Midget lettuce grows well in 4-inch or larger pots and is especially popular for window box gardening. Make outdoor plantings every two weeks in separate small containers. Start 2 to 4 weeks before the last killing frost in the spring. Inside, plant anytime. You can easily grow lettuce on a windowsill or under lights.

TOM THUMB	Tennis ball–sized, medium green heads. Seed source: GUR HEN HIG LED NIC ORG ORN PIN POR SEE SEED SHE SOU TIL VER

Baby Melons/Pumpkins

Plant 3 seeds per 5-gallon container. When about 5 inches high, cut 2 of them out with a pair of scissors. Let the remaining plant grow to maturity.

BUSH MUSKETEER	3- to 4-pound melons, heavily netted, orange flesh. Seed source: HEN JUN MEY PAR STO
BUSH SUGAR BABY	An oval, 8- to 10-pound watermelon, scarlet flesh. Seed source: BURP BURR
GARDEN BABY	A round, 6- to 7-inch diameter watermelon. Grows on bush-type vines. Seed source: DEG VER
MUNCHKIN	Bright orange, 3- to 4-inch flattened pumpkin. Good cooks like to stuff these little guys. Seed source: JUN SHE

Tomatoes

Start indoors 6 to 8 weeks before you intend to plant in your containers. If you're planting on a patio, don't move the seedlings outside until the weather has warmed up. These tomatoes will grow in 8- to 10-inch pots. See Figure 1-17.

BURPEE'S PIXIE	Determinate plant that grows about 16 inches high. The fruit is 1¼-inches in diameter. Seed source: ALL PON TOM TOMA
PATIO	This is a 24- to 26-inch plant. The fruit grows to about 2 inches in diameter. Seed source: ALL COM DEG LED LIB TOM TOMA WIL
PIXIE HYBRID II	An 18-inch tall plant. Produces bright scarlet, 1½-inch fruit. Seed source: JUN ORN TOMA WIL
TINY TIM	This really is a tiny plant that grows to about 6 inches tall. It produces ¼-inch bright red tomatoes. Seed source: ALL BURG COM GLE LED SEE STO TOM TOMA WILL

Baby Zucchini

Plant 2 to 3 plants in a 10-gallon container. Wrap your container with a wire cage to help support the plant.

AMBASSADOR	Pick the green fruit when it is small. Seed source: COM LEB MEY PIN WIL
GOLDEN DAWN II	Golden yellow fruit. Pick when small. Seed source: GAR PAR

Now that we've explored some of the things that you should consider in planning the layout of your IPS garden, we can turn to the soil itself—what it's like and how to convert it into good fertile earth that will turn out an abundance of vegetables.

CHAPTER TWO

What Goes into Your Soil?

I t's a beautiful day. There's not a cloud in the sky. The temperature is in the mid-80s. And there you are in your backyard, picking loads of vegetables from your own small garden tucked away in the corner of your property. Tomatoes, peas, onions, corn, you've grown them all—in fact, more than you ever dreamed possible from such a small space.

Impossible?

Of course not. That's exactly what an intensive postage stamp garden is intended to do and what you will learn to do in the next few chapters.

The condition of the soil can actually make or break the productiveness of your garden. It is, in effect, the motor; and if you expect to grow a lot of vegetables in a small space (as we do), it's extremely important to build the very best motor possible.

Look at it this way. Suppose you buy a Lincoln Continental, and after you get it home, you remove its engine and install one from a Volkswagen. Then you go on a trip. You wouldn't expect to rip up the road getting to your destination, because you know that a Volkswagen engine can't handle a Lincoln Continental.

Or suppose instead of replacing the Continental engine with one from a Volkswagen, you simply leave the original engine in place and take off on your trip. Now, if you want to, you can beat most of the cars on the road.

On the other hand, imagine that you take the Continental engine out and put it in a Volkswagen body. Chances are you'll be able to beat anything in sight . . . and then some. That's something like what we're trying to do.

We want to squeeze every last bit of productivity out of the soil in our IPS (intensive postage stamp) garden. What we are doing in effect is installing a Lincoln engine in a Volkswagen body. We're going to make the soil in your garden super productive.

If you'll take the time in the beginning to build your soil right, your IPS garden will reward you (from then on) with some of the greatest vegetables you've ever seen. Now, as a starter, let's take a peek at what's under the ground in your backyard.

How Soil Works

Most people look at their soil and see a bunch of dirt. It's the stuff that comes in on the kids' clothes, that has to be swept off the back porch, or that has to be cleaned up off the kitchen floor. Actually, soil is a lot more than that.

Every square foot of soil swarms with millions of bacteria and other microorganisms. The organic material that's in the soil or the raw material that you deposit there—leaves, grass clippings, garbage, and so forth—contains essential elements that plants use to grow. These elements are tied up in such a way that vegetables need help to reach them—the soil bacteria break them down and convert them into forms that plants can build with. How fast the soil bacteria act on this raw material depends on the nature of the material itself, the temperature, the amount of air available, and the soil moisture.

In the spring, when the soil warms up, the number of bacteria in the soil and the bacterial action increase tremendously. When you add fresh organic material, the bacteria immediately attack it, breaking it down into food for your plants. The bacterial organisms themselves need nitrogen to grow. And if you don't have nitrogen in the material that you put in the garden, the bacteria will steal it from the vegetables you're trying to grow.

You can get around this problem by building a compost pile of organic material. This pile lets the initial bacterial decomposition take place outside the soil. Then when you turn the material into your soil, the nutrients are in a form that plants can use immediately.

How Soil Is Structured

Basically, there are three kinds of soil: clay, sand, and loam. Clay soil has particles so small that you can't see them without a microscope. They are extremely close together and take in water slowly. Once the clay particles absorb water, they hold it so tightly that it's almost impossible for plants to utilize it; and air can't get in. When clay dries, it's even worse. Plant roots have difficulty penetrating it, and the soil itself contains little air and water.

Sand, on the other hand, has particles many times larger than clay. Air penetrates deeply, and water moves through it too rapidly, dissolving away many of the nutrients.

Loam is somewhere between these two extremes. Loam has clay, sand, and a good supply of decomposed organic material called humus. The grains have good structure. The soil drains well, yet retains enough water for plant growth. Air can circulate, and the soil provides plenty of room for roots to grow easily.

Don't worry if your backyard isn't loam. As we mentioned in Chapter 1, we completely renovate the soil so that it doesn't really matter what you start with.

We might also mention here something that some gardeners seem to worry about a great deal: the pH of their soil. This is the measure of whether your soil is sweet (alkaline) or sour (acid). The pH scale runs from 0 for extremely acid to 7 for neutral to 14 for extremely alkaline. Most vegetables prefer soils that are neutral or slightly acid, that is, with a pH of 6.5 to 7.0. There's no doubt the pH is important. Generally, however, when we make up our IPS beds, we automatically make them just about right for vegetables. Unless you have a really unusual problem, like trying to garden near alkali flats or salt marshes (alkaline soil) or in a peat bog (acid soil), just forget about the pH problem and simply make up your garden according to the instructions given in this book. If you do have one of those problems, contact your local nursery and ask how other gardeners in the area have handled it. Once you've answered that question, then you can proceed to make up your IPS garden in the regular manner.

TABLE 2-1. OPTIMUM pH RANGE FOR VEGETABLES	
pH	VEGETABLE
6 to 8	Beets, cabbage, melons
6 to 7.5	Peas, spinach, summer squash
6 to 7	Cauliflower, celery, chives, endive, horseradish, lettuce, onions, radishes, rhubarb
5.5 to 7.5	Corn, pumpkins, tomatoes
5.5 to 6.8	Beans, carrots, cucumbers, parsnips, peppers, rutabaga, winter squash
5.5 to 6.5	Eggplant, watermelon
4.8 to 6.3	Potatoes

Getting the Ingredients for your IPS Garden Soil

I don't have to tell you that plants need to eat just like you do. That's not technically correct, of course, but everybody knows that plants need certain soil conditions and nutrients—sixteen of them—in order to be healthy and vigorous. There are three major nutrients—nitrogen (N), phosphorus (P), and potassium (K)—and a number of minor and trace elements, including calcium, zinc, iron, manganese, copper, sulfur, magnesium, among others. To provide these nutrients and organic material in our IPS gardens, we add compost, manure, blood meal, bonemeal, and wood ash, or a substitute (as discussed later in this chapter). Sometimes we add a fifth ingredient, fish emulsion.

Compost—and a Temporary Substitute

Probably the most important ingredient that you can add to your IPS bed is compost—the mixture of decayed leaves, grass clippings, garbage, and other organic matter that you prepare yourself in piles and then add to the soil (you can also buy compost in quantities from a landscape supply firm). In composting, the organic matter is broken down by bacterial action into food that your vegetable plants can use immediately. Without it (or some good substitute), you'll get only mediocre vegetables. With it, the ground seems to come alive. Also it helps to give the soil a lighter texture, letting the soil breathe.

You can prepare compost very easily. Detailed instructions for different types of composting are given in the appendix. Most composting, though, takes time. It can take a few weeks or even a few months for the raw organic material in a compost pile to break down into compounds that vegetables can use. For this reason you should begin as soon as possible to build a compost pile for your garden.

In the meantime, don't let a lack of compost stop you from preparing an IPS garden. Simply buy some and work it into your garden. Or you can substitute rotted manure.

Animal Manures

Animal manures are a must in your garden, for they add many needed nutrients, especially nitrogen. And just to make the matter more complicated, every type of manure has different properties and varying amounts of nitrogen, phosphorus, and potassium.

Generally, you should use rotted manure, not fresh. The bacteria in the soil needs extra nitrogen to break down fresh manure, and this process can use up some of the nitrogen that would otherwise go to the plants. Moreover—like organic materials that have been composted—plants can easily use rotted or decomposed manure. We get ours from a nearby stable; they put it out in January, and it's well rotted by March—when you need it for your garden.

Dried manure, which you can buy from a nursery or a landscape materials firm, is also usually just right. It can be worked into your garden soil directly from the sack.

Do not buy steer manure, however, because its high salt content offsets any benefit that it might have. Although the salts can be leached out by watering, leaching also washes out the nitrogen.

Hen, horse, sheep, and rabbit manures are known as "hot" manures because of their high nitrogen content. Cow and hog manures are called "cold" manures because they are low in nitrogen and break down fairly slowly. We prefer using horse manure, since we think it gives us the best results. You can also buy compost or soil with manure in it directly from a landscape materials supplier.

We suggest you start out by using whatever you have available (given the cautions mentioned) and then later experiment to see what gives you the best results in your particular garden. If you prefer not to haul your own manure, we suggest you call a landscape materials supplier and see what they have available. Most of these firms will deliver.

		\ TABLE 2-2. NATURAL PLANT FOODS		
TYPE	**SOURCE**	**COMPOSITION (%)**		
		N	**P**	**K**
Animal manures	Cattle	0.53	0.29	0.48
(fresh)	Chicken	0.89	0.48	0.83
	Horse	0.55	0.27	0.57
	Sheep	0.89	0.48	0.83
Animal manures	Cattle	2.00	1.80	3.00
(dried)	Horse	0.80	0.20	0.60
	Sheep	1.40	1.00	3.00
Organic nutrients	Dried blood meal	9–14	-	-
	Bone meal	1.6–2.5	23–25	-
	Fish emulsion	5–10	2.0	2.0
Pulverized rock	Rock phosphate	-	38–41	-
powders	Greensand	-	1.35	4.1–9.5
Vegetable	Cottonseed meal	6.7–7.4	2–3	1.5–2.0
	Seaweed	1.7	0.8	5.0
	Soybean meal	6.0	1.0	2.0
	Oak leaves	0.8	0.4	0.2
	Wood ashes	-	1.5	7.0

Nitrogen

Blood meal, which you can buy at nurseries, contains up to 15 percent nitrogen and usually some phosphorus and potassium. Activated sewerage sludge (Milorganite) contains up to 6 percent nitrogen and is processed and sold by a number of cities. Cottonseed meal contains about 7 percent nitrogen.

TABLE 2-3. MAJOR NATURAL SOURCES OF NITROGEN		
MATERIAL	NITROGEN (PERCENT)	APPLY PER 100 SQUARE FEET
Blood meal	15.0	5–10 pounds
Cottonseed meal	8.0	10 pounds
Fish meal	8.0	5–10 pounds
Bat guano	10.0	5 pounds

Phosphorus

Generally we supply phosphorus (one of the major nutrients) to our plants by adding bonemeal. Bonemeal has a whopping amount of phosphoric acid—20 to 25 percent or more—as well as 1 to 2 percent nitrogen; and vegetables love it. You can buy steamed bone meal where garden products are sold.

TABLE 2-4. MAJOR NATURAL SOURCES OF PHOSPHORUS		
MATERIAL	PHOSPHORUS (PERCENT)	APPLY PER 100 SQUARE FEET
Phosphate rock	16.0	5 pounds
Bone meal, steamed	11.0	5 pounds

If you like, you can substitute rock phosphate or superphosphate for bonemeal. This is a finely ground rock powder, and it contains up to 30 percent phosphoric acid.

Potassium

Wood ash supplies the potassium needed by your plants. Most wood ash contains 7 to 8 percent potassium and can be obtained simply by burning wood outdoors or in a fireplace. (Wood ashes should not be allowed to stand in the rain, because most of the potassium will be leached away.)

If you have trouble getting wood ash, it's possible to substitute greensand and granite dust, which you can buy at many nurseries. Both of these materials contain about 6 to 8 percent potassium. Both also contain a number of minor and trace mineral nutrients.

You can now buy commercial organic fertilizers containing these ingredients (already mixed for you) from most nurseries. Many gardeners start out this way rather than trying to handle the individual ingredients.

TABLE 2-5. MAJOR NATURAL SOURCES OF POTASH		
MATERIAL	POTASH (PERCENT)	APPLY PER 100 SQUARE FEET
Wood ashes	8.0	5 pounds
Green sand	7.0	5 pounds
Granite dust	5.0	5 pounds

Fish Emulsion

Fish emulsion generally has 5 to 10 percent nitrogen and sometimes phosphorus and potassium, although many brands are marked on the bottle 5-0-0, which, in nursery language, means respectively 5 percent nitrogen, no phosphorus, and no potassium. We use fish emulsion in our IPS garden about every two weeks to add nitrogen to those plants that are pretty heavy feeders.

Some gardeners prefer to use liquid seaweed in place of fish emulsion. It contains nitrogen, phosphorus, and a number of minerals.

Any of these fertilizers can be added to your soil to give your feeding plants an extra boost.

However, avoid all chemical fertilizers; reasons are given.

The Earthworm

Earthworms, like bacteria, are great for the soil; they are extremely helpful in keeping your IPS bed in good shape. By burrowing, feeding, and excreting, earthworms let air and moisture in and break up the soil particles. They usually don't burrow very deep, but when the plant roots start going deeper, the earthworms go with them, making the soil even better.

The gray pink ones (*Helodrilus caliginosus* and *Helodrilus trape-zoides*) are important to your garden. The red one (*Eisenia foetida*), the fishworm, is not as good, since it stays in damp spongy places instead of getting down to work in garden soils. You'll find *Eisenia foetida* works great in compost piles, however, and you may want to buy a few to add when you make your own compost.

The earthworm improves the soil by swallowing it and later expelling it in the form of castings. The earthworm takes in the soil, grinds it up, mixes it with calcium carbonate, pulverizes it, sends it on through its intestine to be digested by enzymes, and then excretes it. These final earthworm castings contain nitrogen, phosphorus, and potassium, all elements that vegetables need. And when the earthworm dies, its body adds a good nitrogen fertilizer to the soil.

It is important to note that chemicals and earthworms don't mix, at least not well. Chemical fertilizers seem to decrease the number of earthworms in the soil, killing them or driving them off; ammonium sulfate is particularly harmful. Many insect sprays also are toxic to earthworms and will cause the population in the soil to dwindle.

Earthworms actually are a little finicky about the soil in general. You can't put them in infertile or hard, clay soils and expect good results. They like rich soil; and if they don't have it, they just take off.

Earthworms make a good soil even better. So, when possible, dig up earthworms from other parts of the yard (or anywhere else) and deposit them in your future vegetable garden. You may have to keep turning dirt over with a shovel until you find them—generally there are fewer of them in most flower beds. Or you can order earthworms through many seed catalogs.

Creating the kind of soil that bristles with the right organic nutrients is the most important thing that you can do in your garden. And your vegetables will love you for it.

CHAPTER THREE

Getting Your Soil Ready

Postage stamp gardens, in general, aren't very difficult to grow, nor do they take very much work. Getting the soil ready in the first place takes more effort than anything else you'll do.

In a conventional garden, you must dig up the soil and then, throughout the season, cultivate and weed. In an IPS garden, you dig up the ground—the big push, but a fairly easy one—but after that, except for watering, you more or less coast. And, believe me, that's the kind of gardening we really like.

As stated in Chapter 2, the whole purpose of the IPS garden is to create a super fertile, well-textured soil that will support the growth of a large quantity of vegetables in a small space. To accomplish this goal, you can choose from two ways of preparing the soil: You can use either the general intensive method or the modified French Intensive method.

With the general intensive method, you can plow a small bed in about ten minutes, using a rototiller (a small one is probably best for small beds). After that, you simply spade in your compost, manure, and other nutrients and rake over the soil. The rototiller method is easy and can produce good results. It has only one general drawback. Because the rototiller breaks down everything in the soil to about the same consistency, it does tend to destroy some of the soil structure and the layering effect that helps create soil fertility. We suggest when planting beds 25 square feet (5 by 5) and under that you use one of the minitillers. Besides, a large tiller is hard to handle in spaces that small.

The modified French Intensive method, on the other hand, employs hand tools only, such as a spade and a rake; and these methods structure the soil in a special way. You can make up most beds with a D-handled square shovel. The advantage is that you can dig equally deep along the edge of the bed.

If you have a lot of rocks or tough soil, a four-pronged garden fork will let you penetrate the soil easily. As you dig, sift the soil to remove the rocks. To move partially decomposed compost, straw, and leaves, you'll need a manure fork. This lets you pick up large quantities of materials easily. A rake helps in leveling beds and breaking up clods. A hoe can handle most other garden chores. You will also need a small garden trowel for planting seedlings or roots and doing other kinds of small digging.

In all cases we recommend that you not buy the cheapest tools on the market. They'll bend or break easily and cost you more in replacements in the long run. Invest in good sturdy tools.

We used to dig our IPS beds with a shovel, and it did take a while. But when one of our friends, who stands 5 feet 2 inches tall and weighs 96 pounds, got her beds ready quickly and easily with a rototiller, we changed our ways. If you intend to garden in an area where the soil is hard and clayey and, therefore, difficult to spade, it may be an especially good idea to rototill the first year. In subsequent years the soil will be looser, and you can spade it up if you like. In any case, here is the procedure:

1. Rototill your bed at least 1 foot deep.
2. If you have clay soil, use a spade or spading fork to turn sand and compost into the soil until your bed consists of $1/3$ compost, $1/3$ sand, and $1/3$ original soil. For sandy soils, turn compost into your bed until you have $1/3$ to $1/2$ compost, the rest original soil. For in-between soils, just estimate how much you'll need of one thing or another in order to end up with a mixture that contains at least $1/3$ compost that is loose and fairly fine and that has good air space and is easy to work. You can purchase sand from most building supply or garden centers.
3. Level the bed with a rake.
4. Spread a 2-inch layer of rotted manure (or compost) over the entire bed. Add blood meal (4 pounds per 50 square feet), a sprinkling of bonemeal (4 pound per 50 square feet), and a small dose of wood ash (3 pounds per 50 square feet)—or any of the substitutes mentioned in Chapter 2. Using a rake, turn this into the top portion of the s[...] light texture. Most garden c[...] that contains these ingredie[...] this fertilizer and spread it i[...]

Modified French Intensive M[...]

The modified French Intensive me[...] to achieve superfertilization becaus[...] ture. They help condition the soil [...]

from below, gases—produced by bacterial action—come up from the roots, and air goes down, thus allowing the soil to breathe.

You can start the soil breathing by simply opening it with a shovel. But to achieve good water conduction, the soil generally must be coarse below and fine textured above. When you get dirt clods in the surface soil or fine grains below the surface, you interfere with water conduction.

General Hand Method

In the general hand method, you achieve a partial layering of nutrients and get a very fertile topsoil and loose subsoil. Here's how it goes:

1. For heavy clay soils, cover the entire with bed 6 to 8 inches of $1/2$ compost and $1/2$ sand. For sandy soils, cover the bed with 4 to 5 inches of pure compost. Your goal is a soil composition of $1/3$ compost, $1/3$ sand, and $1/3$ other soil ingredients. Therefore, adjust your addition of compost and sand to meet the needs of your own soil, whether clay or sand or something in between. Just estimate. You want a soil mixture that contains at least $1/3$ compost, that is loose and fairly fine, and that has good air space and is easy to work. (While you're preparing your soil, you should take out all rocks.)

2. Start at one end of the bed and dig a trench along the entire side. Make the trench one spade (about 9 to 10 inches) wide and deep. Put the excavated topsoil (along with the compost-sand mix) where you can get it later.

3. Loosen the subsoil in the trench that you've just created one spade depth more—to about 18 to 20 inches below the original surface. Make sure that this subsoil is nice and loose, but not too fine. You want the soil to grade from a fairly coarse texture at the bottom to a fairly fine texture at the top.

4. Remove topsoil, the depth of one spade (including the compost-sand mix), from the strip of bed directly beside the trench that you've just opened, and fill in your trench, making sure that you mix in the topsoil and compost-sand mixture.

5. You now have a new trench next to the original one that you just filled up. As before, loosen the subsoil in this trench, and then fill the trench with the topsoil (and compost-sand mix) from the adjacent strip.

6. Now, in the same manner, dig one trench after the other across the width of your bed until you've finished. After you've worked trench by trench and reached the very last row of your garden, take the topsoil with the compost-sand mixture that you laid aside originally from the first trench and fill in the last trench.

7. Let the soil surface stay rough a few days so that air can get into the soil. Then, using a spade and a rake, work the topsoil to a fine texture. Make sure that you break up all clods.

8. Over the entire surface spread about 2 inches of rotted manure, blood meal (4 pounds per 50 square feet), a small amount of bone meal (4 pounds per 50 square feet), and a small amount of wood ash (3 pounds per 50 square feet)—or any substitute mentioned in Chapter 2. Work these materials into the top 5 or 6 inches of topsoil and rake smooth. As mentioned before, you can buy a good organic fertilizer, already mixed, that contains all of these ingredients. In many cases it makes the job much easier.

Because you've added extra material to your bed, you'll end up with a slight mound. You'll also have a soil that's rich in nutrients, takes in air easily, lets fertile gases come up, and drains perfectly.

The Expert Method

The expert method is similar to the previous modified French Intensive method, except that the various ingredients are added to the soil at certain depths. The reason for this more precise layering is that plants seems to grow toward food they like. Cantaloupe roots, for instance, will race straight toward a pile of manure seven to fifteen feet away. Similarly, every plant root seems to know exactly what's going on below and will grow a lot faster to get there to the right nutrients. The plant root also seems to like different kinds of nutrients at different depths. It's almost as if plants want variety, and when they find something different, they say, "Breakfast, oh boy! . . . lunch wow! . . . dinner, great!" When the layering is done right, root growth speeds up.

With the expert method, the bed is made up in two stages. In the first stage, the bed is dug up, sand is added to the soil, and then the bed is left rough for a few days. In the second stage, occurring several days later, all other ingredients—compost and other materials—are added to the soil. Now let's take a look at the individual steps:

1. For clay soils, cover the entire bed with 2 to 3 inches of sand. Adjust the amount of sand to meet the needs of your own soil, whether clayey, sandy, or something in between. When this stage is finished, you should come out with soil that is roughly $\frac{1}{2}$ sand and $\frac{1}{2}$ original soil.

2. Start at one end of the bed, and dig a trench along the entire side. Make the trench one spade (again about 9 to 10 inches) wide and deep. Put the excavated topsoil (along with the sand) where you can get it later.

3. Loosen the subsoil in the trench that you've just created—again, one spade wide and deep—to about 18 to 20 inches below the original surface. Make sure that this subsoil is nice and loose, but not too fine. As we said before, the soil should grade from a fairly coarse texture at the bottom to a fairly fine texture at the top.

4. Remove topsoil to the depth and width of one spade (including the sand) from the strip of bed directly beside the trench that you've just opened, and fill in your trench. Make sure that you mix the sand and soil well in the trench that you're now filling up.

5. You now have a new trench next to the first one that you filled up. In this new trench, loosen the subsoil in the same manner as before. Again, fill in the trench with topsoil (and sand) from the adjacent strip.

6. Dig one trench after another across the width of the bed, always loosening the subsoil and mixing the topsoil and sand, until you've finished the entire bed. Into the very last trench put the topsoil (and sand) that you laid aside originally from the first trench.

7. Leave the garden rough for a few days.

8. Now go back and excavate the topsoil from each strip again, one by one. As you then return the topsoil to each trench, you add different nutrients at different levels. First, spread a small amount of blood meal (4 pounds per 50 square feet) and bone meal (4 pounds per 50 square feet) at the bottom of the topsoil. Add some topsoil. Second, spread a 4-inch layer of compost. Add more topsoil. Third, add about 2 inches of rotted manure. Add some more topsoil. Fourth, add a small amount of wood ash (3

pounds per 50 square feet). Spread over the remaining topsoil. If you prefer, use the substitute nutrients cited in Chapter 2).

9. Rake the soil at the top (don't disturb the strata) until it has a very fine texture.

This method also gives you a slight mound. It generally produces the best results because it stimulates root growth by providing different nutrients at different levels. It also takes more work.

Variations on the Intensive Methods

There are a number of variations possible with all the intensive methods. Here is one that you might want to try: Some gardeners simply like to dump all the ingredients together into the finished or ripe compost (including premixed organic fertilizer) so that they don't have to work with the fertilizing ingredients separately. Simply add one part rotted manure for every two parts of ripe compost. Add one cup of blood meal, one cup of bone meal, and one cup of wood ash (or their substitutes) for each cubic foot of compost. Work the mixture into the bed (again you can add a prepared organic fertilizer here if you prefer).

Again, if you don't have compost yet—and you probably won't if you're a beginning gardener—you can start your garden using only rotted manure.

Putting Moisture into the Soil

After you've dug up the soil and added the nutrients, you can begin planting any time. You should, however, soak the soil a day or two before you actually sow your seeds or set out your seedlings. If it hasn't rained recently, you may have to water for a long while in order to get moisture down to a depth of at least 10 inches.

Refeeding

In the course of a growing season, every time you take out a crop you have to refeed the soil before planting anything new. It's no big deal. To revitalize the soil, simply spread a couple of inches of rotted manure and a couple of inches of compost on top of the garden bed and work it in as thoroughly as possible. Because you really worked up the bed the first time, you won't have much trouble now. Also add small amounts of blood meal (4 pounds per 50 square feet, bone meal (4 pounds per 50 square feet), and wood ash (3 pounds per 50 square feet)—or the substitutes.

Every new year in the spring, of course, you should completely spade or rototill your beds again, according to the intensive methods described in this chapter.

Crop Rotation

In addition to adding compost and other ingredients each growing season, you should rotate the crops to keep the soil healthy. Some vegetables make heavy demands on the soil (heavy feeders); others take out very little (light feeders); and a few (the legumes) restore soil fertility. By moving these various kinds of vegetables around in your IPS beds, you can keep the soil in good shape throughout the years and even add vigor to it as you go along.

When possible, heavy feeders should be followed by legumes (beans and peas), which restore the soil fertility. After the legumes, you then plant the light feeders. In an IPS garden, this rotation is a little difficult because taller vegetables are planted to the north and smaller ones to the south. But if you want to give the soil a break, you must restore the balance whenever possible.

In sum, as you continue gardening the IPS way, your soil will get better and better. If there's a secret to turning brown thumbs into bright green ones, the IPS method is it. When you create the right soil conditions and continue to add compost and other nutrients each growing season, your soil will continually grow vigorous, healthy vegetables, with only a minimum of additional effort.

TABLE 3-1. SOIL NUTRIENT DEFICIENCY

SYMPTOM	CAUSE	NUTRIENT SOLUTION
Yellow leaves starting with the lower leaves; stunted growth	Nitrogen deficiency	Apply blood meal at the rate of 10 ounces per 100 square feet
Bluish green leaves followed by bronzing or purpling, drying to a greenish-brown or black	Phosphorus deficiency	Apply phosphate rock at the rate of $3/4$ pound per 100 square feet, or test soil and follow recommendations
Dry or scorched leaves; dead areas along margins; plants stunted; rusty appearance	Potash (potassium) deficiency	Apply wood ashes or greensand at the rate of $1^{1}/_{4}$–$1^{1}/_{2}$ pounds per 100 square feet, or test soil and follow recommendations
Mottling of lower leaves at margins or tips or between veins; leaves wilt from bottom up	Magnesium deficiency	Use 1 pound of Epsom salt per 1000 square feet, or test soil and follow recommendations
Mottled yellowing leaves; stunted growth	Manganese deficiency	Use manganese sulfate, or test soil and follow recommendations
Dark green, olive gray leaf edges; edges curl upward	Copper deficiency	Use 6 ounces of copper sulfate per 1000 square feet, or test soil and follow recommendations
Mottling, yellowing, or scorching of the tissues between veins	Zinc deficiency	Use 8 ounces of zinc sulfate per 1000 square feet, or test soil and follow recommendations
Yellow leaves; green veins	Iron deficiency	Use a soluble iron complex, iron sulfate, or chelated iron, or test soil and follow recommendations
Young leaves turn pale green to yellow; older leaves remain green	Sulfur deficiency	Most soils contain adequate amounts of sulfur; if not, test soil and follow recommendations
Stem tips die; distortion of young stems	Calcium deficiency	Spray plants with calcium nitrate or add calcium sulfate (gypsum), or test soil and follow recommendations
Leaves turn pale green or yellow; leaves crinkled, stunted	Molybdenum deficiency	Use about 1 teaspoon of sodium or ammonium molybdate per 1000 square feet, or test soil and follow recommendations

CHAPTER FOUR

When
and
How to
Plant

J ust how do you know when to plant so that everything comes up rapidly and keeps right on going to maturity? I really become frustrated when I turn a seed package over to read the planting instructions and they merely say, "Plant after all danger of frost has passed." Unfortunately, although this advice is good as far as it goes, it is inadequate because different classes of vegetables need different amounts of growing heat. Let's begin by looking at the question of cool and warm seasons.

Mother Nature's Time Clock

Vegetables are divided into warm season and cool season crops. Generally, plants that we harvest for their fruit—such as tomatoes, squash, peppers, eggplant, melons, and lima beans—need a lot of heat and long days to grow well. If there isn't enough heat during the day to satisfy a plant's heat requirements, it will just sit there and do nothing. We've planted tomatoes in April, for instance, and wondered why they weren't growing. Then suddenly the days started to turn warm and the plants took off. Since then, I've experimented with planting tomatoes at one week intervals starting in March. Our early plants never seem to reach maturity any faster than the plants set out later, because their development is held back by cool weather.

Cool season plants, on the other hand, do quite well when the weather is on the cool side. These are generally the leafy and root vegetables: carrots, beets, spinach, cabbage, and lettuce. You also have to include peas as a cool season plant, even though you harvest the fruit. When the weather is cool and the days short, these plants put all their effort into forming leafy or root materials, but when the days begin to warm up, they stop producing leafy material and eventually go to seed. As a result, you

---

TABLE 4-1. COOL-SEASON CROPS—ADAPTED TO 55° TO 70°F

TOLERANT OF SOME FROST:
Asparagus, beets, broccoli, Brussels sprouts, cabbage, kale, mustard greens, New Zealand spinach, onions, radishes, spinach, turnips, and rutabagas.

INTOLERANT OF FROST AT MATURITY:
Carrots, cauliflower, endive, lettuce, peas, rhubarb, Swissh chard.

WARM SEASON CROPS—REQUIRING 65° TO 80°F DAY AND NIGHT
(AND READILY DAMAGED BY FROST):
Beans, corn, cucumbers, eggplant, melons, okra, peppers, squash, tomatoes.

generally have to plant cool season vegetables early so that they can achieve the right size before the weather becomes too hot. You can also plant them late so that they mature in the cooler days of fall.

Besides warm season and cool season vegetables, we also have early and late varieties of most vegetables. The early varieties require less heat to mature than the late. If you want to start your vegetables early, start with one of the early varieties, then follow through with a late variety for that particular type of vegetable. Or, if you live in an area that is continually cool throughout the summer, never rising above temperatures in the 70s, you might plant only an early variety, because it requires less heat to mature than the late variety.

TABLE 4-2. VEGETABLES BY GROWING SEASON

SPRING	SUMMER	FALL
Beets	Beans	Beets
Broccoli	Cucumbers	Broccoli
Brussels Sprouts	Corn	Carrots
Carrots	Eggplant	Kohlrabi
Cabbage	Melons	Lettuce
Cauliflower	Peppers	Radishes
Onions	Pumpkins	Spinach
Radishes	Squash	Turnips
Scallions	Tomatoes	
Turnips		

All of this means that you have to watch the heat requirements of particular plants to know when to plant in your area. Experienced gardeners know exactly when to plant for best results. For the rest of us, nature provides a guide that we can use effectively to know when to plant. This guide relies on the blooming of fairly common plants, and since mother nature does all the juggling herself, the system is far more accurate than arbitrary planting rules or a good guess. Here's what to watch for:

TABLE 4-3. MOTHER NATURE'S PLANTING GUIDE

CONDITION	PLANT
Development of color in flowers from spring bulbs, such as tulips or narcissus	Plant beets, carrots, leaf lettuce, onions, peas, radishes, and spinach
Appearance of plum and cherry blossoms	Plant head lettuce
Appearance of apple, cherry, quince, and strawberry blossoms	Plant everything else—cucumbers, melons, squash, tomatoes, and so on

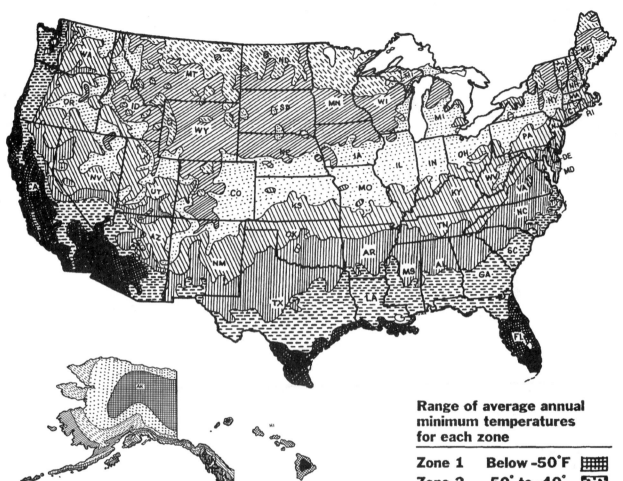

Range of average annual minimum temperatures for each zone

Zone 1	Below -50°F	
Zone 2	-50° to -40°	
Zone 3	-40° to -30°	
Zone 4	-30° to -20°	
Zone 5	-20° to -10°	
Zone 6	-10° to 0°	
Zone 7	0° to 10°	
Zone 8	10° to 20°	
Zone 9	20° to 30°	
Zone 10	30° to 40°	
Zone 11	Above 40°	

Last Frost Dates

Zone 1: June 15
Zone 2: May 15–31
Zone 3: May 1–15
Zone 4: April 15–30
Zone 5: April 1–15
Zone 6: March 15–31

Zone 7: March 1–15
Zone 8: February 1–28
Zone 9: January 15–31
Zone 10: January 1–14
Zone 11: Frost free

Figure 4-1. Agricultural zone map.

Planting with a Frost Map

The only problem in referring to a frost map is that it's impossible to group the entire country into clearly defined climatic regions. Within each region you'll find many different miniclimates, where the average date of the last killing frost varies. Spring nighttime temperatures, for instance, are warmer near the ocean, cooler in inland valleys, and still cooler at higher elevations inland. Geographical points only a few miles apart may have radically different temperatures. This means that you can only generalize. A frost map can be helpful, however, in determining approximately when to plant in the spring.

To use the frost map, simply pick out your zone on the map to determine the average date of the last killing frost. The vegetable planting list below will then tell you approximately on what date to plant particular vegetables. For instance, if you live in Zone 3, the average dates of the last killing frost fall between May 1 and May 15. Referring to the vegetable planting list, you will find that you can plant kale sometime between April 1 and April 15, carrots between May 1 and May 15, and tomatoes after May 15, when the ground has warmed up.

TABLE 4-4. PLANTING WITH A FROST MAP

1. In Zones 6, 7, 8, and 9, plant these vegetables from fall to early spring. In all other zones plant these vegetables 2 to 4 weeks before the last killing frost in spring: **Broccoli, Brussels sprouts, kale, lettuce, mustard greens, onions, peas, radishes, rutabagas, turnips.**

2. Plant these vegetables on approximately the date of the last frost. They tolerate cool weather and very light frost: **Beets, cabbage, carrots, cauliflower, Swiss chard.**

3. Plant these vegetables after the ground has warmed up: **Beans, corn, cucumbers, eggplant, melons, okra, peppers, squash, tomatoes.**

Planting by Moon Cycles

Planting by moon cycles sounds like an old superstition, doesn't it? Yet we know, for instance, that both the moon and the sun affect the tides and that the pull is greater at certain times than at others. If you watch the growth of your garden awhile in relation to various phases of the moon, you'll see some startling things. There seem to be noticeable spurts of growth in the garden that coincide with the new moon and the full moon. Some gardeners swear by this and will plant only at times when they feel that the gravitational effect is best.

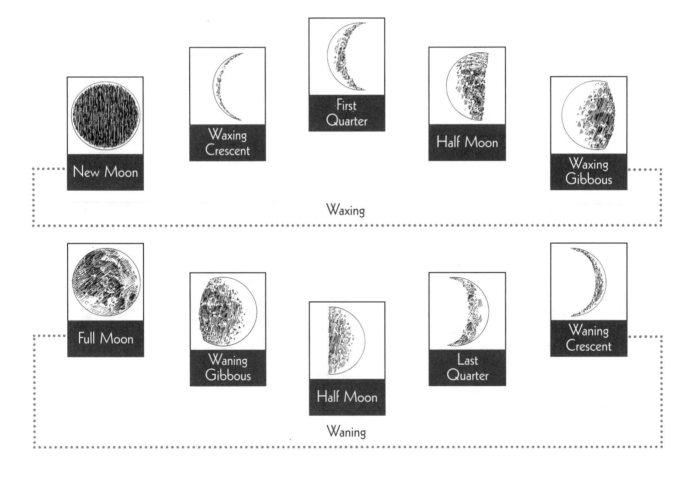

Figure 4-2. Moon cycles.

There was an old woman from the hills of South Carolina who claimed that she could grow green things better than anybody else. Actually she did a good job. She swore by moon cycles and wouldn't plant unless everything was right. At that time we were skeptical, but she would have seeds sprouting up in four or five days while it would take us two weeks or longer. For anybody who'd like to give this method a try, here are her rules:

1. Plant vegetables that grow above ground (such as tomatoes, squash, and lettuce) two nights before the new moon or in the first quarter of the new moon. (She said that this is the first impulse of magnetism.) You can also sow when the moon is waxing from half to full. She also said that when you sow during the waning moon (from full to smaller size), the seeds won't germinate at all but will wait over to the next period.
2. Plant root crops (such as carrots, beets, radishes, and onions) in the third quarter of the moon, when it is waning.
3. Transplant on the waning moon. That way the root will take immediately.

TABLE 4-5. WARM- AND COOL-SEASON CROPS

COOL SEASON*	WARM SEASON**	INTOLERANT OF FROST AT MATURITY
Asparagus	Beans	Carrots
Beets	Corn	Cauliflower
Broccoli	Cucumbers	Endive
Brussels Sprouts	Eggplant	Lettuce
Cabbage	Melons	Peas
Kale	Okra	Rhubarb
Mustard greens	Peppers	Swiss Chard
Onions	Squash	
Radishes	Tomatoes	
Spinach		
Spinach, New Zealand		
Turnips		
Rutabaga		

*Adapted to 55°–70°F. Will tolerate some frost.
**Require 65°–80°F day and night. Readily damaged by frost.

How Far Apart to Set Plants

No matter where the moon may be, you had better know where your plants are. Spacing is very important in the IPS bed. The object is to set out the plants so that their outer leaves just touch one another when the plants are about ³/₄ mature and so that the leaves virtually carpet the bed when fully mature. Thus, the plants shade their own root zones, allowing the bed to retain moisture (calling for less watering) and ensuring that almost no weeds come through. This area beneath the leaves also creates its own fertile microclimate. At maturity there's virtually a little greenhouse under those leaves. Wind bounces off the foliage, and sunshine glances off. The area doesn't become too hot or too cold or dried out by the wind. Many gardeners claim that the micro-climate is extremely important to good intensive garden beds.

When planting vegetables in the IPS garden, space the plants a little closer than generally recommended on seed packets or on instructions for seedlings. Corn, for instance, does quite well planted 8 inches apart in IPS gardens (as opposed to the 12 inches usually recommended for conventional gardens).

TABLE 4-6. INTENSIVE PLANT SPACING IN INCHES

VEGETABLE	SPACING	VEGETABLE	SPACING
Asparagus	12	Leeks	3
Bean, fava	4	Lettuce, head	10
Bean, lima (pole)	10	Lettuce, leaf	6
Bean, lima (bush)	8	Muskmelon	12
Bean, snap (pole)	6	Okra	16
Bean, snap (bush)	4	Onions, bunching	2
Beets	3	Onions	3–4
Broccoli	15	Parsnip	4
Brussels sprouts	15	Peas	2–3
Cabbage, Chinese	10	Peppers	12–24
Cabbage	14	Potatoes	4–10
Carrot	2	Pumpkins	12–18
Cauliflower	15	Radishes	2
Celeriac	8	Rutabaga	6
Celery	6	Shallot	2
Collards	12	Spinach, New Zealand	10
Corn	8	Spinach	4
Cucumbers	6	Squash, summer	12
Eggplant	24	Squash, winter	12–24
Garlic	3	Swiss chard	6
Horseradish	6	Tomatoes	18
Kale	8	Turnips	3
Kohlrabi	6	Watermelon	12–18

How to Start the Vegetables

You have a choice as to how you can start your vegetables:

1. For some vegetables, such as carrots, beets, and other roots, you should sow seeds directly in the ground.
2. For broccoli, cabbage, cauliflower, lettuce, onions, tomatoes, and several other vegetables, you can buy seedlings from the nursery and transplant them directly into your garden.
3. For most vegetables, you can plant seeds in containers indoors and then later transplant the resultant seedlings outdoors, when the weather warms up.

Now let's take a closer look at each of these methods to see how they work into your own gardening plans.

Sowing Seeds Directly

Where do seeds come from? For most of us, they come from the seed racks found in hardware stores, nurseries, grocery stores, and elsewhere. Just look over every seed rack you find and pick out the vegetables that look good to you. The varieties found on racks in your area are generally fine for your particular climate.

There are other places to find seeds. Some of us are incurable seed catalog fans. Seed catalogs are good dream material. (In the appendix you'll find the addresses of companies that will mail you seed catalogs.)

To get good results with certain plants, you must start with seeds. Such plants as bush beans, beets, carrots, dwarf peas, radishes, rutabagas, spinach, and turnips don't transplant very well, so you'll want to sow their seeds directly into the garden bed. Here's how to do it:

1. Soak the soil the day before planting.
2. Scatter the seed evenly across the bed (or a portion of it), and try not to miss the corners. Try to space the seeds roughly according to the spacing table. The bigger seeds—such as those for radishes and spinach—won't be any problem. You can see exactly where they are; and if you get too many in one spot, you can just move them around. With tiny seeds—such as those

for carrots—you'll have more of a problem, but you can get the hang of it by practicing with coffee grounds over a piece of paper.

3. Cover the seeds with fine soil. Different vegetable seeds require different depths below the soil surface (consult the instructions in Chapter 5).

4. Later, if too many plants come up, crowding one another, don't worry about it. Just thin them out a bit, pulling up a number of the plants so that the ones that are left are more evenly distributed according to the desired spacing. (You'll get a dividend here: The small beets and carrots that you pull up can be extra tender and delicious.)

Not all the seeds will come up. Germination is never 100 percent— a few seeds in any collection will be sterile. Even the germination of fertile seeds is affected by soil moisture, depth of planting, and other conditions that are rarely perfect.

Unused seeds, by the way, can be saved for the next year. The germination rate will drop only slightly from year to year. Simply seal the seed packets airtight with tape, and store them in a very cool place.

Buying Seedlings and Transplanting

Some vegetables—such as broccoli, Brussels sprouts, cabbage, cauliflower, eggplant, peppers, and tomatoes—seem to get off to a better start if they are first grown from seed indoors and then later transplanted into the garden as seedlings. (Lettuce, melons, and onions seem to develop well either way—from seeds sown directly in the garden or from transplants.) In general, transplanting gives you a head start because you have little plants already developed by the time that it's warm enough outdoors to plant. Also, you avoid having to thin plants, since you space the seedlings directly.

If you decide to buy vegetables as small plants, you can generally find most of the popular varieties at your local nursery or garden center.

When planting seedlings, dig a hole in your IPS bed big enough to avoid bending or squeezing the root mass. Try not to disturb the roots any more than possible when transferring to the ground, and, once the plant is in, make sure that the soil is firm but not packed around the roots.

For transplanting, you can probably get by with a small trowel. But there are other tools that can be useful. One of the best is a pointed stick, just a small dowel with a rounded point. Use it in your left hand to poke in the soil. With your right hand hold the seedling in the hole, and then, with the stick, fill in around the roots and push the soil back.

Starting Seeds Indoors in Containers

Why bother to start your own seeds indoors at all when it's a lot easier to just go down to the nursery, pick out what seedlings you need, and come back and plunk them in your garden? The reasons for developing your own seedlings are both psychological and practical. The psychological reason is purely the joy and feeling of accomplishment of having grown entirely yours.

TABLE 4-7. WHEN TO START SEEDLINGS INDOORS		
1 MONTH*	**2 MONTHS***	**3 MONTHS***
Celeriac	Broccoli	Brussels Sprouts
Eggplant	Cabbage	Lettuce
Leeks	Cauliflower	Pumpkins
Onions	Melons	Squash
Peppers	Tomatoes	

*Before you intend to plant in garden

The practical reasons are several. First, buying seeds is cheaper than buying seedlings. Second, only a relatively small selection of vegetable varieties are sold at nurseries; thus, if you want to experiment with new or unusual varieties, you must grow your plants from seeds. And third, seedlings (whether you grow them yourself or purchase them from a nursery) are a great advantage for such warm-weather crops as cucumbers, melons, squash, and tomatoes. These crops don't do well until the weather warms up and outdoor temperatures stay in the 60s or above. So, by planting them indoors early and transplanting them later, you can get a head start on the weather.

Here are some methods for starting vegetables indoors:

Metal Foil Pans.
1. Purchase metal foil pans at a variety or grocery store. To fill them, make up a soil mix of equal parts sand, loam (soil with

a lot or organic material), and compost or peat moss. Screen this mixture so that the particles are fairly small. You can also buy prepared planting mixes at any nursery.

2. Plant the seeds an inch or two apart, and cover them with soil or vermiculite. Vermiculite—light mineral granules that can be bought packaged at any nursery—is best because it holds moisture well.

3. Place the containers in a warm place (above 60° to 65°F), where they will be in full sun or under a fluorescent light for about twelve hours a day, if possible (just do the best you can). For fast germination of the seeds of eggplant, peppers, and tomatoes, you'll need a soil temperature of 75° to 85°F. Within a couple of weeks, in any event, most plants will have begun to poke through the soil.

4. When the second pair of leaves opens, move each plant to a separate small pot or to a small paper cup, or space the plants 3 inches apart in another loaf pan.

5. Transplant the seedlings outside according to the dates given earlier in this chapter in the vegetable planting list.

Peat Pots

Peat pots are small individual pots or pellets, square or round, made of compressed peat moss or other materials; you can buy them at any nursery. Some types are already filled with soil; others you must fill with potting soil. Into each pot sow a seed or two; and when the plant is several inches tall, transplant pot and all to the garden bed. The roots grow through the walls of the pot, and the plants don't suffer any transplant shock. You don't lose any soil from around the roots, and the nutrients are built right into the pot. These peat pots are especially good for cucumber, melons, and squash, because disturbing their roots by transplanting tends to check their growth.

Figure 4-3. Peat pod containers.

Figure 4-4. Stages of seeds planted in peat pods.

Starter Kits

If using peat pots seems too hard, you can buy starter kits for tomatoes and other vegetables—the kits come with a container, soil, and seeds—already put together. All you have to do is take the lid off the container and water the soil. (Sometimes, though, you'll find the seeds in a separate packet that you sow yourself.)

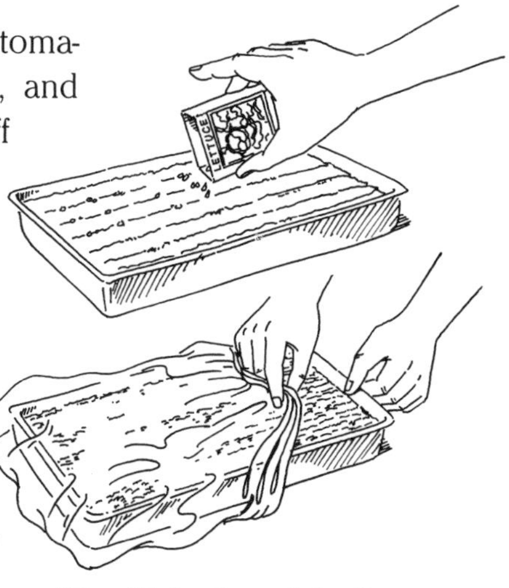

Flats

You can also start seeds in a flat; a good size is a 14-by-24-inch box about 3 inches deep. Again, use the soil mix of sand, loam, and compost or peat moss, or buy big packages of planting soil. Soak the soil in the flat thoroughly. For small seeds, sow gently over the surface, then press in. For larger seeds, make furrows with a pencil—2 inches apart and at the depth required for particular vegetables. Then drop in your seeds, and cover them with planting mix or vermiculite. Place the flat in a warm light spot like that described for metal foil pans. When the first two sets of leaves have developed, transplant the seedlings individually to small pots or to other flats, spacing them 3 inches apart. When transferring seedlings, always be careful to disturb the roots as little as possible.

Figure 4-5. Starting seeds in a flat.

Hardening the Transplants

Before actually planting the young seedlings in the soil outdoors, you should get them used to outdoor conditions. Adjust the young plants to outdoor temperatures by putting them outdoors (in their containers) when it's sunny. Bring them indoors whenever frost seems likely, especially overnight. In one way or another, expose them to the lower temperatures for about two weeks before setting them out in your garden bed.

There are, of course, more complicated methods of growing young seedlings for transplanting. But this book is dedicated to giving you the easiest most hassle-free ways possible.

Other Seeding Methods

By making coverings that intensify heat, it's possible to plant outdoors before the weather really gets warm enough to expose particular plants fully to the elements. For melons, for instance, you can make small frames or boxes, each 1 by 1 foot and 3 or 4 inches high, with a clear vinyl plastic cover, and place them on your prepared garden bed. Plant eight to ten seeds within each frame. Remove the plastic cover on warm days; replace it on cold nights or days. Remove the cover entirely when the danger of frost has passed.

Another idea is to make "jug houses" for your plants. You do this by cutting off the bottoms of gallon bottles and setting the bottomless jugs over your planted seeds. Or you can simply buy commercially made waxed-paper plant protectors (often called hot caps) from a nursery. All of these methods will give your seedlings a faster start. Just make sure that you remove the hot caps, jugs, or plastic sheets on warm days, or your plants are liable to burn.

How to Stretch Your Crops

You probably know gardeners who produce so many vegetables out of their small gardens that you wonder if they aren't hauling them in from the country. They aren't. They've just mastered those little tricks that make mother nature work overtime. These miracle "crop stretchers" are intercropping, succession planting, and catch cropping.

Intercropping

Intercropping simply means planting quick-maturing crops between slowermaturing crops. With intercropping you can plant quick-maturing radishes, green onions, or leaf lettuce between rows of corn or tomatoes. Because you plant corn and tomatoes far apart—8 inches for corn and 18 inches for tomatoes—you will harvest the intercrops before the corn and tomato plants have become big enough to crowd the smaller plants out. That's getting double duty out of your IPS bed.

Succession Planting

In succession planting, later crops are planted as soon as you take out early ones (make sure that you add compost and additional organic fertilizer before you replant). For instance, harvest spinach and then plant beans, or take out broccoli and then plant corn. Or plant early, midseason, and late-maturing varieties of the same kind of vegetable. Any combination of early and late varieties stretches the productivity of your garden. Here are some suggestions for succession planting:

Beets followed by brussels sprouts
Snap beans followed by cabbage, cauliflower, kale, lettuce, or spinach
Peas followed by beans

Catch Cropping

In catch cropping, quick-maturing plants are planted in places from which you've just harvested larger, slower growing vegetables. You can harvest a couple of broccoli plants in late summer, for instance, and then grow radishes or green onions in the very same space.

The basic rule here is simple: Don't leave bare ground unplanted.

TABLE 4-8. SEED GERMINATION

VEGETABLE	MINIMUM FEDERAL STANDARD GERMINATION (%)	SEEDS PER OUNCE (AVERAGE)	RELATIVE LONGEVITY (YEARS)
Asparagus	60	1,400	3
Bean, Lima	70	20–70	3
Bean, Snap	75	100	3
Beets	65	2,000	4
Broccoli	75	8,100	3
Brussels Sprouts	70	8,500	4
Cabbage	75	7,700	4
Cabbage, Chinese	75	7,000	3
Carrots	55	22,000	3
Cauliflower	75	8,600	4
Celeriac	55	50,000	3
Celery	55	76,000	3
Chicory	65	20,000	4
Corn	75	140	2
Cucumbers	80	1,100	5
Eggplant	60	7,000	4
Endive	70	17,000	5
Kale	75	10,000	4
Kohlrabi	75	9,200	3
Leeks	60	9,900	2
Lettuce	80	26,000	6
Muskmelon	75	1,100	5
Okra	50	500	2
Onions	70	8,500	1
Parsnip	60	18,000	1
Peas	80	50–230	3
Peppers	55	4,500	2
Pumpkins	75	200	4
Radishes	75	3,100	4
Rutabaga	75	11,000	4
Salsify	75	2,000	1
Spinach	60	2,900	3
Spinach, New Zealand	40	430	3
Squash	75	180–380	4
Swiss Chard	65	1,500	4
Tomatoes	75	10,000	4
Turnips	80	14,000	4
Watermelon	70	320	4

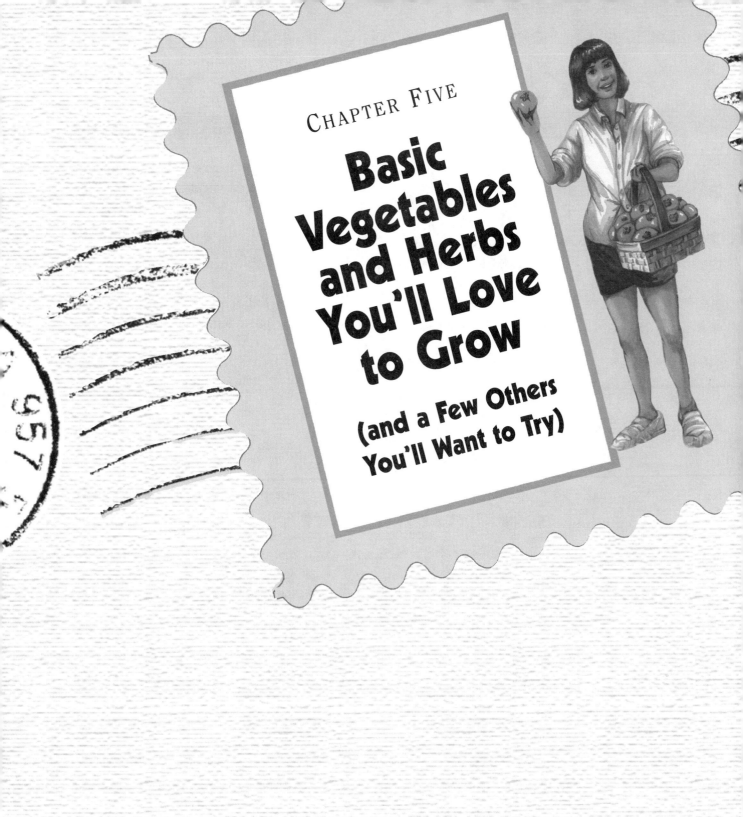

CHAPTER FIVE

Basic Vegetables and Herbs You'll Love to Grow

(and a Few Others You'll Want to Try)

Vegetables

Which vegetables should you grow in your intensive postage stamp garden? That depends a lot on you. When selecting vegetables, consider which vegetables you like and whether those particular vegetables are suited to the space that you have available. It's also important to select varieties that grow well in your geographical area, but generally anything purchased from local seed racks will do reasonably well.

Another important consideration is that some vegetables grow well in small gardens and some don't. For example, if you're planting a 6-by-6-foot garden, a pumpkin vine or a large squash vine just won't do.

In this chapter we include all vegetables that grow well in intensive postage stamp gardens as well as a few that are just marginally acceptable. The marginal ones, like cabbage and asparagus, are here because they're old favorites; they can be grown if you're willing to put up with a few special considerations (which are discussed later).

In an IPS garden you must consider how much ground the vegetables take up and just how long they will tie up that space. Most pumpkins and winter squash, for instance, have large vines that run all over the place. Potatoes take up only about a square foot per plant, but they tie up the ground a good four months. It's better to buy them at the supermarket. The same is true of parsnips (four months), celery (four to six months), and a few others. They are all great vegetables in their own right, but they are just not suitable for the type of high-yield gardening that we're discussing here.

One popular fad has been to grow so-called midget vegetables. The midget vegetables, whose miniature plants are $1/2$ to $1/5$ the size of those for regular vegetables, are space savers all right; and there are now quite a few of them around: cabbage, corn, cucumbers, lettuce, and melons. The only problem is that if you're looking for quantity, you'll have to grow twice or three times as many of these midgets to obtain the same production that you would get from regular-sized plants. Try them if you like, but we'd just as soon plant the other varieties in our own garden.

Harvesting

When considering individual vegetables, you should also think about harvesting them. Actually, when we're ready to eat something, we just go out and pick it. But we probably pay for this haphazardness with a flavor loss. After all, there is a right and a wrong time to pick vegetables. Many plants go through a chemical change converting sugar to starch (this is especially true of corn). The trick is to catch them when the sugar (or flavor) content is highest. The general rule is to try to pick vegetables before they're completely mature and then cook them as soon as possible. Vegetables picked this way are far tastier than anything you can buy in the supermarket, because by the time vegetables travel from the commercial grower, to the wholesale market, to the store, and then to you, the best part of the flavor has already been lost.

In the list of "popular varieties" under each vegetable in this chapter, we give the days to maturity—that is, the average length of time that it takes vegetables to ripen, from planting to maturity. The figures are averages only and are affected by sunniness, cloudiness, temperatures, and other climatic variables in different regions of the country. Moreover, seed catalogs aren't always clear on what the figures mean. For most vegetables, the maturity days denote the period of time from planting seeds outdoors to harvesting. But for some vegetables, such as tomatoes, peppers, and eggplant, the maturity days denote the period of time from planting seedlings outdoors to harvesting; this period has, of course, been preceded by four to eight weeks of indoor growing.

Home Storage

Fresh vegetables can be stored in your home for long periods provided that you have storage areas of proper temperatures and proper dampness or dryness. As a general rule, the cooler you keep vegetables the better. Individual vegetables, however, have their own temperature and humidity requirements.

Beets, carrots, turnips, and rutabagas like lots of moisture and a temperature between 34° and 42°F. You can store these root vegetables in a damp cellar or possibly in a cool garage, preferably in a container like a garbage can, with rags that you wet down occasionally on top of the vegetables.

Cabbage stores best with a moderate amount of moisture and a temperature between 48° and 62°F. Individual squash should be spread out so that air can circulate between them.

Freezing Vegetables

There are a few general rules that you should follow when preparing vegetables for freezing. First, you should wash the vegetables in cold water.

Most vegetables must then be immersed in boiling water for two to four minutes in order to halt the enzyme action that causes vegetables to lose flavor and become tough. The parboiling is called blanching. Immediately after removing the vegetables from the boiling water, plunge them into a pan of ice water, leaving them in the pan until they're cool. Finally, before placing the vegetables in the freezer, pack them in some kind of container. You can use heavy plastic freezer bags, empty milk cartons (or other wax-lined containers) sealed with tape, or simple plastic freezer containers that can be purchased at most supermarkets and variety stores.

Asparagus

Cool season crop. Rated marginal for IPS gardens.

Unlike most other vegetables, which are annuals, asparagus is a perennial plant; once it's planted and gets going, it just keeps right on pouring out a continuous food supply every season for the next fifteen years or so.

Planting

Actually, asparagus is not the best plant for an IPS garden because it tends to take over and eat up space. But if you're an asparagus lover as I am, you'll find a way to sneak it in somewhere. You definitely, however, don't want your asparagus in a small IPS bed with other vegetables. You can successfully grow it alone in a 4-by-4-foot IPS bed surrounded by a frame. Grown this way, it stays fairly well within boundaries. Asparagus also does extremely well in a flower bed because its ornamental fronds blend in nicely.

You can start asparagus from seed, but if you do, you'll throw away a whole year right there. Grown from seeds, it will not produce its first crop until the third year. Therefore, you had best buy one-year-old roots from your local nursery and transplant them directly into the garden. Even using roots, you will not get a crop until the second year.

In some ways, asparagus and the IPS bed were made for each other—asparagus demands rich, loose soil that's nice and deep. In early spring, just plant the roots about 12 inches apart. That's pretty close for asparagus, but it seems to work out all right. For each plant, make a hole about 5 inches in diameter and 8 inches deep. At the bottom of the hole, spread out the roots, crown side up, and cover with 2 inches of soil. As the plant grows, simply keep filling the hole with additional soil; but do not cover the crown tip. Two to three months after planting, the hole should have been filled to ground level.

Unfortunately, asparagus doesn't grow nearly as fast as other vegetables. Although you'll get some spears the first year, don't cut them, but let them go to foliage. When they turn brown in the fall, cut them to the ground. The second year, though, you can harvest spears for about four weeks. The year after, you can cut spears for eight to ten weeks.

Feed asparagus with fish emulsion a couple of times a year (apply according to the instructions on the bottle).

Crop Stretching

Asparagus is extremely prolific without much help.

Popular Varieties

Be sure to choose rust-resistant varieties of asparagus. Here are a few that are successful:

JERSEY GIANT	$\frac{1}{2}$-inch diameter. Widely adapted. All plants are male. Seed source: BURP JUN SHE THO TWI
MARY WASHINGTON	A prolific variety. Thick, heavy, dark-green shoots. Seed source: ALL BURG BURP BUT DEG FAR FIS GAR GUR HEN HIG JUN LED MEY PIN RED ROS SEE TILL VER
WALTHAM	Tighter heads than most other varieties. Easy to grow. Seed source: GUR HEN

Typical Problems

You'll have few problems with asparagus—except for insect pests (which we take up in Chapter 8).

Harvesting

When the asparagus spears are 8 to 10 inches long and when the buds at the tips are still compressed, you can harvest by cutting the spears at ground level or a few inches below. You can also snap the spears off by bending them over sharply until they break.

To freeze asparagus, use only the tender portions (the tops and smaller shoots) and prepare them immediately. Blanch them in boiling water two to four minutes, cool rapidly, place in containers, and freeze.

Asparagus Growing Tip

Better Production: To grow more asparagus, strip off the green peppercorn-size berries as they appear on the fronds of the female plants. This increases the yield almost immediately.

Beans

Warm season crop. Rated good to excellent for IPS gardens.

Bean plants are literally small food factories that really give you your money's worth in the IPS garden. In addition, they do double duty, because they're one of the legumes (peas being the other major vegetable) that help to improve the fertility of the soil. That is, bacteria living in the nodules on the roots of legumes take soil nitrogen in unusual forms and combine it with sugars from the legumes to produce ammonia, a nitrogen compound that plants can use. Legumes thus actually conserve and restore the soil.

Primarily there are two types of beans grown by home gardeners: snap and lima. (Snaps are also called string beans, green beans, or wax beans. Limas are sometimes called butter beans.) Both snaps and limas come in bush varieties, which grow 15 to 20 inches tall, and in pole or climbing varieties, which grow as vines 5 to 8 feet high. Some people recommend bush beans for small gardens, because they mature in less than sixty days and grow three or four plants in every square foot of space.

Planting

Beans are heat lovers, so plant the seeds after the ground has warmed up in the spring. Plant seeds of bush types 1 inch deep and about 4 inches apart and of pole beans 1 inch deep and about 10 inches apart. Make plantings every two weeks (until about sixty days before the first fall frost) in order to harvest beans all summer long. Beans need lots of water and shouldn't be allowed to dry out while they're still growing.

In an IPS garden the nutrients that you've already put in the soil will carry your beans through the season, but they'll do better if you give them some fish emulsion just as the pods begin to form (apply according to the instructions on the bottle).

Crop Stretching

Although horizontal space in the IPS garden is tight, you have almost unlimited vertical space. Therefore, the more you can get your plants up in the air the more food your garden will crank out. Here are some methods that work well for beans:

1. Set up four 6-foot posts (preferably 2 by 2s) at the corners of one square foot of space. Plant two seeds per pole; the vines twine up the pole. It's possible to place two or three of these setups around the garden.
2. Set up a 6-foot post (again a 2 by 2), and at the top affix two 1-foot cross arms at right angles to each other. From the ends of these cross arms, run strings or wires to the bottoms of the post. Plant 4 to 6 seeds around the post. The vines twine up the strings or wires.
3. Between two 6-foot posts (preferably 4 by 4s), spaced about 6 feet apart, run a sheet of chicken wire, creating a kind of trellis or fence. Along the fence, plant seeds about 8 inches apart, and train the vines up the chicken wire.

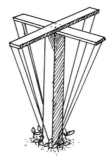

Figure 5-1. A simple bean post.

Popular Varieties

Bush green

BLUE LAKE BUSH	52 to 60 days 6½-inch, round, dark green pods. Seed source: ABU ALL BURR DEG FIS HIG MEY ORN POR ROS STO TIL
CONTENDER	42 to 55 days 5- to 7-inch, medium green pots. Seed Source: BOU BURR DEG FAR HEN LED PON POR RED SOU STO VER WIL
E-Z PICK BLUE LAKE BUSH	49 days 6- to 6½-inch dark green pods. Seed source: GUR POR
ROMA II	59 days 4½-inch, flat, medium green Italian-type. Seed source: BURP COM JUN LED MEY ORN PAR POR TWI VER WIL
TOPCROP	48 to 52 days 6-inch, medium green pods. Seed source: BURR DEG FAR FIS GUR HEN JUN MEY PIN PON POR ROS SOU TWI VER WIL

BUSH WAX

BRITTLE WAX   50 to 58 days 6- to 7-inch, mildly flavored, yellow pod.
                     Seed source: BURP FAR GUR PON TIL

BUSH PURPLE

ROYAL BURGUNDY   50 to 60 days 6-inch, round, curved, purple pod turns
                     green when cooked. Seed source: BURP COM COO DEG
                     GUR HEN JUN LED SEE SHE STO TER TIL TWI VER
                     WILL

Bush Bean Growing Tips

Protecting Beans: Radishes planted around beans enhance the
flavor of the beans and help repel bean beetles. Radishes are ready
every twenty-four to thirty days, so reseed every ten days or so.

POLE SNAP

BLUE LAKE   55 to 66 days 6-inch pods are dark green and oval. Seed
                     source: ABU ALL BOU BURG BURR GAR GUR HEN JLH
                     JUN PAR PON POR ROS SEE SHE STO TER THO TIL
                     VER WILL

KENTUCKY WONDER   58 to 74 days 7- to 9-inch, oval, silvery green pods. Seed
                     source: ABU ALL BURG BURR BUT COM DEG FAR GAR
                     GUR HEN HIG MEY NIC ORG PIN POR ROS SEE SEED
                     SOU STO TER THO TIL VER WIL WILL

ROMANO POLE   64 to 70 days 5½-inch-wide, flat pods. Italian variety. Seed
                     source: ABU ALL BURP BUT COM DEG FAR GAR HEN
                     LED NIC ORG PIN PON RED SEE SEED THO TIL VER
                     WILL

Pole Bean Growing Tips

Bush Pole Beans: To miraculously turn pole beans into bushlike
vines, pinch out the growing tips every time they exceed 12 inches.
This keeps them at easy-picking height and doubles the crop over comparable bush beans.

Bean Tower Power: Beans go mad when properly supported by a
bean tower. This tower of bean power grows up to 20 pounds of
Kentucky Wonder string beans a season. Construct the tower from ³/₄
inch PVC pipe. Drill ¹/₈ inch holes, 6 inches apart, in the bottom cross-
pieces. By hooking them up to a hose, you can irrigate the root zones
of the plants below ground.

BUSH LIMA

BABY FORDHOOK BUSH	67-70 days 2³/₄-by-³/₄-inch dark green, slightly curved pods. Small seeds. Seed source: BURP MEY VER
FORDHOOK 242	75 to 85 days 3- to 4-inch pods. Plump seeded. Seed source: ALL BURP BURR COM DEG GUR HEN JOH JUN LED MEY ORN PAR PON POR SEE STO TWI VER WIL
HENDERSON BUSH	65 to 81 days 3-inch, flat, dark green, slightly curved pod. Small seeded. Seed source: ALL BURP GUR MEY PAR PIN POR ROS SEE TWI VER WIL

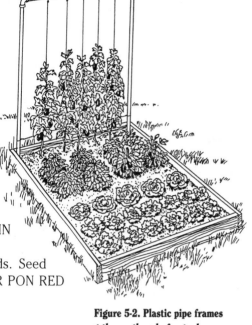

Figure 5-2. Plastic pipe frames at the north end of a garden are great for beans.

POLE LIMA

CAROLINA	79 days 3¹/₂-by-2-inch wide, flat, medium green pods. Seed source: BURP HEN MEY PIN RED WIL
KING OF THE GARDEN	88 to 90 days 5- to 8-inch dark green pods. Seed source: COM DEG GUR JUN LED MEY PAR PON RED SEE SOU STO TWI VER

Lima Bean Growing Tips

Peak Flavor: The large white or speckled lima beans are at their peak flavor when the beans are fully formed in the pods. To test, simply shell several pods you think are full, then choose pods that have a similar feel. This test will not work for baby limas or baby butter bean pods.

Early Harvest: You can gain a couple of weeks on the season by sprouting lima bean seeds on a windowsill inside wet paper towels. When they start to sprout, set them outside with the sprout tips showing above the soil. Stick the sprouting seeds in the ground the minute the soil warms up.

BUSH SHELL BEANS

RED KIDNEY	95 to 100 days 20- to 22-inch plants set large, flat, green pods that produce pinkish red to mahogany seeds. Seed source: ALL BUT COM DEG FAR GAR GUR HEN LED PAR PON VER WILL

A NOVELTY TO TRY

YARD LONG BEAN	80 days Pick at 12 to 15 inches for best flavor. Seed source: BURP COM GLE LED LEJ NIC RED SEE SOU STO SUN TIL VER WILL

Typical Problems

My vines don't produce well. Sometimes the bean ends shrivel up. They are probably not getting enough water. Beans need considerable water and shouldn't ever dry out while growing. When there isn't enough moisture in the soil, the bean ends will sometimes shrivel up. Also, you may not be picking the young beans as they mature; old pods left on the vine will cut the production of new ones.

My beans didn't come up at all. You probably planted before the soil warmed up. Bean seeds won't germinate in cold soil, nor will they come up well if the soil has crusted over. A sprouting bean seed must push the small stem and leaves through the soil; if the ground is too hard at the surface, it can't do this. (This generally isn't a problem in an IPS garden because we made it nice and loose and grainy before planting.)

Beans can also get in trouble if they are not well fertilized. If you give them a little supplement of fish emulsion, that should do the trick.

Harvesting

Pick beans when they're fairly small. The flavor of small beans is better, and keeping the plants picked helps extend the bearing season.

Freeze only the small tender beans. Remove their ends, cut them in small lengths, blanch in boiling water for one-and-a-half minutes, cool, place in containers, and freeze.

Beets

Cool season crop. Rated excellent for IPS gardens.

Beets are double-barreled vegetables; that is, you can eat both the roots and the leaves, and both are delicious. Beets are probably an almost perfect vegetable for the IPS garden because they don't take up much room and they grow like mad. (We've produced as many as four hundred beets in a 4-by-4-foot area.)

Planting

Beets generally like cool weather, but they're also fairly tolerant of a wide temperature range. Once started, beets need to grow rapidly without stopping, which means that you've got to keep them watered.

In an IPS bed you scatter seed 1 inch apart and $\frac{1}{2}$ inch deep, but be careful with beet seeds because, unlike most other vegetables, they come in clumps of three or more seeds (called seedballs) that produce three or more plants. This means that it's awfully easy to sow too many. Simply thin out the little plants as you go along, and cook up the young beet greens. You'll probably also want to divide your beet area into quarters, planting each quarter five to ten days apart to ensure a continuous harvest.

Crop stretching

Plant beets in any spot where you've taken out another vegetable—corn, for instance.

Popular Varieties

You have a choice of globe-shaped, semiglobe-shaped, long-rooted, red or golden beets, as well as beets used mostly for greens.

RED GLOBE

DETROIT DARK RED   55 to 60 days 3-inch diameter, dark red. Excellent for greens. Seed source: ABU ALL BURP BURR DEG FAR GAR GUR HEN LEJ ORG PIN PON POR SEE SEED SOU STO TIL TWI VER WIL WILL

RED ACE   51 to 53 days Deep red, smooth, round roots. Seed source: COM JOH JUN LED MEY PAR PIN STO TER TIL TWI VER

SEMIGLOBE

EARLY WONDER   48 to 55 days Dark red, all-purpose beet. Seed source: ABU ALL BURP BURR BUT COM COO DEG FAR FIS GAR GLE GUR HIG JOH LED MEY PIN PLA PON SOU TER TIL TWI VER WIL WILL

CYLINDRICAL

CYLINDRA   55 to 60 days Dark red, 8 inches long, 2 to 3 inches across. Seed source: BURP BURR COM FAR FIS GAR GOU HEN JUN PAR PIN PON SEE SHE TIL TWI WILL

BABY BEETS

LITTLE BALL   43 to 58 days Red, 3-inch diameter ball that forms rapidly. Harvest when 1^1/$_2$ inches. Seed source: BURP HIG ORN PAR PIN SEE SHE STO TER TIL TWI WILL

BEETS FOR GREENS

GREEN TOP BUNCHING 65 days Round, bright roots, medium-size tops. Seed source: DEG STO

NOVELTIES TO TRY

CHIOGGIA	50 to 55 days Italian heirloom variety that has rings of cherry red and creamy white interior. Seed source: COO JOH NIC ORN PIN SEE SEED SHE SOU
GOLDEN BEET	50 to 60 days Golden orange, small round beet. Seed source: ABU BURP COO FIS GLE GUR HIG JUN LED NIC ORN PIN PON SEE SHE STO SOU WILL

Typical Problems

My beets tasted woody. The plants are not getting enough moisture. As with most other vegetables, you have to keep beets growing full blast until they mature. Lack of water will slow them down and make them taste woody.

My beets didn't get very big. You sowed too many seeds and forgot to thin. Thin the small plants, leaving only one plant every inch or so.

Harvesting

Pick beets when small (just pick one to see how big they have grown). Big beets get tough and taste blah.

For freezing, pick small beets, peel them, blanch in boiling water four-and-a-half to five minutes, cool, place in containers, and freeze. Large beets can also be frozen, but they usually lack flavor.

Beet Growing Tip

Redder Beets: To produce bright red beets, sprinkle the bed with a light scattering of common salt, about a spoonful per foot. This improves the growth and color of the roots and eliminates white rings.

Broccoli

Cool season crop. Rated good for IPS gardens.

You might call broccoli the IPS gardener's best friend in the cabbage family. It's big. After all, it can grow 3 or 4 feet high and branch prolifically. Also, it's easy to grow, and once it gets started it just keeps right on producing for a month or two. All you have to do is cut off the terminal head and the side shoots start to develop in small clusters right away. It's also possible to grow some of the other members of the cabbage family in our IPS garden, but they tend to be overlarge, and we have to be very selective in handling them.

Planting

Being a cool weather plant, broccoli can be a problem because it's pretty sensitive to heat. It'll grow like mad, then all of a sudden—during a heat wave—begin to flower. After that, it's all over as a vegetable.

Buy broccoli from your nursery as small plants. This is the standard planting method, because starting from seeds will take you several weeks longer to get a mature vegetable. Four to six plants are about all that an IPS garden can handle because they must be spaced 15 inches apart. You can plant them in the spring a couple of weeks before the last frost, then again in midsummer. Midsummer is probably the best time because the weather will have cooled by the time the plants reach maturity.

If you prefer starting from seeds, plant them indoors in peat pots $1/4$ inch deep about five to six weeks before you intend to set the plants outside. (The other indoor planting methods described in Chapter 4 can also be used.)

Broccoli, like other members of the cabbage family, is a heavy feeder, so give it some fish emulsion at least once before the heads begin to form (apply according to the instructions on the bottle).

Crop Stretching

Replace harvested broccoli with carrots, beets, or radishes.

Popular Varieties

CALABRESE	70 to 85 days 6-inch-diameter bluish green head. Many side branches. Seed source: ABU BOU FAR JLH NIC PIN RED SEE SOU
PACKMAN	58 to 80 days 10-inch head, excellent side shoots. Seed source: DEG GUR HEN JOH JUN LED LIB MEY NIC PAR PIN POR STO TER TWI WILL
WALTHAM 29	74 to 80 days 4- to 8-inch, slate green head. Lots of side shoots. Seed source: ABU ALL BURR BUT COM DEG LED LIB MEY ROS SEE SOU TIL

Typical Problem

My broccoli flowers before the heads are ready to harvest. You're getting too much heat. If you're having trouble with your spring crop, try planting in midsummer for a fall crop. In mild winter areas, where the temperatures generally don't drop below freezing, you can plant broccoli from early fall through late winter.

Harvesting

Broccoli is ready to cut when the tops are hard and green, just before the buds begin to open. You simply cut the stem a few leaves below the main head. The bud shoots that subsequently form in the leaf joints below the cut will never get more than an inch or two across, but they can be harvested and eaten. If your plants are kept picked, your growing season will continue until warm weather arrives—or, in the fall, until frost.

For freezing broccoli, use the tender portions only. Trim off the woody parts, cut the clusters into small pieces, blanch them in boiling water for two to three minutes, cool rapidly, place in containers, and freeze.

Broccoli Growing Tips

Fully Packed: Broccoli often produces premature, small scattered heads when young plants are subjected to temperatures below 40°F, before or shortly after planting. Solve this by protecting plants in early spring with hot caps or other protective devices.

Broccoli Factory: Some gardeners keep producing edible broccoli buds like they're running a production line. To duplicate this, after harvesting the main head, pick the developing buds every three or four days as long as the plant continues to produce. Once you let a few developing buds flower, the action stops and you're out of business until next season.

Brussels Sprouts

Cool season crop. Rated fair for IPS gardens.

One brussels sprouts plant will keep producing sprouts until you wonder if it's ever going to stop (one plant will produce seventy-five to a hundred sprouts). Brussels sprouts are a member of the cabbage family and are an erect plant that produces ever-growing clusters of sprouts or buds in the axils of the leaves. They're easy to grow—if you live in the right climate.

Planting

Brussels sprouts are a cool weather plant. They do extremely well for you if you in an area of summer fog or in an area where the climate is nice and moist and summer daytime temperatures generally average 65°F or less. They don't do well where the climate is hot and dry.

Because brussels sprouts take quite a lot of space, you probably won't want more than one or two in any single IPS garden. Set the plants out in early summer so that they mature in the colder fall weather. If you have mild winters, with above-freezing temperatures, you can also plant them in the fall for winter harvest.

Most gardeners buy young plants from their local nursery. Set the plants 16 inches apart. As the plants mature, remove all excess leaves except those at the top of the plant.

You can grow brussels sprouts from seed if you like, but you should start them indoors, planting your seeds $\frac{1}{2}$ inch deep in peat pots five or six weeks before you intend to set them outdoors.

Crop Stretching

Interchange brussels sprouts with early maturing crops, such as radishes and leaf lettuce.

Popular Varieties

JADE CROSS	80 to 95 days 24-inch plant yields copiously, oval, blue-green sprouts that grow all the way up the stalk. Seed source: COM GUR HEN JUN PAR PIN PON POR STO WILL
LONG ISLAND IMPROVED	85 to 95 days $\frac{1}{4}$-inch sprouts cover most of the stalk. Seed source: ABU ALL BURR BUT COM DEG FIS GAR HIG LED LEJ LIB MEY PON RED ROS SEE SOU TIL WIL WILL
RUBINE RED	90 to 105 days Red foliage and red sprouts that won't fade when cooked. Seed source: BOU COO GLE GUR HEN ORN PAR PIN SEE VER WILL

Typical Problems

Practically none, other than the weather restrictions already noted.

Harvesting

Pick the lowest sprouts each time you pick, and break off any leaves left below the "sprout." Don't remove the top leaves.

For freezing, first wash the brussels sprouts and then soak them a half hour in salted water (1 teaspoon salt per quart of water). Place them in clear water and bring just to a boil, then drain, chill rapidly, and freeze.

Brussels Sprouts Growing Tips

From Bottom to Top: To harvest brussels sprouts properly, start at the bottom, snapping them off as you go up. Always remove the leaves below the picked sprouts. Leave the small sprouts at the top and those that are smaller than $1/2$ inch in diameter.

Cabbage

Cool season crop. Rated marginal for IPS gardens.

Cabbage often turns out to be a big show-off. It comes in green, red, and purple varieties and is a great conversation piece grown singly in a prominent spot. The only complaint that I have about cabbage is that it takes an awful lot of space for what you get out of it. If you insist on cabbage, you might plant three or four IPS gardens, or put one by itself in a flower bed where it can be ornamental.

Planting

Cabbage is a cool weather plant, so you want to time your plantings so that the plants reach maturity before or after the hot summer months. Put the plants out in the early spring or in late summer.

Most gardeners buy small seedlings from a nursery rather than start from seeds. The seedlings should be set 12 inches apart in your IPS bed. If you want to start cabbage from seed, sow the seeds $1/2$ inch deep in flats or peat pots about six to eight weeks before you intend to set the plants outdoors.

New cabbage plants should never be set where other cabbages or any cabbage relatives have been grown in the past two or three years. This precaution is necessary in order to reduce the risk of being plagued by common cabbage diseases.

Crop Stretching

You can follow beans with a planting of cabbage. Also you can make successive plantings of cabbage to stretch the season.

Popular Varieties

EARLY

COPENHAGEN MARKET 68 days $3^1/2$ pounds, suited to small gardens. Seed source: BURP BURR COM DEG GUR HEN HIG LEJ MEY STO TIL WIL

| GOLDEN ACRE | 58 to 65 days 2- to 3-pound, gray-green head. Seed source: ABU ALL BURR DEG FAR FIS GAR GUR JUN LED LEJ LIB PON ROS SEE STO TER TIL WIL |
| STONEHEAD | 50 to 70 days 3½ pounds, 6 inches across, blue-green head. Seed source: COM FAR GUR HEN JUN LED LIB NIC PIN POR STO VER |

LATE

| DANISH BALLHEAD | 100 to 105 days 3 to 8 pounds, dark green head. Seed source: BURR COM FAR FIS GAR JUN LED LIB PIN SEE TER TIL WILL |

RED

| RED ACRE | 75 to 85 days 2 to 5 pounds, 6 to 7 inches, reddish-purple round head. Seed source: ALL BURR COM FAR FIS GUR HEN HIG LIB PON POR ROS SEE SOU TIL |
| RUBY BALL | 65 to 80 days 3- to 6-pound head. Japanese variety. Seed source: BURR COO DEG LED LIB MEY NIC PIN POR TER VER |

SMALL

| FLASH | 65 days 2 to 3 pounds, deep green head. Seed source: LED PIN |

SAVOY

| CHIEFTAIN SAVOY | 80 to 90 days 5 to 7 pounds, 8-inch, blue-green head. Seed source: ABU COM GAR HEN LED MEY SOU STO TER TIL VER |
| SAVOY KING | 82 to 120 days 4 to 5 pounds, dark green, semiflat head. Seed source: DEG LIB NIC PAR PON TWI WILL |

Typical Problem

My cabbage heads split badly. Cabbage needs a good steady supply of water. Any time that the watering becomes irregular, growth becomes irregular—slowing down, resuming, slowing down again. This causes the cabbage to crack. Therefore, you should make sure that you keep your cabbages supplied with water. If you haven't, however, you can try a reverse trick. You can delay growth and halt cracking by holding off on the water when cracking begins, or you can twist the plant to break off some of the roots and thereby slow the growth process.

Harvesting

Pick cabbage heads as soon as the heads feel solid. If you let them mature on the plant, the core gradually lengthens until it bursts through the top and uncurls into a long stalk. Cabbage does not freeze well.

Cabbage Growing Tip

Cut-and-Come-Again: You can easily turn your cabbage plants into a vegetable factory. When you remove the head, cut squarely across the stem leaving four or more leaves. Then cut a shallow slit across the top of the stump. The cabbage plant will produce up to five smaller cabbage heads within six weeks after cutting the first head.

Carrots

Cool season crop. Rated excellent for IPS gardens.

When the ancient Greeks and Romans used carrots for medicine but wouldn't eat them for food, they really goofed because carrots supply more food in our gardens over a longer period of time than practically anything else. They're also super-packed with vitamins—A, B_{12}, small amounts of B_2, and C—as well as sugar and iron.

Carrots, like beets, need to grow fast. So make sure that they have plenty of water and never dry out.

Planting

Carrots are more tolerant of garden mistakes than almost any other plant that I can think of. They are generally considered a cool season crop—best for spring and fall—but they do pretty well in summer, maturing sixty-five to seventy-five days after initial planting.

For a season-long crop, divide your planting area into quarters, and then scatter seed in each quarter ten days apart. Cover the seeds with $1/2$ inch of soil or planting mix. When the tops show, thin the plants to 1 inch apart; a couple of weeks later, thin to 2 inches apart. The tender young carrots are delicious, cooked or raw.

Crop Stretching

As you pull out a few heads of cabbage or broccoli, plant a few carrots in the same space.

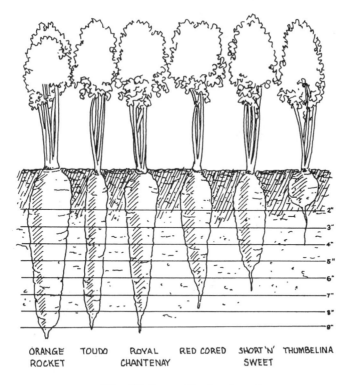

Figure 5-3. Comparative size of carrots.

Popular Varieties

With carrots you can go wild and plant almost any shape you desire—from very small and almost round to long and slender.

SMALL

BABY SPIKE 52 days 3 to 4 by ½ inches long. Seed source: GUR HEN PAR POR

LITTLE FINGER 50 to 65 days 2 to 3 by ½ inches, small core and extra sweet taste. Seed source: BOU COM GUR JLH JUN ORN PIN VER

OX HEART 70 to 75 days 6 by 4 inches long, deep orange color. Seed source: ABU FIS GAR SEE

MEDIUM, PLUMP

CHANTENAY 68 to 72 days 6 by 2¼ inches long. Bright orange. Seed source: ALL BOU LEJ NIC SEE

| RED-CORED CHANTENAY | 68 to 72 days 6 by 2 inches, red-orange color. Seed source: ABU DEG FAR FIS GAR GUR HEN JUN MEY NIC PIN PON ROS SEED SOU TIL WIL WILL |

MEDIUM, SLENDER

| DANVERS HALF LONG | 73 to 85 days Deep orange color, 8 by 2 inches long. Seed source: ALL BURP DEG FAR FIS GAR GUR HEN LEJ MEY PIN PON ROS SEE SOU THO TIL WILL |

LONG, SLENDER

| GOLD PAK | 65 to 80 days $8^1/_2$ by 1 inches, deep orange color. Seed source: COM DEG GUR HEN PON POR |
| IMPERATOR | 64 to 80 days 10 inches long, $1^1/_2$ inches thick, orange-red color. Seed source: BURP FAR LED MEY PON ROS VER |

A NOVELTY TO TRY

| BELGIUM WHITE | 75 days White carrot with mild flavor. Seed source: BOU NIC |

Typical Problem

My carrots just don't germinate well. I'll get a few in a clump in one area and none in another. Carrot germination can be a problem. Some of this problem is due to the seeds drying out. To reduce evaporation, some gardeners recommend placing a black plastic sheet over the carrot bed immediately after sowing, then removing it as the seedlings start to break through. You must watch carefully, however, in order to make sure to remove the plastic before it stunts the seedlings.

Harvesting

Pick carrots when relatively small. Big carrots produce woody cores. For real flavor, plant a few more than you need, then thin them when they're big enough to eat.

For freezing, small carrots are best, but you can cut the big ones into small pieces. Blanch the carrots in boiling water about three minutes, cool quickly, pack in containers, and freeze.

Carrot Growing Tips

Sprout Them Fast: To ensure uniform carrot germination, try covering your carrot seed bed with a sheet of clear plastic. Carrots are a cool weather crop but won't germinate well in early spring when the soil temperature is below 40°. Clear plastic heats up the soil and maintains moisture. Uncover the seed bed on warm sunny days to keep the soil temperature from exceeding 95°F.

Pot Magic: To take the guess work out of growing carrots, try starting in clay or plastic pots. Fill several 4- to 6-inch pots with a good potting mix to within 1 inch of the rim. Sow ten to twelve seeds evenly over the surface. When each plant has two to three fernlike leaves, thin back to six to eight evenly spaced carrots per pot. When the plants reach 6 to 9 inches high, remove the entire root mass from the pot and plant, intact, in the garden. Ten pots planted close together (intensive style) yields about seventy carrots.

Cauliflower

Cool season crop. Rated marginal for IPS gardens.

Cauliflower can be a bit finicky about the weather. In the area where we live, it can be cool for a period during the spring, then suddenly hot; and under these conditions, cauliflower just doesn't do very well. But if you live in an area of cool or gradually warming springs or cool summers, your cauliflower should do fine.

Planting

If you live where the spring is fairly cool, but frost free, you can set out the plants in early spring. If summers are very warm where you live, then you may want to grow your cauliflower in the fall; just set out the plants in late July or early August.

You can grow cauliflower indoors from seed in flats if you like, but it generally takes about fifty days before the plants are ready to set out—an awfully long time. For this reason you should probably buy seedlings from a nursery. Plant them 2$\frac{1}{2}$ feet apart.

When the cauliflower begins to head, you must "blanch" the buds—that is, keep them from turning green—by shielding the head from the sun. You do this by pulling a few outer leaves over the head completely, gathering the tops of these leaves together, and tying them together loosely with a string or rubber band. For purple-headed cauliflower, this blanching is unnecessary.

Crop Stretching

If you plant cauliflower in an IPS bed, be sure to grow something else between the plants—radishes or lettuce, for instance. When the radishes or lettuce come out, plant bush beans. Your cauliflower will be out of the way before your beans are ready to harvest. This way you'll use all the space efficiently.

Popular Varieties

EARLY

SNOW CROWN	50 to 68 days 2 pounds, 5- to 9-inch head. Seed source: BURP COM FAR JOH JUN LED LIB MEY NIC ORN PIN PON POR STO TER TWI VER WILL
SUPER SNOWBALL	55 to 60 days 6½-inch, ivory colored head. Seed source: ALL BURP FAR FIS HEN

MIDSEASON

SELF-BLANCHE	68 to 71 days 6½- to 8-inch thick, white head. Seed source: FAR FIS GAR GUR HEN JUN LIB MEY PON SEE
SNOW PAK	62 to 85 days 9- to 12-inch white head. Seed source: BURR LED WILL

SMALL

MINI CORGILL	82 to 86 days Easy to grow plants don't mature all at once. Seed source: THO

A NOVELTY TO TRY

BURGUNDY QUEEN	70 days 6½-inch thick, 19-ounce purple head. Seed source: ORN STO

Typical Problem

My cauliflower heads are always small. You probably have a watering problem. It's important that you don't check the growth of cauliflower at any time. This can happen if you water irregularly or don't water for long periods of time. You must water consistently and fairly deeply, and in very hot weather a gentle overhead misting is beneficial too.

Harvesting

Pick cauliflower as soon as the heads fill out; otherwise they will lose quality.

To freeze cauliflower, break the buds into small pieces, blanch them in boiling water for three minutes, cool, place in containers, and freeze.

Cauliflower Growing Tips

Blanching Made Easy: To blanch cauliflower easily, place aluminum foil over the heads when they are about the size of a softball. Start with a square of aluminum foil approximately 14 by 14 inches and crinkle it up. Unfold and loosely place the foil over the head, allowing as much air space as possible. Tuck the edges around the head. At harvest time your heads will be nice and white.

Healthy Cauliflower: Select seedlings with about four green leaves, a short straight stem, and plenty of root. Reject seedlings with a bluish tinge, since they will produce only small curds. Seedlings with six or more leaves have grown too old too quickly and will die, as will blind seedlings—those with no growing point.

Corn

Warm season crop. Rated fair for IPS gardens.

What we call corn today is a far cry from the maize that the Pilgrims found the Indians growing when they first arrived in America. The reason: Corn loves to crossbreed; and unlike some other plants, every time you cross one kind of corn with another you get something different—something in between. As a result, over the last 150 years corn hybridizers have developed countless varieties, and today you have a huge choice: You can plant tall varieties, short varieties, whites, yellows, blacks, popcorn, early varieties, late varieties, and seemingly everything else.

Planting

Corn is a heat lover, so plant the seeds or seedlings after the ground has warmed up. It also needs plenty of water throughout the growing season, and it's a heavy feeder. Generally, IPS soil has enough nutrients to carry corn through a full season; but just to make sure, we sometimes give one feeding of fish emulsion when the plants are about 15 inches tall (apply according to the instructions on the bottle).

Corn isn't terribly good in an IPS garden because it takes up a lot of space from two-and-a-half to three months or more. If you like corn as much as we do, however, you can make up a special 4- by 4-foot bed for corn and plant seedlings in it 8 inches apart. (If you use seeds, plant them 1 inch deep, 8 inches apart.) If possible, you might distribute about three of these 4- by 4-foot squares somewhere around the yard, planting each square a couple of weeks apart for a continuous crop. Each square will yield about seventy-two ears.

The 4- by 4-foot beds are good because corn is a wind pollinator, and small blocks like these are better than a long row. The reason: Corn is a member of the grass family; the tassels contain the male parts, and the silks that come out of the ears are part of the female flowers. Wind-borne pollen from the tassels of one plant falls on the silks of another plant, and each silk that receives pollen produces a mature kernel. Because the pollen can't float very far, the plants must be fairly close together to pollinate one another. Supersweet corn, however, must be kept isolated from regular corn.

Crop Stretching

Fast-maturing crops such as radishes and lettuce can be planted between your corn, and they'll be harvested before the corn gets tall. Corn and pole beans can be planted at the same time, close together; and the bean vines will then twine up the corn stalks.

Popular Varieties

You'll generally want to plant either a white variety or a yellow one or both, but not both in the same bed, because if pollen from white corn lands on the silks of yellow (or vice versa), you'll get a crazy mixed-up ear with a muddle of whites and yellows.

If you've got a sweet tooth, try the Extra Sweet, Super Sweet, and Early Sweet varieties. This sweetness is in the genes. "Sugary enhanced" corn has a gene (labeled "se") that modifies the normal gene for sweetness. Each tasty kernel has a higher sugar content than normal corn, making them tender and sweeter. The *supersweet variety* (sh2 shrunken gene types) has two or three times the content of normal sugary types. Both sugary enhanced and supersweet come in yellow, white, and bicolor varieties. You must keep the varieties separate and isolated.

A great variety for IPS gardens is Golden Midget. It has 4-inch ears on a 3-foot stalk. Seed source: ABU GAR SEED VER.

If you're an experimenter, try one of the two-tone varieties (yellow and white together), such as Butter and Sugar, which has 8-inch ears on a 6-foot stalk. Seed source: ALL COM DEG FAR JUN

If you want to play around with something wild instead of producing food, try ornamental Indian Squaw corn, which produces large, decorative ears in an array of color combinations. Seed source: ALL BURR COM HEN LED LIB POR SEE STO TWI VER WIL

Here are a few varieties:

YELLOW (NORMAL "SU" GENE)

EARLY SUNGLOW	63 days 4½-foot stalk, 7-inch ears. Yellow kernels. Seed source: BURP BURR FAR FIS GUR HEN MEY NIC PAR POR SHE SHOU TIL VER WIL
GOLDEN BANTAM	78 to 83 days 7-inch ears, 6½-foot stalk. Yellow kernels. Seed source: ABU ALL BOU BURR BUT GAR GUR HEN JOH LED ORG SEE SOU WIL
GOLDEN QUEEN	88 days 9-foot stalk, 8- to 9-inch ears. Yellow kernels. Seed source: LED MEY PAR TWI WIL
IOCHIEF	86 to 93 days Two 10-inch ears per 6½-foot stalk. Yellow kernels. Seed source: BURR FAR GUR HEN LIB VER
NK 199	84 days 8-foot stalk, 8-inch ears. Yellow kernels. Seed source: BURR GUR HEN JUN LIB MEY ORN TWI
SENECA CHIEF	86 days 6½-foot stalk, 8-inch ear. Yellow kernels. Seed source: ALL BURR PAR STO WILL
SENECA HORIZON	65 to 75 days 8-inch ears. Yellow kernels. Seed source: ALL BURR LIB MEY STO TWI WIL WILL

WHITE (NORMAL "SU" GENE)

PLATINUM LADY	75 to 85 days Two 8-inch ears per 7-foot stalk. Seed source: BURP BURR COM GAR GUR MEY NIC ORN PIN STO TIL TWI VER
COUNTRY GENTLEMAN	73 to 100 days 7½-foot stalk, 9-inch ears. Seed source: ABU BOU BUT HEN RED SEE SOU
SILVER QUEEN	94 days 8-foot stalk, 9-inch ears. Seed source: ALL BURP COM DEG FAR GOU GUR HEN JOH JUN LED LIB MEY PAR PON POR ROS SHE STO SOU TWI VER WIL
TRUCKER'S FAVORITE	78 days 9-inch ears. Seed source: FAR ROS SEE WIL

BICOLORED (NORMAL "SU" GENE)

HONEY AND CREAM	78 days 7½-inch ears. Seed source: ALL BURP GUR LIB PIN PON WIL

YELLOW (SUGARY ENHANCED "SE, SE+" GENE)

BODACIOUS — 75 days 6½-foot stalk, 8-inch ears. Seed source: BURR COM GUR HEN LIB NIC PAR STO TER TIL VER WIL

EARLY XTRA-SWEET — 71 to 85 days 6-foot stalk, 9-inch ears. Seed source: BURP FAR GOU GUR HEN PON VER WILL

KANDY KORN — 89 days 8½-foot stalk, 8-inch ears. Seed source: BURP BURR DEG FAR FIS GAR GUR HEN JUN LIB MEY ORN PON POR STO TIL TWI VER WIL WILL

MIRACLE — 78 to 100 days 6½-foot stalk, 9½-inch ears. Seed source: BURP BURR COM FAR GOU GUR HIG LIB NIC STO TER WILL

SUGAR BUNS — 65 to 72 days 6-foot stalk, 8-inch ears. Seed source: COM FAR JOH LIB TER TIL WIL

WHITE (SUGARY ENHANCED "SE, SE+" GENE)

ALPINE — 76 days 7-foot stalk, 8-inch ears. Seed source: FAR JOH LED LIB MEY TWI

DIVINITY — 75 days 6-foot stalk, 9-inch ears. Seed source: LIB STO

SNOW QUEEN — 87 days 8-foot stalk, 10-inch ears. Seed source: FAR

BICOLORED (SUGARY ENHANCED "SE, SE+" GENE)

AMBROSIA — 75 days 8-inch ears. Bicolored bodacious. Seed source: STO VER

BURGUNDY DELIGHT — 73 to 84 days 9-foot stalk, 8-inch ears. Seed source: JOH ORN PIN STO

PEACHES AND CREAM — 78 days 6½-foot stalk, 8-inch ears. Seed source: SHE WILL

YELLOW (SUPERSWEET SH2 "SHRUNKEN" GENE)

ILLINI GOLD EXTRA SWEET — 85 days 6½-foot stalk, 8-inch ears. Seed source: BURP DEG FAR GUR HEN JUN MEY VER WIL

NORTHERN XTRA-SWEET — 71 days 5-foot stalk, 9-inch ears. Seed source: FAR JOH JUN VER WILL

SUPERSWEET JUBILEE — 82 days 7- to 9-foot stalk, 9-inch ears. Seed source: JUN NIC TIL TWI

WHITE (SUPERSWEET SH2 "SHRUNKEN" GENE)

HOW SWEET IT IS — 87 days 7-foot stalk, 8-inch ears. Seed source: GUR HEN JUN LED MEY NIC ORN PAR PIN POR TIL TWI VER WIL

BICOLORED (SUPERSWEET SH2 "SHRUNKEN" GENE)

HONEY AND PEARL — 78 days 7-foot stalk, 9-inch ears. Seed source: BURP JOH JUN PAR TWI VER

IVORY AND GOLD — 75 days 6-foot stalk, 9-inch ears. Seed source: STO VER

There are, of course, many, many more varieties. If in doubt, ask your nurseryperson which ones are best for your area.

Typical Problems

I just didn't get very many ears from my few plants. Corn is a wind pollinator, so it's best to plant a lot together rather than just a few plants.

The lower leaves of my corn turned yellow. This doesn't happen often if you've made up your IPS soil right, because this condition indicates a nitrogen deficiency. You might give the plants a feeding of fish emulsion (apply according to the directions on the bottle).

When I husk the ears to cook them, quite often some of the kernels have been eaten by a fairly large worm. This is the corn earworm. We'll take this up in Chapter 8 when we talk about pests in the garden.

Harvesting

Corn is one of the hardest vegetables to pick properly. You want to catch it in the milky stage. For best results, just take your thumbnail and squeeze a kernel; if it's just right, it'll squirt a milky juice. Corn reaches a peak of sweetness, then holds it only two to five days. After that, the sugar starts to turn to starch. Moreover, the minute you pick corn, the sugar in the ear starts to turn to starch. Thus, if you're really looking for top flavor, you've got to pop it in boiling water almost immediately.

For freezing, pick slightly immature yellow corn. If you're freezing corn on the cob, blanch in boiling water six to eight minutes, cool, put in freezer bags, and freeze. If you're going to cut the kernels off the cob, blanch the cob first for one-and-a-half minutes, then cut the kernels off the cob, cool them, package, and freeze.

Corn Growing Tips

Baby Corn: If your mouth waters for those "baby" 3-inch ears of corn used in Chinese cooking and as pickled appetizer goodies, don't bother to plant special varieties. Just place the corn seed close together (6 inches or so), then harvest the tiny ears when the silks start to emerge from the husks. At this point the cobs will be about 3 inches long with perfect, but barely developed, kernels.

Peak Flavor: To pick corn ears at the peak of their flavor, try this. Pop a kernel two inches from the top of the ear with your fingernail. If the fluid is watery, wait a few more days, if the fluid is milky, pick immediately. If the fluid is gummy or starchy, you've waited too long.

Cucumbers

Warm season crop. Rated good to excellent for IPS gardens.

Here's a vegetable that undoubtedly is a contender for best actor on the vegetable circuit. Cucumbers have a thousand faces, and if you grow enough different kinds, you'll eventually come up with every shape imaginable. Some are warty, some are smooth, some are prickly, others aren't; they're crooked, straight, balloon-shaped, cigar-shaped, blackjack-shaped, peanut-shaped, and more. Moreover, they're big or small or anything in between. In short, cucumbers really perform in your garden. We love them. After all, who wouldn't love a vegetable that is such a big ham.

Cucumber vines are one of those crazy mixed-up plants that drive some of us to fits of frustration. They're what botanists call monoecious; that is, all male flower parts are in one flower, and all female parts in another (though every plant has both male and female flowers). The first ten to twenty flowers that are produced on any plant are males. Even after that, there are ten to twenty male flowers for every female. The cucumbers themselves come only from the female flowers; thus we have these plants producing all those non-productive flowers before they really get down to the business of making vegetables.

Planting

Cucumbers are heat lovers, so wait until the ground has warmed up before planting. Seeds should be planted 1 inch deep and about 4 inches apart if the vines are going to be trained in the air. To get a head start, you can sow the seeds ½ inch deep in peat pots or flats two to four weeks before outdoor planting and then transfer the seedlings into your IPS bed.

Crop Stretching

Cucumbers ordinarily take a lot of space. In fact, they'll run all over the ground if you let them. That's something that you just can't afford in a good postage stamp garden. So you've got to take to the air if you want to grow cucumbers effectively in a small area. There are a lot of ways to go:

1. Run a fence of chicken wire between two 6-foot posts, and let the vines grow up the wires. Generally the north side of the garden is best for this so that the vines won't shade other plants. Allow the main stem of each plant to grow as high as possible; pinch back some of the lateral shoots, but let some shoots grow into branches. Train the branches on the fence, using plastic tape. You can grow the plants about 4 inches apart along the fence.

   If you pick the cucumbers when they're fairly small, you won't have to support them with cloth slings or strings. If they get too big, however, they'll drop off or drag down the vine, if they aren't supported somehow.

2. Sink a 6-foot post (preferably a 4 by 4) in your garden, and on it space small 18-inch crossbars up and down the sides. Plant four seeds or seedlings around the post. As the vines grow, tie them to the crossbars.

3. You can also use several types of trellises: rectangular trellises 2 or 3 feet high and 2 or 3 feet wide, X-shaped trellises about 3 by 3 feet, and so on. Buy a ready-made trellis from a local nursery, or make one of your own.

Popular Varieties

With cucumbers you have a choice of those for eating raw or cooked and those for pickling, as well as midget varieties and some in rather unusual shapes, colors, and sizes.

SALADS

AMIRA	55 to 62 days 6-inch long, thin-skinned cucumber. Seed source: BURR COO FAR LED NIC PIN TER WILL
MARKETMORE 76	58 to 68 days 8-inch long, glossy, dark green cucumber. Seed source: ABU BURR COM DEG FAR GAR GUR HEN LIB MEY ROS STO TER TWI VER WIL WILL
STRAIGHT 8	60 to 67 days 8-inch, white spined cucumber. Small seed cavity. Seed source: ABU ALL BURP COM DEG FAR FIS GUR HEN MEY POR SEE VER WIL WILL

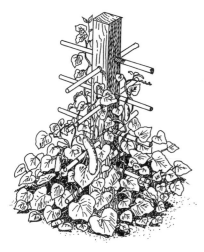

Figure 5-4. A cucumber pole.

SWEET SUCCESS	54 to 58 days 14-inch, thin, smooth-skinned cucumber with no bitterness. Seed source: BURP DEG GUR HEN LED NIC PAR PIN TIL TWI VER

SALADS, SPACE SAVERS

SALAD BUSH	57 days 8-inch long cucumber on compact plant. Seed source: BURP COM DEG HEN JUN LED LIB NIC PAR PIN POR SHE TIL TWI VER WILL
SPACEMASTER	60 days 8-inch long, slender cucumber; 18- to 24-inch bush. Seed source: ALL COM DEG FIS GAR GUR LIB ORN PIN PLA POR SEE SOU VER WILL

PICKLERS

CALYPSO	56 days 6-inch long, dark green cucumber. Seed source: ALL DEG LIB STO TWI VER WIL
GHERKIN	60 days 2-inch long cucumber, chunky and covered with tender spines. Seed source: GUR RED TIL
NATIONAL PICKLING	48 to 50 days Medium green cucumber. Seed source: DEG FIS GUR JUN LEJ PIN STO TIL WIL WILL
PIONEER	48 to 55 days Medium green with black spines. Good short season variety. Seed source: BURR COM JUN STO TIL WILL
SMR 58	56 days 6$\frac{1}{2}$ by 2$\frac{1}{2}$ inches, medium green with black spines. Seed sources: ALL BURG BURR GUR HEN JUN MEY NIC PON POR ROS STO TER WILL
WHITE WONDER	58 days 6 inch long cucumber, a Southern heirloom that turns ivory when mature. Seed source: BURG SOU

BURPLESS

BURPLESS HYBRID	62 days 10-inch long cucumber, curved and nonbitter. This variety makes a good bread and butter pickle, or use in salads. Seed source: BURP DEG FAR FIS LED LEJ PIN PON POR TIL
SWEET SUCCESS	65 days 12-inch long cucumber, dark green and bitter free. Seed source: BURP HEN JUN LED LIB MEY NIC PIN POR TWI VER WILL

NOVELTIES TO TRY

ARMENIAN YARD LONG	65 to 75 days 3-foot-long, gray-green cucumber with unique fluting. Seed source: ABU BURR DEG GOU NIC PLA POR RED ROS SEE TER
LEMON	64 days 3 inches in diameter, round, yellow, and flat on the stem end. Good in salads. Seed source: ABU BOU

COM COO DEG FIS GAR GUR JUN LIB NIC ORG ORN
PLA POR SEE SEED SHE STO TER

Typical Problem

My cucumbers taste terribly bitter. Some gardeners say that this is due to uneven watering; others believe it is due to temperature fluctuations of more than 20° daily. If you're having considerable trouble getting a good-tasting cucumber, there are bitter-free cucumbers you might want to try.

The plants just stopped producing new fruit all of a sudden. You probably left some of the cucumbers to mature on the vines. This can stop a cucumber plant from setting new fruit. Pick cucumbers as soon as they reach usable size.

Harvesting

Pick cucumbers when they're young and green, before the seeds get large and tough.

Cucumber Growing Tip. Compost Ring: For cucumber salads all summer long, try planting a few cucumbers in a compost ring. Bend a section of wire 4 feet wide and 10 feet long into a cylinder and fasten the wire where the ends meet. Locate in full sun.

Fill the ring with leaves, grass clippings, wood chips, sawdust, and other organic matter, alternating with a few shovels full of soil and a handful of blood meal. Near the compost ring mound two hills opposite each other outside the ring, and plant two to four seeds in each hill. As the plants come up, remove all but the two healthiest ones from each hill. Train the remaining plants to climb the wire. Add grass clippings and other plant waste to the heap during the growing season.

Eggplant

Warm season crop. Rated fair for IPS gardens.

Here's a garden show-off if we ever saw one—widely grown in the warm regions of the Mediterranean and in India. Eggplants grow on treelike bushes about 2 to 3 feet tall, and most varieties produce beautiful shiny, plumpish, purple-black fruit. Actually, eggplant fruit comes in other shapes and sizes and in colors ranging from purple to yellow to white. The plants are often grown as ornamentals in a garden.

Planting

Eggplant is actually not a good plant for IPS gardens because it takes up so much space, but most gardeners insist on growing one or two. You can plant a few in your flower beds, or you can put a few in a 4-by-4-foot framed bed.

Because of the long period of time required to develop eggplants from seeds, most gardeners buy seedlings from nurseries. In your IPS bed set the young plants 25 inches apart, well after the soil has warmed up in the spring.

If you grow from seeds, you need a lot of patience, for the seeds sometimes take three weeks or more to germinate and another eight to ten weeks before they're ready to be set out. If this is what you decide to do, though, simply sow the seeds $^1/_3$ to $^1/_2$ inch deep in peat pots, and transplant the complete unit—seedling, soil, and pot.

Eggplant is a heat lover and needs to grow steadily and unchecked throughout the summer. This means regular watering. Eggplants are also heavy feeders, and it helps if you give them some fish emulsion about every six weeks (apply according to the directions on the bottle).

Crop Stretching. Grow radishes, lettuce, and similar fast-maturing vegetables in the space around eggplants. They are harvested long before the eggplants mature.

White Egg

Popular Varieties
BELL-SHAPED

BLACK BEAUTY	73 to 80 days Dark purple with a small seed cavity. 24- to 28-inch plant. Seed source: ABU ALL BURP BURR BUT COM DEG GUR HEN LED LEJ MEY ORN PON POR RED ROS SEE SOU VER WIL WILL
BLACK BELL	68 to 70 days 6 inches long, oval, glossy, dark purple. 28- to 30-inch plant. Seed source: LED STO TWI VER WIL

Osteri

LONG, CYLINDRICAL

DUSKY	56 to 68 days 8-by-3$^1/_2$-inch, dark purple. 36 inch plant. Seed source: BURR COM FIS HEN JUN LED LIB MEY NIC PIN STO TER TIL TWI VER
ICHIBAN	58 to 65 days Up to 12 inches long, purple. 36- to 40-inch plant. Seed source: BURR COM DEG GUR LED PAR PIN POR TWI VER

Blacknite

SMALL

BAMBINO	45 days Ornamental that grows 12 inches tall. Seed source: BURP GUR LIB SHE STO TER
EARLY BLACK EGG	65 to 75 days 4-by-2-inch, shiny black fruit. Bushy plant. Seed source: GAR GLE SOU

A NOVELTY TO TRY

ALBA	60 days Full-size, pure white eggplant. Seed source: BOU
CASPER	70 days 6 by 2³/₄ inches, shiny, ivory eggplant. Seed source: SEE SEED STO
LISTADA DE GANDIA	75 days 6 to 10 inches long, white with purple stripes. An Italian variety. A real beauty. Seed source: ORN SEE SEED SOU
TURKISH ITALIAN ORANGE	85 days 2-ounce, orange-red fruits that look like tomatoes. Seed source: ABU DEG SEE SOU

Imperial Black Beauty

Casper

Typical Problem

I planted a few plants in the spring, and they just sat there and did nothing. You probably planted before it was warm enough. You can protect your small plants by putting a cut-off jug over them or a wall-o-water, or by covering them with "hot caps" bought at a local nursery.

Harvesting

Pick your eggplants before they start to lose their glossy shine; after that, they'll be tough. Be sure to keep picking the fruits as they become ready so that the plants will continue to bear.

Eggplant Growing Tip

Large Fruit: For bushy, fully packed plants that produce a number of larger fruits, pinch out the growing tips when the plants are 6 inches high. This encourages several branches to form. After a number of fruits have started to form, clip out several branches. This encourages the plants to produce larger and fewer fruits.

Kale

Cool season crop. Rated good for IPS gardens.

Other members of the cabbage family may be a little hard to grow, but not kale, if you grow it in the right season. Kale is a great flower bed crop too because the leaves are so beautiful. They're curled and fringed and range from dark green to bluish purple.

Planting

Kale is a cool weather plant like other cabbage crops and does best under cool conditions. If your summers are cool, with average daytime temperatures of 75°F or less, you have no problem. Otherwise sow your seed in midsummer so that the plants grow in the cool days of fall. Or if your frost-free days begin early in the spring, sow seed for a late spring or early summer crop.

Sow the seeds ½ inch deep, about 16 inches apart. To keep kale coming along well, you should generally give it a feeding of fish emulsion about midseason (apply according to the instructions on the label).

Crop Stretching

You can stretch your harvest by planting kale in place of any crop that matures by midsummer—early corn, for instance.

Popular Varieties

DWARF BLUE CURLED VATES	55 to 70 days Finely curled, bluish-green leaves. Seed source: ABU BURP BUT COM DEG GAR GUR HEN JUN LED LIB MEY NIC ROS SEE SOU STO TIL TWI WIL
RUSSIAN RED	40 to 60 days Wavy, red-purple leaves. 2-foot plant. Seed source: ABU BOU GAR JLH JOH NIC ORG ORN PIN SEED SHE SOU

Typical Problem

My kale isn't doing very well by midspring. Kale is a cool weather crop, remember. It generally does best as a fall crop and doesn't like heat very well.

Harvesting

You can cut the outer leaves as they mature or cut the entire plant. Generally, the inside leaves are more flavorsome and tender than the outer ones.

Kale Growing Tip

More Kale: To make kale really produce, just harvest the loose crowns in the spring, on leaf and spear varieties. Remove the leaves from the top down. Without crowns or leaves, side shoots will develop; just pick these like broccoli.

Lettuce

Cool season crop. Rated excellent for IPS gardens.

What a vegetable! You can grow lettuce almost without effort, tuck it in anywhere, take your choice of color or type, and spend hours at the seed racks looking at varieties that you've never seen before.

Lettuce, of course, is well known as the dieter's friend. It is chocked full of vitamins A and B and yet contains almost no calories. What more could you ask for?

Planting

You can start lettuce from either seeds or plants (the plants can be purchased from a nursery). If you want head lettuce as soon as possible in the spring, start seeds indoors in a pot ($^1/_4$ to $^1/_2$ inch deep) about two weeks before the last frost. When all danger of frost has passed, start setting the plants out in the garden. At the same time, you can plant more seeds in the garden bed itself ($^1/_4$ to $^1/_2$ inch deep) for a later crop.

Set head lettuce about 10 inches apart, butterhead 4 or 5 inches apart. The spacing for leaf lettuce and romaine can vary. If you intend to pick the outer leaves over a period of time (letting the core of the plant continue to grow), then plant the lettuce 10 inches apart. If you intend to pick the entire plant at once, 4 inches is okay—you'll get more that way.

When summers are hot, plant lettuce in partial shade or give it protection with a lath or gauze on a frame. Lettuce, remember, is a cool-season crop. In hot areas, the longer days and warmer nights of summer encourage flowering (bolting to seed). You can correct this problem somewhat by planting varieties that are slow to bolt.

Crop Stretching

You can plant loose-leaf lettuce where you intend to grow corn, then harvest it before the corn has grown very large.

Popular Varieties

Basically there are four main types of lettuce: head lettuce, butterhead (also known as Boston or bibb lettuce), loose-leaf lettuce, and romaine (also called cos lettuce). Here are a few varieties you might like to try:

Head Lettuce

HEAD LETTUCE

ALL-YEAR-ROUND	72 days Pale green leaves. Seed source: ABU FAR ORN POR SEE
GREAT LAKES	90 to 100 days Bright green large, dense head. Seed source: ALL BURP COM DEG HEN MEY NIC PIN SEE TIL
ICEBERG	85 days Wavy, light green leaves, tinged brown. Slow to bolt. Seed source: ALL DEG GUR LED LEJ MEY POR ROS SUN WIL WILL
RED GRENOBLE	55 days Light green leaves, tinted red. Seed source: COO GOU SHE

BUTTERHEAD/BIBB

BUTTERCRUNCH	49 to 75 days Smooth, dark green leaves. 6-inch center rosette. Seed source: ABU ALL BOU BURP BURR BUT COM COO DEG FAR FIS GUR HEN HIG JOH JUN LED LIB MEY NIC PAR PIN PON POR ROS SEE SOU STO TER TIL VER WIL WILL
CONTINUITY	67 to 70 days Wavy dark green leaves overlaid with brown. Seed source: BOU GUR HEN SEED TER
MARVEL OF 4 SEASONS	50 to 72 days Wavy green leaves with ruby tips. Seed source: COO GOU HIG JLH ORG ORN PIN RED SEE SEED SHE TER

SMALL

BUBBLES	65 days Very crinkly leaves. Romaine type. Seed source: THO
LITTLE GEM	50 days Miniature romaine with bright green, slightly wavy leaves, 5 to 6 inches tall. Seed source: BOU GAR ORN PAR SEED TER
TOM THUMB	52 to 65 days Tennis-ball-size buttercrunch with medium green, crumpled leaves. Seed source: GUR HEN HIG LED NIC ORG ORN PIN POR SEE SEED SHE SOU TIL VER

LOOSE-LEAF

BLACK SEEDED SIMPSON	45 days Light green, frilled outer leaves. Seed source: ABU ALL BURG BURP BURR BUT COM COO DEG FAR FIS GAR FUR HEN HIG JOH JUN LED LEJ LIB MEY NIC ORG PAR PIN PON POR ROS SEE SEED SOU STO TIL VER WIL WILL

OAK LEAF	38 to 50 days Medium green leaves shaped like an oak leaf. Seed source: ABU ALL BURG BUT COM DEG FAR FIS GAR GOU GUR HEN HIG JLH JOH LED LIB MEY NIC ORN PIN PON POR RED SEE SOU VER
SALAD BOWL	45 days Wavy, light green deeply lobed leaves. Seed source: ABU ALL BOU BURP BURR BUT COM COO DEG FAR FIS GAR GUR HEN HIG JOH JUN LED LIB MEY NIC ORN PAR PIN SEE SOU TER WIL WILL

ROMAINE

PARRIS ISLAND COS	70 to 75 days 9-inch tall, dark green leaves. Seed source: BURP COM GAR HEN JOH LIB MEY PIN POR RED SEE SEED SOU STO TIL VER WIL WILL
ROUGE D'HIVER	60 days Bronze to deep red, broad, flat leaves. Seed source: COO JLH ORN SEE SEED SHE
WINTER DENSITY	54 to 65 days 10 inches tall, dark green leaves. Seed source: ABU BOU JOH SEE SOU TER

Typical Problems

My lettuce keeps going to seed before it's big enough to eat. Your lettuce is getting too much heat. You can solve this problem in any of several ways: (1) plant earlier in the spring, before hot weather sets in, or in late summer; (2) shade your garden with lath or gauze; or (3) plant one of the varieties that are slow to bolt.

I always get poor heads and sometimes no heads at all. You probably didn't thin out your plants enough. IPS beds let you plant a little closer than conventional gardens, but you must still thin a little to space out your heads.

My lettuce turns brown at the tips. This is tip burn, due to hot weather. Again, you can prevent this by shading your garden.

Harvesting

Head lettuce should be picked when the heads are nice and crisp. But in general, the leaves of all types of lettuce remain edible at almost all stages; pick them as you need them.

Most IPS gardeners like to pick loose-leaf lettuce a leaf or two at a time. If you intend to do this leaf picking, be sure to allow enough spacing (as mentioned previously); otherwise, you're likely to wind up with bitter leaves.

A Lettuce Substitute for IPS Gardens—Endive

Endive makes a great lettuce substitute, but it's actually a member of the chicory family. You'll find it a little lacier than most lettuce and slightly bitter. Grow it just as you would lettuce. Endive is more heat and cold resistant than lettuce, and many gardeners find that they do best by planting it in the summer for fall or early winter harvesting. A good variety to try is Green Curled; it is 18 inches wide and has finely cut, green curled leaves. Seed source: ALL BOU BURP JUN LED NIC RED SEE STO TWI WILL.

You generally need to "blanch" endive to lessen its bitterness and improve its flavor. Two or three weeks before you intend to start picking your endive, simply draw the outer leaves over the heart and center leaves until they come together at the top; then tie the bunched leaves together with string or a rubber band. Be sure that the center leaves are dry when tied; otherwise they may rot.

Lettuce Growing Tips

Summer Lettuce: Try planting in shaded ground beneath pole beans or cucumbers. As soon as the little sprouts poke through the warm soil, tuck mulch around them to keep the roots cool. Keep well watered.

Bigger Heads: As your head lettuce starts to grow, pick the outer leaves a few at a time just as you would leaf lettuce. This doesn't affect the heading, since the heads grow from the center out. Removing the outer leaves, however, makes the plant smaller in comparison with the root structure. This gives the roots time to gain the strength needed to produce stronger, larger tops.

Melons

Warm season crop. Rated fair to good for IPS gardens.

Melons take a lot of space, since they're determined to wander just about anywhere they please. Each vine stem may creep 6 to 10 feet or more, and each plant will have several stems. Nevertheless, cantaloupes (also called muskmelons), watermelons, and other melons are the sentimental favorites of a lot of people; so if you insist on these fruits in a small garden, good luck. Actually, they're not that bad if you don't insist on watermelon (unless you plant the midget kind).

Planting

Melons are hot weather plants and can be planted about two weeks after the last frost. Plant seeds or seedlings 24 inches apart and train them up posts or other supports. (If you don't train them into the air, you'll be obliged to plant them 4 to 10 feet apart, because they'll spread out all over the place.)

Melons are heavy feeders and should be given a feeding of fish emulsion about every six weeks (apply according to the instructions on the bottle). Also—this is crucial to their success—make sure that the ground never dries out while the plants are growing. Give them steady watering.

Crop Stretching

There's no reason at all why you can't grow cantaloupe and other small melons in quantity in a small portion of any good IPS garden. All you have to do is to grow the vines in the air. There are several ways:

1. Sink a 6-foot post (preferably a 4 by 4) in the ground and stagger small crossbars on both sides up to the top. Tie the vines as they reach the crossbars, and support the fruit with cloth slings.
2. Put up a construction-wire fence on one side of the garden and tie the vines and fruit.
3. Use a construction-wire island. Just form a circle of wire about 2 feet in diameter, and train three melon plants up this wire, tying the fruit as before.

Popular Varieties

CANTALOUPE (ORANGE FLESH)

ALASKA	65 to 80 days Short season variety that produces $4^1/_2$-pound football-shaped melons. Pick when netting turns light reddish brown. Seed source: COM FAR GAR GUR HEN LIB NIC PIN VER WILL
AMBROSIA	83 to 86 days 4- to 5-pound, $6^1/_2$-inch melon with thick orange flesh and small seed cavity. Seed source: BURP LED LIB ORN PAR PIN POR TWI VER
EARLISWEET	73 to 75 days $5^1/_2$ by $5^1/_2$ inches, salmon-colored flesh. Produces well into fall. Seed source: BURR FAR NIC STO TWI WILL

HALE'S BEST JUMBO   85 days 4½ pounds, 7½ by 6 inches, deep salmon-colored flesh. Seed source: BURR BUT DEG LED PON POR ROS SEE SOU VER WIL

IROQUOIS   90 days 7 to 8 pounds, small seed cavity. Salmon-colored flesh. Seed source: COM DEG FAR GUR HEN JUN LIB PON STO TER TWI VER WIL

SPACE SAVERS

BUSH MUSKETEER   90 days 3- to 4-pound, 6-inch melon with orange flesh. Can be grown in containers or pots. Seed source: HEN JUN MEY PAR STO

JENNY LIND   75 days 1 to 2 pounds, with green flesh. Grows on a 5-foot vine. Many have knobs on the end. Seed source: ABU LED PIN SEE SOU

CANTALOUPE (GREEN FLESH)

ISRAEL   80 days Pale yellow rind, small seed cavity. Seed source: ABU BOU ORG SHE

ROCKY FORD GREEN FLESH   84 to 92 days 2½-pound, 5-inch oblong melon. Seed source: BURR DEG ROS SOU WIL

NOVELTIES TO TRY

BANANA   90 to 95 days 7-pound, 18-by-24-inch long melon looks like a giant banana. Yellow rind and sweet, spicy salmon colored flesh. Seed source: DEG JUN LIB MEY POR SEE VER WIL

GOLDEN CRISPY   85 days 12-ounce golden yellow melon you eat like a pear, skin and all. Seed source: DEG GLE NIC THE VER

HONEYDEW (GREEN AND ORANGE FLESH)

EARLI-DEW   70 to 86 days 3 pounds, 5 to 6 inches. Smooth skin, sweet green flesh. Seed source: COM FAR HEN JOH JUN LIB NIC PIN PON STO TER TWI VER WIL WILL

HONEYDEW (GREEN)   110 to 112 days 6 to 8 pounds, 7½ inches. Smooth, ivory rind with light green flesh. Seed source: BURR DEG LEJ MEY NIC ORG SEE

HONEYDEW (ORANGE)   110 days 5 to 6 pounds, creamy white rind when ripe. Small seed cavity and salmon-colored flesh. Seed source: ROS

OTHER TYPES

CRENSHAW   90 to 110 days 5 pounds, 6 by 8 inches. Rough, dark green rind turns yellow when ripe. Salmon-colored flesh. Seed source: BURR DEG HEN GLE ROS SEE

JUAN CANARY	105 days Casaba melon, 8 to 9 pounds, 8 by 6 inches, egg shaped. Yellow rind, very sweet whitish yellow flesh. Seed source: BURR SEED WIL

WATERMELON

BUSH JUBILEE	95 days 13 pounds, bush variety space saver melon. Seed source: LED MEY PON POR
CHARLESTON GRAY BUSH	90 days 22 to 40 pounds, gray rind, deep red flesh. 3- to 5-foot vine. Seed source: DEG
YELLOW DOLL	70 to 75 days 5 to 8 pounds, green striped rind, bright yellow flesh. Semicompact vines. Seed source: BURG COM HEN JUN LED LIB NIC ORG POR TER TWI WIL WILL

Typical Problems

My melons taste bitter. Usually this bitterness occurs when there is cold, wet weather during the ripening period. Melons need nice warm weather to be at their best. Or the problem could be uneven watering. Never let the soil dry out completely. Ideally, you should water deeply; then don't water again until the soil has dried out to about 8 inches from the top.

I have blossom drop and no fruit setting. Like the blossoms on cucumber vines, the first blossoms on melon vines are male. These will naturally drop. You should simply be patient until the female flowers come along; then you'll have small fruit developing.

Harvesting

Cantaloupes are ready to eat when the stems pull off easily—usually with a slight touch of the thumb. If they don't pull off easily, they should stay on the vine. You can also tell when they're ready because the skin begins to look like a corky net and the stem cracks a little all the way around.

For testing Persian melons, smell the blossom ends. If the smell is fruity and sweet, the melons are probably ripe. Honeydew and casaba melons are ripe when the rinds have turned completely yellow.

For testing watermelons, there's nothing like thumping them with your knuckle. They have a *bonggg* . . . sound (that is, a dull rather than a sharp sound). This is a great test for early morning, but once the watermelons get hot late in the day, it's pretty hard to tell whether or not they're good and ripe because the *bongg* gives way to a dull thud.

Another test is to look at the discolored spots where the melons touch the ground. If they're ready, these spots have turned from white to a pale yellow. If the stem slips easily from the vine, the melon is ready.

Melon Growing Tips

More Melons: To turn your vines into a melon factory, pinch out the growing tip when the main stem has produced five large leaves. Nip out subsequent side shoots when the growing tip develops three leaves. This stops the plant from producing leafy growth and forces more fruit production. When the plants are growing vigorously, keep them well watered and give them a liquid organic food as the first young fruits reach walnut size.

Mustard Greens

Cool season crop. Rated good for IPS gardens.

Mustard greens have long been a Southern favorite, and yet they've never really caught on in other sections of the country. There's no reason, however, why everybody can't enjoy this versatile vegetable. They're great as cooked greens and tremendous in salads. In addition (an important consideration for most gardeners), they grow to maturity fast.

Planting

In virtually every climate, you can take out several crops of greens every year. Sow seed early in the spring, then again in late summer. If you live in an area of mild winters, plant again in the fall. Sow seeds $\frac{1}{2}$ inch deep and 2 inches apart, and later thin the plants to 4 inches apart. (Be sure to cook up the tender thinned greens. They're delicious.)

Make sure that the plants get a continuous supply of water throughout the season.

Crop Stretching

Plant mustard greens in succession. Divide your mustard greens section into four subsections, planting each subsection three weeks apart.

You can also plant greens among tomato seedlings; the greens will be ready for harvesting before the tomato vines have grown large enough to shade them out.

Popular Varieties

FLORIDA BROAD LEAF	43 to 50 days Broad, smooth leaves with flattened greenish-white ribs. 16- to 22-inch spread. Seed source: BURR COM DEG MEY POR RED ROS SEE STO SUN TWI VER WIL
SOUTHERN GIANT CURLED	40 to 60 days 18- to 24-inch spread. Wide, crumpled, bright green leaves. Seed source: BOU BURR DEG JUN LED MEY PAR POR ROS SEE SUN TIL TWI WIL
TENDERGREEN	34 to 40 days Large, broad, thick dark green leaves. 16- to 22-inch spread. Seed source: ALL BURG COM DEG FAR GUR HIG MEY PAR ROS SEE SUN VER WIL

Typical Problem

My mustard greens keep going to flower very early. Mustard greens are a cool weather crop. If you keep having trouble with spring plantings, try planting in August for fall use.

Harvesting

Pick the leaves just before they mature. Be sure to keep the plants cut back to hold off flowering. After flowering, the leaves become tough and bitter.

Okra

Warm season crop. Rated fair for IPS gardens.

If you're from the South, you probably know and love okra, but for some reason, people in the rest of the country often ignore okra (except for a few pieces in commercially prepared soups), at least as a garden vegetable. If you'd like a delicious vegetable that will add flavor and body to soups and stews, you've got to include this one.

Unfortunately, the okra plant is too big to be a really good vegetable in our IPS gardens. But there are several dwarf varieties that you can put in your flower borders, and it'll give you all the okra you'll need.

Chinese Okra

Planting

This is a warm weather plant with about the same requirements as corn. Plant only after the ground has warmed up. Soak the seeds overnight before planting, then plant them $1/2$ to $1^{1}/_{2}$ inches deep, about 8 inches apart. Thin the seedlings to 15 inches apart.

Give okra a feeding of fish emulsion at least once, six to eight weeks after planting (apply according to the directions on the bottle).

Crop Stretching

Stick okra in odd corners of flowerbeds to use extra space that would ordinarily not be productive for vegetables.

Popular Varieties

CLEMSON SPINELESS	55 to 60 days 4- to 5-foot plant produces 6- to 9-inch rich green pods. Seed source: BOU BURP BURR COM DEG GUR JLH JUN LED LEJ MEY PAR PIN POR RED ROS SEE SOU VER
DWARF GREEN LONG POD	50 days 3-foot plant produces 7-inch-long pods. Seed source: ALL DEG LED MEY POR SEE

Typical Problems

The buds keep dropping off, and no pods come. This usually results from a lack of adequate moisture. Thus, make sure that you water regularly during the growing season.

I planted my okra early in the spring, and the plants didn't do well for a long time. Okra is a warm season crop. Don't plant until the soil has warmed.

Harvesting

Pick the pods young, before they become too large—within a few days after the flower petals have fallen. Overripe pods, if left on the plants, will cause the plants to cease producing.

To freeze okra, cut the stems off the pods, blanch the pods in boiling water two to three minutes, cool, place in containers, and freeze.

Okra Growing Tip

Cut, Don't Pull: Instead of straining to pull off okra pods, just cut with scissors. It's best to harvest when they are young and tender with half grown, immature seeds. If left on the plant, they become hard and unpalatable.

Onions

Cool season crop. Rated excellent for IPS gardens.

Onions comprise a happy family of vegetables for gardeners and cooks. They're grown the world over and used as seasoning for meats, vegetables, and salads and as vegetables alone. Although they're mainly a cool weather crop, they'll do fine in moderately warm weather.

Planting

Onions can be grown from seeds, seedlings, or sets (small bulbs or roots). Seeds should be scattered about 1 inch apart and covered with $1/2$ inch of soil. As the plants rise, harvest the small onions so that the remaining plants are spaced about 2 or 3 inches apart; then let the mature bulbs develop. Seedlings, purchased from a nursery, should be planted 1 inch apart and then thinned to 2 to 3 inches apart as they grow larger.

Sets, which are tiny bulbs, are probably the best way to grow onions, because they're good sized and easy to handle. Some varieties, however, can't be grown from sets but must be grown from seeds; and generally, in fact, the variety of onions that you'll find available as sets is pretty limited. In any case, plant sets 1 to 2 inches apart; then harvest green onions until the plants are spaced 2 to 3 inches apart, letting the remaining bulbs develop to maturity.

Seeds, seedlings, and sets should all be planted in early spring. In areas of mild winters, they can be planted all winter long.

Onions need lots of moisture, especially during bulb formation (tops grow during cool weather, bulbs during warmer weather). A good general rule is to never allow the soil to dry out. Onions are also heavy feeders, but they do pretty well in our IPS soil without extra feeding.

Crop Stretching

Plant green onions between tomatoes, corn, eggplant, or other large plants, and harvest them before the later crops get big.

Popular Varieties

The two most popular kinds of onions are ordinary bulbing onions and bunching onions. Bunching onions are usually called green onions (or scallions).

The green onions listed below are varieties especially intended to be harvested as green onions. However, dry bulb onions can be harvested as small green onions just twenty to thirty days after planting; only if you leave them in the ground for the length of time noted will they become bulb onions.

Green onions

Evergreen Long White	65 to 120 days Long, silvery white stems. Don't form bulbs. Seed source: ABU BURP DEG FIS JLH PAR PON SEE SUN TWI WILL
He Ski Ko Evergreen	60 to 80 days Winter-hardy perennial. White, pungent flesh without bulbs. Seed source: ALL BOU COM FAR GUR HEN JLH JUN NIC PIN SEE STO THE VER

Dry bulb onions
Globe-shaped

Early Yellow Globe	98 to 114 days Deep yellow scales, clear white flesh. Mild flavor. Seed source: ABU DEG FAR JUN PIN SOU STO TER VER WILL
Redman	105 days Deep burgundy scales, with red interior. Medium pungency. Seed source: JOH STO TER WILL
Southport Red Globe	100 to 120 days Deep red scales, pink tinged white rings. Pungent flavor. Seed source: JLH LIB PIN THO
Southport White Globe	100 to 110 days Clear white scales, white rings, mild flavor. Seed source: BOU DEG LED MEY PIN

Bermuda

Red Burgundy	95 days Soft, mild red onion. Also called the hamburger onion. Seed source: BURP DEG FAR GUR HEN NIC POR ROS SEE WIL
Yellow Bermuda	92 to 185 days Straw-colored scales. Mild flavor. Seed source: BURP DEG POR

Typical Problem

My onions didn't get very big. You probably let the soil dry out during bulb enlargement. Make sure that you water regularly.

Harvesting

When the tops of ordinary bulb onions begin to dry and yellow, bend them over to a nearly horizontal position on the ground or break them off. This will divert all growing energy to the bulbs. When all the tops are dead, dig the bulbs up and let them dry on top of the ground for a few days; then store them in a dry, frost-free place indefinitely.

Vidalia

Yellow Grano

Green onions can be harvested as needed. But you should recognize that they don't keep long after harvesting, even with refrigeration.

Onion Growing Tip

When onions flower: Sometimes onions planted from sets form flowers and fail to produce mature bulbs. Avoid this by selecting and planting smaller sized onion sets. When flowers appear, break off the flower buds and use these poorer onions first.

White Sweet Spanish

Peas

Cool season crop. Rated good to excellent for IPS gardens.

Peas are nearly always a star performer in the garden. They come up right away, bloom fast, and produce lots of food within sixty to eighty days. Peas are a cool-season crop, thriving in soil and air filled with cool moisture. Although they'll continue growing and producing when the days become somewhat warmer and longer, they do not do well in hot dry weather.

Planting

Pea plants grow only from seeds planted directly in the bed where they're going to remain. Plant the seeds in the spring as soon as the ground can be worked, sowing them 2 inches deep, 2 inches apart. Use successive plantings, five to ten days apart, for a continuous crop.

Crop Stretching

Peas grow either as bushes or as vines. The vines can—and should—be trained in the air, and you can do this a number of ways:

1. Place chicken wire fence along the north side of your garden, and train your vines on it.
2. Sink a 4-foot post (preferably a 2 by 2) in the ground with a 1-foot cross nailed to the top. Run pea vines (about 12 plants) up strings stretched from the ground to the cross. You can station several of these crosses around the garden.
3. Make a construction wire island: Form a circle of wire about 2 feet in diameter and 5 feet high and plant and train pea vines inside it. When harvest time comes, you can pick the pods through the wires.

Popular Varieties

The common green peas, also called garden peas or English peas, are grown for their edible seeds; they grow as vines or bushes. Peas grown for their edible pods, popular in Oriental cooking, are known as Chinese snow peas or sugar peas and grow as vines.

BUSH GREEN PEAS

ALASKA
52 to 58 days 29-inch vine, 2½-inch pods, 6 to 8 peas per pod. Seed source: ABU BURR BUT DEG FAR MEY PIN SEE TIL VER WIL

GREEN ARROW
62 to 100 days 28-inch vine, 4-inch pods, 8 to 12 peas per pod. Seed source: ABU ALL BOU BURP BURR COM COO DEG FAR FIS GAR GUR HEN JOH JUN MEY NIC PAR PIN PON POR STO THO TWI VER WILL

LAXTON'S PROGRESS
60 days 20-inch vine, 4½-inch pods, 7 to 9 peas per pod. Seed source: ALL BURR FAR FIS GUR HEN JUN LED MEY TIL TWI VER WIL WILL

LITTLE MARVEL
58 to 64 days 18-inch vine, 3-inch pods, 7 to 9 peas per pod. Seed source: ABU ALL BURP BURR DEG FAR GUR HEN JUN LED MEY PON POR SEE SOU STO TIL WIL WILL

MAESTRO
57 to 61 days 24-inch vine, 4-inch pods, 9 to 10 peas per pod. Seed source: BURP GAR GUR HEN HIG JOH JUN ORN PAR TER

VINE GREEN PEAS

ALDERMAN
75 days 6-foot vine, 5-inch pods, 8 to 9 peas per pod. Seed source: ABU ALL BOU COM FAR GAR LED ORN PIN SEE STO TER TIL VER WILL

FREEZONIAN
60 days 2½-foot vine, 3½-inch pod, 7 to 9 peas per pod. Seed source: ALL BURG BURR DEG FAR LED TIL VER

EDIBLE PODDED PEAS

DWARF GREY SUGAR
65 to 70 days 2½-foot vine, 3-inch pods. Seed source: ABU BOU COM FIS GUR HEN JLH LEJ POR RED SEE SUN WILL

SUGAR ANN
56 days 18-inch vine. Seed source: ABU BURG GAR GOU HEN HIG JOH JUN LED MEY NIC PIN PON POR STO SUN TER TWI WILL

SUGAR SNAP
6-foot vine, 3-inch pods. Seed source: ABU ALL BOU BURG BURP BURR BUT COM DEG GAR GUR HEN HIG JOH JUN LED MEY NIC PAR PLA POR RED ROS SEE SOU SUN TIL TWI VER WIL WILL

Typical Problems

My vines are lush and bushy but produce few peas. To start them producing, simply pinch back the growing tips of the various stems, thereby thinning out the vine a little.

My pea pods are hard when I pick them. You're letting them stay on the vines too long. Pick them regularly.

My peas aren't growing well; the tips of the leaves seem to be dying. Peas need lots of water when the weather is warm and the atmosphere dry. If the days are extremely hot, there's not much you can do; you must grow peas in cool weather.

Harvesting

Pick off all the pods as they mature in order to keep the plants producing vigorously. It is best to harvest only in the morning; this seems to preserve their flavor. After picking, shell them and store them in the refrigerator as soon as possible.

For freezing peas, shell them, blanch the seeds in boiling water about three minutes, cool, place in containers, and freeze.

Pea Growing Tips

Pollinating peas: When peas produce a profusion of blossoms but no pods, it means the pollen isn't being transferred from the male parts to the female parts of the flower. Peas are self-pollinating, but once in awhile they get lazy and need a little help. Just shake them a couple of times a day for about a week, then get ready for a bumper crop.

Pre-sprouting peas: To ensure that peas will come up fast, pre-sprout them by laying a paper towel on a waterproof surface. Scatter peas evenly over it and cover with another paper towel. Dampen this pea sandwich, roll it up, and put it in a plastic bag in a warm room. A few days later, unroll and remove pre-germinated seeds. Plant outdoors. They'll grow even in cold soil.

Peppers

Warm season crop. Rated excellent for IPS gardens.

Pepper plants are very pretty. It's not the flowers that make them so attractive, however; it's the fruit and foliage, and they make great ornamentals.

Snow Peas

Peppers originally came to the attention of the Western world when explorers landing in the New World tasted the native chili and mistook it for the spice "pepper," one of the trading spices from the Orient. The New World "pepper," however, tasted only vaguely like the East Indian pepper that they were looking for. In fact, the various sweet and hot peppers native to the New World are related to the tomato and eggplant.

Planting

Peppers are classified as hot weather plants; thus they like temperatures above 60°F. On the other hand, they also like temperatures below 90°F. Anywhere out of this temperature range, from 60° to 90°, seems to keep the fruit from setting.

You can start peppers either from seeds or from plants purchased from your local nursery. If you're going to use seeds, you should start them indoors in peat pots—two to four seeds, 1/2 inch deep, in each pot—about ten weeks before you intend to set the plants out. In your garden bed, space the seedlings 14 inches apart.

Peppers need lots of regular watering. They are also heavy feeders and should be fed fish emulsion about the time that the first blossoms open (apply according to the instructions on the bottle).

Popular Varieties

There are a lot of different kinds of peppers—all shapes and sizes and colors—but generally the most common can be divided into two classes: sweet and hot (the sweet we know as bell peppers).

SWEET PEPPERS
GREEN

BELL BOY — 63 to 70 days 3¼ by 3½ inches, glossy green pepper. 24-inch plant. Seed source: COM DEG FAR GUR HEN JUN LED MEY PIN STO TOMA VER WIL WILL

CALIFORNIA WONDER — 75 days 4½ by 4 inches, glossy green. Seed source: ALL BURG COM DEG FAR GUR HEN LEJ MEY NIC ORG PIN PON POR RED ROS SOU STO TIL VER WIL WILL

YOLO WONDER — 77 days 4 by 4¾ inches, 4 lobes, thick walls. Seed source: BOU DEG LEJ STO

RED

EARLIEST RED SWEET — 55 to 60 days 3 by 4 inches, 2 to 3 lobes, red pepper. Seed source: HIG PIN STO

ITALIAN RED MACARONI	75 days 12 by 3 inches, 3 lobes, bright red. Seed source: ABU COO

HOT PEPPERS

ANCHO	65 to 100 days Also known as Poblano. 4 inches long, red when ripe. 36-inch plant. Seed source: BURP HEN HOR NIC PIN PLA RED SEE SEED SHE
FRESNO	78 days 2½ by 1 inch long. Very pungent. 24-inch plant. Seed source: HOR SEED
HUNGARIAN YELLOW WAX	60 to 68 days 6 by 1¼ inch long, light yellow that matures to red when ripe. 14 to 22-inch plant. Seed source: BOU BURG BURP BURR COM DEG GAR GUR HEN HIG HOR JOH LED LEJ LIB MEY NIC PAR PIN POR ROS SEE SEED SOU STO TER TIL TWI WIL WILL
JALAPENO	72 to 80 days 3⅓ by 1½ inches long. Goes from green to red when ripe. 26- to 36-inch plant. Seed source: BURR BUT COM COO DEG FIS GLE GUR HEN HOR NIC PLA PON POR RED ROS SEE SEED SOU STO SUN

**Serrano
Chili**

Habanero

Ancho

Typical Problem

The blossoms dropped off, and I stopped getting fruit. This could be the result of a couple of things. The night temperatures may have become too hot or too cold; if so, there's not much you can do. Or you may not be picking the ripe peppers regularly; pepper plants usually won't continue producing more blossoms when the plants have all the fruit they can handle.

Harvesting

Pick bell peppers when they are firm and crisp. Most people believe that they have a better flavor when picked green, not red, unless they are a red variety. Let hot peppers completely ripen on the vine.

For freezing, first dice or slice them and then freeze them one hour on an uncovered cookie sheet. Then put the pieces in small bags and return to the freezer.

Pepper Growing Tips

Increasing pepper production: To double and triple pepper production, plant only the stockiest of seedlings with well-developed root systems. Leggy, already blossoming seedlings will not produce like the younger, fuller plants. When they begin to produce, pick off the first

Jalapeno

Yellow Cayenne

pepper—the "crown set." This encourages a higher production of big fruits over the entire season.

Night temperatures: Spring planted peppers sometimes just sit there with the leaves turning yellow. The reason: Peppers need nighttime temperatures above 55° to grow properly. To solve this, wait until the weather turns warm before popping your peppers into the ground.

Helping hand: If peppers are slow setting fruit in hot weather, syringe the plants with water. Then give a dose of liquid fish fertilizer every seven to ten days when the first fruits start to swell. This helps produce larger, heavier crops.

Radishes

Cool season crop. Rated excellent for IPS gardens.

The radish is a quick-maturing, here-today-and-gone-tomorrow plant. Some varieties of radish mature in as few as twenty-two days; others average about a month—which is fast for most vegetables. They're also ridiculously easy to grow; give anyone a package of radish seeds, and you make him or her an instant gardener.

Planting

Just pop your radish seeds into the ground as soon as it can be worked; after that, sow more seeds every week or so to assure a continuous crop. It is best to plant only what you can eat in a week or so; then you won't get overloaded with radishes. Because radishes are a cool-weather crop, halt the sowing in early summer and then resume about a month before the first frost. The seeds should be scattered about 1 inch apart, $\frac{1}{2}$ inch deep.

Crop Stretching

Radishes can be sown early in places where you will be planting such later crops as corn and tomatoes. Because of the speed with which radishes grow, you can plant them between any vegetables that require a 4- or 5-inch spacing; the radishes will be harvested before the main crops get very big.

Popular Varieties

There are two main kinds of radishes: the ordinary ones (though of many shapes and hues), which are small and quick maturing, and the winter ones, which are usually large and require cool weather at the end of their growing season. Usually these are the Oriental varieties. The winter varieties should be sown in midsummer. Although both the skin and flesh of ordinary radishes are edible, the skin of winter radishes should be peeled to reveal the edible white flesh.

ORDINARY RADISHES

CHAMPION	25 to 28 days Bright scarlet, round. Seed source: BURG BURP COM DEG FAR FIS GAR GUR HEN HIG JUN LED LIB MEY POR SEE STO VER WIL
CHERRY BELLE	20 to 24 days $3/4$-inch round radish, resembles a cherry. Seed source: ABU ALL BOU BURP BURR COM DEG FAR FIS GUR HEN JUN LED LEJ LIB MEY NIC PIN PON POR SEE SEED SOU STO TIL TWI VER WIL WILL
FRENCH BREAKFAST	20 to 30 days $1^3/4$ inches oblong, rose-scarlet with white tip. Seed source: ABU ALL BOU BURP COM DEG FAR FIS GUR HEN JUN LED MEY NIC ORG ORN PIN PON POR ROS SEE STO TER TIL WILL
WHITE ICICLE	27 to 30 days 4 to 5 inches long, all white. Seed source: ALL BURG BURP BURR COM DEG FAR FIS GAR GUR HEN JLH JUN LED LIB MEY NIC ORN PIN PON POR SEE SOU STO TER TWI VER WIL WILL

WINTER RADISHES

BLACK SPANISH ROUND	53 to 80 days Globe, $3^1/2$-inch diameter. Black skin, pungent white flesh. Seed source: BOU COM DEG FAR GUR JLH JUN LED LIB MEY SEE SOU STO VER WILL
CHINESE ROSE	52 days 7 by 2 inches. Rose to light pink skin, white pungent flesh. Seed source: DEG HEN JLH JUN LED MEY NIC PIN POR SEE SOU STO SUN VER

Typical Problems

I get lots of leaves but no radish bottoms. You sowed the seeds too close together. Thin the plants to at least 1 inch apart.

My radishes taste so hot I can hardly eat them. Sometimes this happens when the soil becomes hot and dries out. Keep watering regularly.

Harvesting

Pick radishes when they're still fairly small and young (pull up a couple to see). They'll be tender, succulent, and full of flavor at this stage. Later on they'll be somewhat pithy.

Radish Growing Tip

Plant Radishes with Carrots. Mix carrot and radish seeds together and scatter across the bed. The radishes will come up quickly. Harvest them before the carrots need their first thinning.

Rhubarb

Cool season crop. Rated fair for IPS gardens.

If you like big-leaved plants, you'll love this one. It looks almost like a tropical growing in your garden, and it compares favorably with any of the broad-leaved plants grown primarily as ornamentals. Rhubarb, however, is a perennial, like asparagus, and will spread out and take up an awful lot of space. It's therefore not the best thing for IPS gardens. That shouldn't rule it out, though, because it'll do very well in its own separate bed or especially in your flower beds, where it'll look tremendous.

Planting

Rhubarb doesn't do well in most subtropical regions of the United States because it needs a winter dormant period, although it can do well in mild winter areas. You should purchase root crowns from your nursery and plant them 12 inches apart in the spring or fall (36 inches apart if you want giant plants). Dig holes and set the plants in so that the tops of the roots stand 3 or 4 inches below ground level; cover with soil. Wait two years after planting before you begin to pull stalks for eating. From then on you'll have ample yield for the next eight or nine years.

Water rhubarb regularly and deep, and give the plants a feeding of fish emulsion once or twice a year (apply according to the instructions on the bottle).

Crop Stretching

Put rhubarb in odd flower bed space not suited for other vegetables.

Popular Varieties

CANADA RED	90 days Stalks are deep red. Seed source: FAR GUR HEN JUN
VALENTINE	90 days Deep red stalks measure 22 by 1½ inches. Seed source: BURP GUR HEN JUN
VICTORIA	90 days Deep red, with slight green shoulders. Seed source: DEG LED PAR PIN ROS VER WILL

Typical Problems

Practically none.

Harvesting

Select the larger outside stalks; grasp them firmly near the base and snap them off. Use only the stalks for eating; discard the dark green leaves, which are poisonous. For freezing rhubarb, wash the stalks, cut them in ¾-inch slices, put in containers, and freeze.

Rhubarb Growing Tip

Early Rhubarb: To get a jump on the season, force rhubarb during the winter months (cooler climates only), place a 2-foot-high barrel, wooden box, or large pot over the plant, and cover with a lid to keep out the light. Cover the whole thing with grass clippings, straw, dead leaves, or garden compost. The rhubarb in the barrel will produce rhubarb stalks early in the season before the exposed rhubarb starts to grow.

Spinach

Cool season crop. Rated fair to good for IPS gardens.

Spinach is one of those on-again, off-again vegetables. We live in one of those areas where it may be cool in March and April and 90° a few weeks later in May. That's what you might call a spinach grower's nightmare, because spinach must have cool weather, or else. Give it long days and hot temperatures, and all of a sudden it's gone to seed.

Planting

Spinach grows best from seeds, set directly in the ground where they're to grow. Sow the seeds in early spring and again in late summer, placing them about ½ inch deep and 2 inches apart. Thin the seedlings to about 6 inches apart. For a long crop, make successive plantings ten days apart.

Spinach is a heavy feeder, so give the plants a feeding of fish emulsion about halfway through the season (apply according to the directions on the bottle).

Crop Stretching

You can harvest your early spinach in the late spring and then plant beans. Later, when it cools off, you can follow the beans with another planting of spinach for a fall crop.

Popular Varieties

BLOOMSDALE LONG STANDING	39 to 48 days Very crinkled, glossy, dark green leaves. Seed source: ABU ALL BURP BURR BUT DEG FAR GAR GUR HEN HIG JLH JUN LED LIB MEY NIC PAR PIN PLA RED SEE SOU STO TIL VER WIL WILL
MELODY	42 days Dark green leaves. Seed source: BURP FAR GOU HEN JUN LED MEY NIC PAR PIN POR STO TWI VER
NOBEL GIANT	46 days Huge, thick, smooth, pointed leaves with round tips. Seed source: BURR DEG HEN JLH SEE TIL

Typical Problem

My spinach flowers every spring before I get a good crop. The problem is that spinach tends to flower (bolt) quickly, especially as the days get longer and the temperatures a little higher. The only solution is to grow a variety, like Bloomsdale Long Standing, that is slow to bolt. Or, if you live in an area of mild winters, plant in late summer or in the fall for a late crop.

Harvesting

Harvest the outer leaves when the plants are full size (when the outer leaves are at least 3 inches long). If you pick just the outer leaves, the inner ones will become the next crop.

For freezing spinach, pick the tender leaves only, blanch them in boiling water one-and-a-half minutes, cool, put in containers, and freeze.

A Spinach Substitute for IPS Gardens—New Zealand Spinach

New Zealand spinach is not a true spinach but a succulent plant from New Zealand that resembles spinach in appearance and is highly heat and drought resistant. For this reason you can grow it all summer long, when spinach would be impossible.

New Zealand spinach is a low-growing, ground-cover type plant that spreads 2 to 4 feet across. Seeds can be started indoors or outdoors. Indoors, sow them in peat pots 1 inch deep and then transplant the seedlings to the garden after the last frost. Outdoors, simply sow the seeds 1 inch deep, about 8 inches apart.

Harvest New Zealand spinach by cutting the young tender stems when you need them. Seed source: ALL BOU BURP BUT COM DEG FAR GAR GOU HEN JLH JUN LED LIB MEY NIC PIN POR RED ROS SEE SOU STO VER WILL

Spinach Growing Tip

Cut Back: Some gardeners stop spinach flowering by cutting the plant back to the ground when there are just four or five leaves on the plant. As soon as new leaves appear, harvest and cut back again. If you wait too long, hoping the leaves will become nice and big, you end up with less spinach.

Squash

Warm season crop. Rated good for IPS gardens.

Traditional gardeners grow both summer squash and winter squash. Summer squash is harvested and cooked in summer while immature and soft-skinned; it will not store for long. Winter squash, which is left on the vines until the shells are thoroughly hardened and leaves turn brown, stores well for fall and winter use. IPS gardeners should prefer summer squash because it produces smaller fruit with thinner skins, grows usually as bushy compact plants, and doesn't take up much space.

Winter squash has runner-type vines that can require lots of space. Nevertheless, although IPS gardeners probably should stick to summer squash, they can grow the vines of winter squash in the air, as we do cucumbers. The heavy fruits must be tied up with cloth supports.

Planting

Squash is extremely easy to grow, but it's a heat lover and shouldn't be set outdoors until nighttime temperatures regularly stay above 55°F.

Use seeds or seedlings purchased from a nursery. Plant seeds 1 inch deep, 18 inches apart. Set seedlings 18 inches apart.

Crop Stretching

Small-fruited winter squash can be trained up in the air on the same kind of structures as those used for cucumbers. Be sure to support the fruit with cloth slings.

Popular Varieties

Among the varieties of summer squash, zucchini is a wonder, because it can be prepared in so many ways: You can stuff it, fry it, bake it in a casserole, or cut it up for salads. Generally you'll find two or three zucchini plants enough because the plants are so prolific. We swear that you can find it in bloom one morning, then come back two days later and pick a full-blown zucchini. You should also try some of the other summer varieties. As I said, most winter varieties are too big for IPS gardens; we're listing some you might try.

SUMMER SQUASH

BLACK BEAUTY	58 days Blackish-green zucchini. Pick at 6 to 8 inches. Seed source: BOU COM DEG HIG LED SOU TER TIL WIL
EARLY PROLIFIC STRAIGHTNECK	50 days Creamy yellow straightneck squash should be picked when 3 to 4 inches long. Seed source: ALL BURP BURR BUT COM DEG FIS GAR GUR HEN LED MEY ROS SOU VER WIL
SUNBURST	50 to 53 days Pick when this bright yellow scallop squash is 3 inches across. Seed source: COM DEG GAR JOH LIB NIC ORN PAR PIN POR SHE TER VER
YELLOW CROOKNECK	42 to 58 days Bright yellow crookneck squash is best picked when 4 to 5 inches long. Seed source: BUT GAR HIG JOH ORG PIN SEE SEED SOU TER

WINTER SQUASH
SPACE SAVERS

BURPEE'S BUTTERBUSH	75 days 1³/₄ pounds, deep reddish flesh. Plant grows 3 to 4 feet long and bears 4 to 5 fruit. Seed source: BURP PIN
BUSH BUTTERCUP	80 to 100 days 3 to 5 pounds, round, thick orange flesh. Seed source: ALL COM FIS LIB TIL
BUTTERNUT BUSH	95 days 10 to 12 inches long, small seed cavity, rich orange flesh. Seed source: PON

Black Beauty

Sunburst Squash

TABLE KING   70 to 80 days 1½-pound acorn squash. 6 to 8 fruit per
                      vine. Seed source: GAR LED TWI

Typical Problem

My zucchini plants start out each year producing some small squash that rot before they get very big. Some female flowers on the plant bloomed before there were male flowers around to pollinate them. These unpollinated flowers result in small fruits that rot. Just wait and you'll get plenty of zucchini that will grow to full size.

Harvesting

Pick summer squash when it's fairly young and small. It's tender and delicious then. Usually, summer squash is too old for eating when the thumbnail doesn't readily pierce the skin with little pressure. Let winter squash mature fully on the vine until its skin is very hard.

Both summer and winter squash can be frozen, but winter squash must first be peeled. Cut the squash into small pieces, blanch the pieces in boiling water one-and-a-half minutes, cool, place in containers, and freeze.

Squash Growing Tips

Summer Squash: Playing Bee: If mature squash plants produce few fruit, the problem may be a lack of bees. Collect the yellow pollen with an artist brush and dust the female flowers (the ones with the tiny miniature squash at the base). Put the pollen on the tip of the small fruit above the flower (the stigma).

Baby Squash: You don't need a particular variety to create a baby squash delicacy. Simply pick miniature size squash with the blossoms still on the fruit. Most hostesses cook and serve whole.

Greater Yields: Few gardeners really want to improve the yields of summer squash. If you do, however, try mulching with alumininized foil. Experiment station research shows it produces significantly greater yields.

Winter Squash: Squash Basics: Before harvesting winter squash for storage, push your thumbnail against the squash as hard as you can. If the outer skin doesn't cut easily, the squash will keep for a long time. If the squash skin cuts easily, it will probably rot in storage. If already picked, cook the squash within a few days.

Swiss Chard

Cool season crop. Rated good for IPS gardens.

If you've tried spinach and failed or are just tired of fighting its special weather requirements, then you'll want to grow Swiss chard, for it can take summer temperatures that would make spinach bolt to seed. Chard, a member of the beet family, but without the bulbous root, has delicious big crinkly leaves and delicious white stalks. That's a double dividend. The leaves are cooked like spinach or other greens. The stalks are cooked and served like asparagus.

Planting

In cold winter areas, plant seeds in the spring about two or three weeks before the final frost; in areas where winter temperatures stay above 25°F, plant in the fall for harvesting the next year. In fact, in regions of very mild climates you can plant almost any time of the year.

Broadcast the seeds about 4 inches apart across the bed and cover with 1/2 inch of soil. When the seedlings come up, thin to stand at least 8 inches apart.

Crop Stretching

Plant Swiss chard in spaces that will later contain corn, tomatoes, and other heat lovers.

Popular Varieties

Fordhook Giant	50 to 60 days Snow-white midribs and heavily crumpled leaves. Seed source: ABU ALL BURP COM FIS GAR HIG JOH MEY ORN PON RED ROS SEE STO TER TWI VER WIL
Rhubarb Chard	55 to 60 days Crimson stalks with crumpled green leaves. Seed source: ABU ALL BURP BURR COM DEG FAR FIS GAR JOH LED NIC ORG ORN PIN SEE SEED SHE STO TER TIL TWI VER WILL

Typical Problems

Almost none.

Swiss Chard

Chard Growing Tip

Cut off the leaves an inch or two above the crowns. The whole plant will take on a new life.

Harvesting

There are two ways to harvest Swiss chard. Every few days you can cut the outer leaves from the plant while it continues growing. (Don't let old and tough leaves remain on the plant, or the plant will stop producing fresh leaves.) Or you can also cut off the whole plant a couple of inches above the root crown, and the plant will produce new leaves.

Tomatoes

Warm season crop. Excellent for IPS gardens.

The tomato is one of those strange vegetables that seem to grow well in spite of what people do to it. One of our neighbors plants a few tomato plants in the backyard, then barely waters or weeds them, yet they always seem to come out great. We have another neighbor, on the other hand, who takes meticulous care of his tomato plants, selects the varieties carefully, plants them at the right time, then sprays and feeds them religiously. His crops turn out great too—which leads us to believe that it's pretty hard to go very far wrong growing tomatoes. Temperature seems to be the crucial factor. As warm-weather plants, tomato seedlings should not be set out in the garden until night-time temperatures begin staying above 58°F.

Planting

You can start your tomatoes from seeds or buy them as seedlings. Buying seedlings is the easiest way, and the one we use. You'll generally have to grow from seed, however, if you want a wide choice of varieties.

To start from seeds, plant them $1/2$ inch deep in compressed peat pots. Then after the weather outdoors has warmed up, plant the pots with the seedlings in your IPS beds 18 inches apart.

There are a couple of rules that you should follow when transplanting seedlings. If you have a bushy plant (which is preferable to a long lean one), bury it so that ¹/₂ to ³/₄ of the stem as well as the root ball is below the soil level; roots will form along the buried stem. For really long-stemmed plants, you still should get ¹/₂ to ³/₄ of the stem underground, but you should be careful not to place the root ball too deep. In a shallow hole, put the root ball almost on its side so that the stem is semihorizontal, or at least not vertical; then you gradually bend the stem so that only the bushy part appears upright above ground level.

Tomatoes generally are deep rooted, often going 6 feet deep or more. The plants should get plenty of moisture during the growing season. Overwatering, however, can stimulate too much leaf growth and cause blossoms to drop. Too much shade or too much nitrogen fertilizer can also cut down blossoming. Despite these apparent problems, tomatoes seem easy to grow.

If you have tomato diseases around (ask your nursery person), avoid them by looking for the letters *V*, *F*, and *N* on the instructions accompanying your seeds or seedlings. The letters stand for varieties resistant to verticillium, and fusarium, and nematode, major tomato diseases.

Tomatoes are heavy feeders. However, in an IPS bed it usually isn't necessary to give them an extra feeding during the season.

Figure 5-5. Tomato growing technique for an IPS garden.

Crop Stretching

There are several ways to adapt tomato plants to an IPS garden:

1. Make a fence of chicken wire stretched between two 5- or 6-foot posts (preferably 2 by 2s). As the plants grow, cut back enough foliage to make each plant easy to tie to the wires, but leave as many stems as possible—say, two to six. (This way you'll get more fruit.)

2. Make a lath framework or trellis for each plant. Pinch off all but two or four main stems and tie them to the frame.

3. The best thing for IPS gardens is to make a circular tomato cage from a 5-foot length of construction wire. (That's the kind used for concrete reinforcing, with a 6-inch mesh.) Just circle each plant in your garden with the wire, and tie the ends of the wire together. You don't have to cut off any plant stems, but you'll probably have to tie the stems to the wire. This tomato cage will give you an extremely productive bushy tomato factory.

Popular Varieties

You've got a lot of choices of tomatoes, so let's divide the varieties into early, midseason, and late; large fruit, small fruit, and container varieties; yellow and other variations. The early varieties set fruit at lower temperatures than later maturing plants; you get tomatoes much earlier in the season.

EARLY

CELEBRITY   70 to 80 days Determinate plant. 7- to 12-ounce red globe fruit. Seed source: BURG BURP BURR COM DEG FAR GUR HEN JOH LED LIB MEY NIC PAR PIN POR STO TER TOM TOMA TWI VER WIL WILL

EARLY GIRL   50 to 62 days Indeterminate plant. 4- to 6-ounce red fruit. Seed source: ALL BURG BURP DEG FAR GAR GUR HEN MEY NIC ORN PAR POR TIL TOM TOMA VER

OREGON SPRING   58 to 70 days Determinate plant. 4-inch diameter red fruit. Seed source: GAR HIG JOH NIC PIN SEE SEED SHE TIL TOM TOMA

MIDSEASON

FLORAMERICA   70 to 80 days Determinate plant. Deep red tomatoes grow up to 1 pound. Seed source: ALL BURG BURR DEG FAR JUN LED LIB MEY POR TOM TOMA TWI VER WIL WILL

MOUNTAIN DELIGHT | 77 days Determinate plant. 8-ounce red fruit. Seed source: BURR GUR HEN LED LIB MEY PAR TOMA TWI

RUTGERS | 73 to 90 days Indeterminate plant. 6-ounce red fruit. Seed source: BOU BURP COM DEG FAR GLE HEN JLH LIB MEY ROS SEE SOU TOM TOMA VER WIL

LATE

FLORADADE | 77 to 83 days Determinate plant. 7-ounce red fruit. Seed source: BURR TOM TOMA

HOMESTEAD 25 | 80 to 83 days Determinate plant. 8-ounce red fruit. Seed source: SOU TOMA WIL

PEARSON A-1 IMPROVED | 80 to 93 days Determinate plant. $\frac{1}{4}$- to $\frac{1}{2}$-pound fruit. Seed source: BURR ORG ROS TOM WIL

LARGE FRUIT

BEEFMASTER | 80 days Indeterminate plant. Up to 2-pound fruit. Seed source: ALL COM DEG GUR HEN LED LIB MEY PAR PIN POR TOM TOMA TWI VER WIL

BETTER BOY | 70 to 75 days Indeterminate plant. Up to 1-pound bright red fruit. Seed source: ALL BURG BURP BURR COM DEG GUR HEN LED LEJ LIB MEY NIC PAR PIN PON POR STO TOM TOMA TWI VER WIL WILL

BIG BOY | 80 days Indeterminate plant. Bright red fruit grows up to 2 pounds. Seed source: BURG BURP COM DEG FAR GUR HEN JUN LED MEY PAR STO TOM TOMA TWI

CONTAINER

PATIO | 50 to 70 days Determinate plant 24 to 30 inches tall. 2-inch, 4-ounce red fruit. Seed source: ALL COM DEG LED LIB TOM TOMA WIL

SMALL FRY | 65 to 72 days Determinate, compact plant. Red, 1-inch cherry tomatoes. Seed source: BURG COM JUN LED LIB STO TOM TOMA

TINY TIM | 45 to 60 days Determinate; 6-by-6-inch plant. $\frac{3}{4}$-inch red fruit. Seed source: ALL BURG COM GLE LED SEE STO TOM TOMA WILL

SMALL FRUIT

GARDENER'S DELIGHT | 50 to 80 days Indeterminate plant. $\frac{1}{2}$- to $\frac{3}{4}$-inch red fruit. Seed source: BOU BURP COO GAR PAR PIN SEE SEED THO TOM TOMA

GOLD NUGGET | 50 to 80 days Determinate plant. $1\frac{1}{2}$-inch diameter golden-yellow tomatoes. Seed source: COO HIG JOH NIC ORN PIN SEE SEED TOM TOMA

SWEET 100 — 65 to 70 days Indeterminate plant. Cherry-size red fruit. Seed source: BURP COM COO GUR HEN LIB MEY ORN POR SHE STO THO TIL TOM TOMA TWI

YELLOW PEAR — 70 to 78 days Indeterminate plant. Yellow pear-shaped fruit. Seed source: ABU ALL BURP COO DEG GAR GLE GOU HEN HIG JOH MEY NIC ORN POR SEE SEED SHE SOU STO TOM TOMA WIL WILL

YELLOW/ORANGE FULL-SIZE FRUIT

GOLDEN BOY — 80 days Indeterminate plant. Large, deep yellow fruit. Seed source: COM LEJ PIN TOM TOMA VER WIL

JUBILEE — 72 to 80 days Indeterminate plant. $\frac{1}{2}$-pound orange-yellow fruit. Seed source: ALL BURP BURR DEG FAR LED LIB NIC ORN POR TIL TOM TOMA WIL WILL

LEMON BOY — 72 to 100 days Indeterminate plant. 8 to 10 ounces, bright yellow fruit. Seed source: BURP DEG HEN JLH LIB NIC ORN POR STO TER TOM TOMA VER WILL

PINK FULL-SIZE FRUIT

BRANDYWINE — 74 days Indeterminate plant. $\frac{1}{2}$-pound, dark pinkish red fruit. Seed source: ABU COO GLE JOH ORG PIN SEE SEED SOU TOM TOMA

LONG KEEPER — 75 to 78 days Semideterminate plant. 4- to 7-ounce pale pink fruit. Seed source: ALL BURG BURP COM FAR GAR GUR HEN HIG JUN LED LIB PIN PON SOU TER TOM TOMA WILL

PONDEROSA PINK — 80 to 95 days Indeterminate plant. 2 pounds, rather rough skin. Seed source: DEG LIB NIC POR TOM TOMA VER WIL WILL

Typical Problems

I planted in the spring, and the plants took forever to start growing. Remember that tomatoes are a warm season plant. They'll just sit there looking unhappy if you put them out while it's still too cold. Nighttime temperatures should be above 58°F. In fact, tomatoes grow best in a fairly narrow temperature range—70 to 75°F at night and 80 to 90°F during the day.

My tomato blossoms keep dropping off instead of producing fruit. This happens when the night temperatures go much below 58°F. The problem corrects itself when the nights become warmer. Excess heat can cause the same problem.

My tomato plants look great; they're nice and bushy; but they're just not producing any tomatoes. This could happen because they're getting too much shade or too much water or because it's too hot at night. Try pinching off the terminal shoots and cut down on the water that you're giving your plants.

Harvesting

Tomatoes are best harvested when they have reached their full color. But they may also be picked when showing only a tinge of red, then stored in a warm, dark place to ripen.

Tomato puree can be frozen. Douse the tomatoes in boiling water for a few seconds so that you can skin them easily; remove the seeds if you wish. Then puree the skinned tomatoes in a blender, package the puree, and freeze.

Tomato Growing Tips

Improving fruit set: To improve the fruit set of your tomatoes, try giving individual tomato flower clusters a daily vibration with a battery operated toothbrush. This scatters pollen from top to bottom. Best time to shake and vibrate is midday, when it is warm and the humidity is low.

Extending the season: To keep from losing tomatoes, peppers, and eggplants at the first frost, lay a wide strip of black plastic over each row or cage at night. It protects the fruit and extends the season as much as three weeks.

Turnips and Rutabagas

Cool season crops. Rated good for IPS gardens.

Turnips and rutabagas aren't grown nearly as often in gardens as are other kinds of root crops, such as carrots and beets, but they really have their own distinctive flavor and a very enthusiastic group of fans. The roots of both plants look alike, both having purplish tops; but turnips have white flesh and are about 2 inches across, and rutabagas have either white or yellow flesh and are about 4 or 5 inches across. Also the leaves of turnips are edible as cooked greens; the leaves of rutabagas are not.

Planting

Turnips and rutabagas are both cool-season vegetables and should be planted as early in the spring as the ground can be worked. Sow the seeds $\frac{1}{8}$ to $\frac{1}{4}$ inch deep, about 1 inch apart; and in stages, thin the resultant seedlings to 2 inches apart for turnips, 6 inches apart for rutabagas.

Turnips can also be planted in spring and midsummer in the cooler northern parts of the country. Where winters are frost-free and mild, they can be planted in the fall. Turnips mature in about thirty-five to sixty days, rutabagas in about ninety.

Be sure that turnips and rutabagas receive a steady supply of water to maturity.

Crop Stretching
Plant turnips and rutabagas between cabbages.

Popular Varieties

TURNIP

PURPLE-TOP WHITE GLOBE	45 to 60 days 5-inch diameter, bright purple top, creamy white bottom. Seed source: ABU ALL BURG BURR BUT COM DEG FIS GAR GUR HEN HIG JOH JUN LED LEJ LIB MEY PAR PIN PON POR ROS SEE SEED SOU STO TER TIL TWI VER WIL WILL
TOKYO CROSS	35 days White globe 6 inches across. Seed source: BURP FIS GUR HEN JUN MEY PIN POR TWI VER WILL

RUTABAGA

AMERICAN PURPLE TOP	89 to 90 days Purple top, buttery yellow bottom. 4 to 6 inches diameter. Seed source: ALL BURR DEG FIS GUR HEN JUN LIB MEY PAR PON POR SEE SOU TIL TWI VER

Typical Problems
Practically none.

Harvesting
Harvest turnip roots when they are 2 to 4 inches in diameter and before they get pithy. For turnip greens, harvest the leaves when they are young and tender. Harvest rutabagas when the roots are about 3 to 5 inches in diameter.

For freezing turnips and rutabagas, peel the roots, cut them into cubes, and blanch them in boiling water one to two minutes. Then cool them, place them in containers, and freeze.

Growing Tips

Seed-saving. Rutabagas will cross with turnips, Chinese cabbage or oriental mustard. So isolate any varieties you want to set seed.

Herbs

Herbs are fun to grow and great for kitchen use. Many gardeners insist that they have beneficial effects in the garden; in Chapters 6 and 7 we'll discuss some of the good effects.

For the kitchen, you can always use herbs fresh; just pick pieces as you need them. You can also dry them for storage, but they should be dried quickly and in the dark, in order to preserve their best flavor. You do this by placing them on a cookie sheet and placing them in the oven for two to three hours at the lowest possible heat setting. The oven door should be left slightly ajar (but without the light on). Store the dried herbs in glass or metal containers that can be closed tightly to preserve the flavor.

Now here are a few herbs that you'll want to try.

Basil

Basil

Most Italian cooks would be lost without sweet basil to flavor pasta and other Italian dishes. It's also great for almost any other kind of cooking. The plant is an annual with light-green foliage that grows 1 to 2 feet high. It also comes in a bush form.

Basil will make an attractive plant set in a sunny corner of your flower beds or stuck into a few odd corners of your IPS garden. Simply sow the seeds about 2 inches apart after the last frost. To harvest basil, cut the stems regularly—the more you cut, the more they grow. When the plants flower, cut them about 6 inches from the ground, dry them, and then strip the leaves and flowers and store these in jars.

Chives

Sweet Basil

Chives are a gourmet's delight. You can buy pots of chives from a nursery and separate them. Plant a clump in your IPS garden, or stuff them in an odd corner of a flower bed. (They prefer full sun but will tolerate filtered shade.) When you need some leaves, just clip off what you need.

Dill

Dill is used in pickles; its slightly bitter taste and unusual fragrance is fascinating. Sometimes the "weeds" or stems are used to flavor salads (especially green salads) and to flavor fish and lamb. Dill is good in cottage cheese or with eggs. The plant itself grows 4 feet high, with flowers in clusters.

Sow dill seeds in spring or late summer in a sunny area, and thin the young plants to about 10 inches apart. Harvest the leaves when you need them. Harvest the seeds from the flower beds when they begin to turn brown.

Dill

Garlic

Garlic is not really an herb but a relative of the onion. It is strong medicine, and many gardeners insist that the plant (and its extracts) can be used to control a wide range of insects (see Chapter 7). There are two types available: regular garlic bulbs, which contain a number of small cloves, and elephant garlic. Elephant garlic has the flavor of regular garlic but none of its strong pungency. You can, for instance, slice elephant cloves right into salads.

Plant garlic cloves 1 to $1^{1}/_{2}$ inches deep, 2 inches apart, base down, in an area of full sun. To harvest, dig the roots up when the tops fall over.

Marjoram

Marjoram is used as a seasoning for zucchini, as a wonderful flavoring for Italian dishes, and as an enrichment for many other foods too. Sweet marjoram is a bushy plant that grows 1 to 2 feet high.

Start marjoram seeds indoors in winter; then, after the last frost, set the small plants in sunny areas in your garden. Harvest the leaves and stem tips at any time, and use them fresh (new leaves and stems will appear after the cuttings). Or pick the leaves just before blossoming, dry, and store them.

**Planting mint
in large pots keeps
roots from spreading.**

Mint

Everybody should have a little mint planted around somewhere—to use for iced tea, lamb dishes, and many other foods and drinks. You

Spearmint

**Orange or
Bergamot
Mint**

can grow spearmint, orange mint, peppermint, and many other flavors. The distinctive flavors in all the mints come from the oils produced within the plants. Spearmint is probably the favorite of most gardeners; it grows from 1 to 2 feet high, producing clusters of flowers on spikes. Orange mint grows to about the same height and has a subtle taste and smell comparable to that of oranges. Peppermint grows to 3 feet, producing spikes of tiny purple flowers.

To start mint, plant roots or runners in the spring, or buy a few plants from a nursery. It needs plenty of water, prefers full sun, but will tolerate partial shade. To harvest, simply cut a few sprigs whenever you need them; the more often you cut, the better the plants grow. You can also dry the leaves for storage.

Oregano

Oregano

Sometimes called wild marjoram, oregano (or origanum) has been an essential seasoning in Latin cooking since ancient times; today it is found in many Italian, Spanish, and Mexican dishes. The plant is a hardy perennial shrub growing 2$\frac{1}{2}$ feet tall.

Start oregano from seeds, or buy small plants from a nursery. Because oregano starts slowly, some gardeners like to begin seeds indoors in winter and transplant the seedlings later, after the last frost. To harvest, pick the leaves as you need them. You can also dry the leaves and store them for later use.

Parsley

Parsley is an old favorite that can garnish almost anything and is especially good in salads. There are three types: curled, plain leaf, and turnip rooted.

Sow parsley seeds outdoors in spring or summer. Soak the seeds in warm water twenty-four hours before planting to hurry them along, since they're slow to germinate. Sow them 1 to 2 inches apart, and then thin the seedlings to 8 to 10 inches apart. To harvest, pick mature leaves whenever you need them.

Rosemary

Pennyroyal

Rosemary is a great seasoning for veal, lamb, and fish and is used in many sauces and breadings. As a plant, it looks like an evergreen shrub, and it can grow to 6 feet tall. Fortunately, there's also a dwarf form, only 2 feet tall. You can use rosemary in your IPS garden if you keep it trimmed back; otherwise, plant it in a flower bed in a sunny spot where it won't spread out to crowd your other plants.

You can propagate rosemary from cuttings taken from a growing plant, or you can buy small plants from a nursery. To harvest, just cut off leaves whenever you need them.

Rosemary

Sage

Sage is good in all kinds of dressings and stuffings, for pork as well as for poultry, and it's often used in making sausage or pate. The plant is a gray-leaved perennial, growing 1 to 2 feet tall, and there are many varieties.

You can grow sage from cuttings taken from existent plants, you can plant seeds, or you can buy small plants from a nursery. If you use seeds, plant them indoors in the winter and later transplant the seedlings. Give sage full sun. To harvest, pick the leaves during the growing season before blossoming. Cut the plant back to the ground as soon as it's stopped blooming; the plant will renew the next year.

Narrow-Leaf Sage

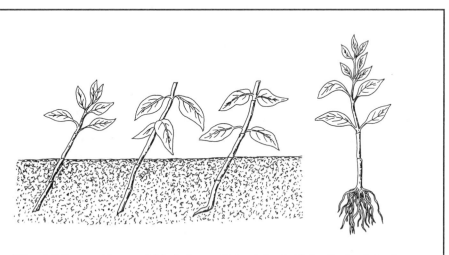

Figure 5-7. To propogate perennial herbs from cutting, cut at a slant below the growing node. Place your cutting in moist sand and move to a warm place. When you see new growth, transplant to a sunny window, then to individual containers.

Savory

Savory is used in cooking beans, other vegetables, and soups and in preparing seasoned salads. There are two kinds: summer savory and winter savory. Summer savory, which is the most popular, is an annual that grows 18 inches high. Winter savory is a perennial, also growing to about 18 inches.

Start summer savory from seed planted in the place where you want it to grow. Start winter savory from cuttings taken from existing plants, or buy plants from a nursery. To harvest, take leaves during the growing season. Cut back winter savory to the ground as soon as it stops blooming; it will arise again the next season.

Tarragon

Tarragon is a seasoning for fish, salad dressings, stews, sauces, vegetables, and many other dishes. Tarragon is a perennial that grows to about 2 feet. Once started, it's good for about two years.

You can grow tarragon from cuttings taken from existing plants, but most gardeners buy small plants from a nursery. To harvest, cut the leaves during the growing season before blooming. Dry leaves for preserving.

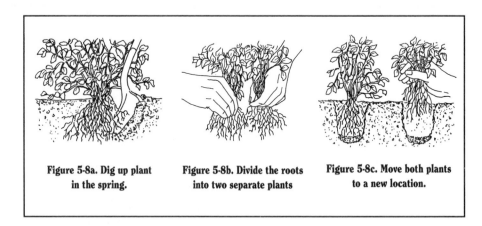

Figure 5-8a. Dig up plant in the spring.

Figure 5-8b. Divide the roots into two separate plants

Figure 5-8c. Move both plants to a new location.

Thyme

There are so many thymes available that you hardly know which one to grow first—lemon thyme, caraway thyme, golden thyme, French thyme, and more. As the names imply, lemon thyme has a lemon scent and caraway a caraway scent. All varieties make good seasonings for vegetables and meat sauces. The plants grow 8 to 12 inches tall.

You can sow seeds indoors in the winter and later transplant the seedlings outside, you can start plants from cuttings taken from existing plants, or you can buy small plants from a nursery. Plant thyme in full sun, 8 to 12 inches apart. Replant every three years. To harvest, cut the plants when in full bloom. After blooming, cut the plants back to the ground; they will arise again the following year.

And that's our roundup on herbs. You can buy the plants or seeds from nurseries, seed catalogs, and garden centers.

Now you're well informed about which vegetables and herbs can be grown in your garden. As you can see, there's really a wide selection. Eventually, as you get more experience and become an avid gardener, you'll want to hunt through the seed catalogs looking for different or unusual varieties that you've never tried before. You can experiment to see just how much you can grow in the space that you have available. That's half the fun of gardening. From now on, the more vegetables that you take out of your own garden, the more the vegetable urge will get you. And that's just the beginning!

Thyme

Lemon Thyme

CHAPTER SIX

Plants That Like Each Other

Today, ecology has become a household word. We recommend a method of gardening that is based on ecological principles—maintaining the balance of nature and restoring to the earth what we take from it. We are practicing applied ecology. An important part of this effort is sometimes called companion planting, which rests on the idea that certain species of plants aid each other by their mere presence together or, conversely, that certain species do poorly when living together.

There is much evidence that plant relationships and dis-relationships are extremely important. In the early 1900s Rudolf Steiner and his followers in Europe developed and explored the companion plant concept. Later, Richard Gregg carried on a great deal of field observation in New York. And still later, E. E. Pfeiffer developed what is called crystalization to determine the relationships between plants.

It is now known from other research that all plants give off chemicals called root diffusates, which affect other plants in various ways. Moreover, the aromas given off by some of the herbs repel or attract certain types of insects.

Which ones do what? It's really pretty hard to tell. This is an area intertwined with superstition and fact. Nevertheless, there is a great deal of truth concerning the compatibility of plants, and the information should help make our gardens healthier and more vigorous; and that, after all, is what we want. In this chapter, we'll give you some of the general beliefs about particular plants, and you can experiment yourself to find out what works best for you in your own garden.

Companion Vegetables

Asparagus

Some gardeners find that asparagus plants like tomato plants and make them grow profusely. It's not that simple, of course, but scientists have indeed isolated a substance, called asparagin, that seems to exert a good influence on tomato plants. Many gardeners thus like to plant tomatoes in the asparagus bed after they've harvested the asparagus in the spring. In the postage stamp bed, you might want to plant asparagus, tomatoes, marigolds, and beans next to each other. Together these offer protection from a number of insect pests. Parsley and basil also do well with asparagus.

Beans

Beans seem very compatible with many vegetables. Gardeners have found that they do pretty well with beets, carrots, cauliflower, cucumbers, corn, and radishes. Pole beans are stimulated by corn and will use the stalks for support. Bush beans grow well with celery. French beans like potatoes and strawberries. Neither pole nor bush beans (all types) seem to grow well with onions, garlic, or other members of the onion family; planted too close together, beans and onions tend to stunt the growth of one another.

Beets

Beets do well with almost everything that we grow in our IPS garden—except pole beans. Here they're set back. They do especially well with lettuce, cabbage, onions, and even bush beans. Why there's a difference in compatibility with the different bean varieties, pole and bush, has not been adequately explained, but apparently the chemistry is different.

Broccoli

Broccoli seems to do well near all the smelly herbs (such as chamomile, dill, sage, and rosemary) and also next to potatoes, beets, and onions. It also prefers to be planted near other members of the cabbage family (such as Brussels sprouts, cabbage, and cauliflower). Keep it away from pole beans and strawberries.

Brussels Sprouts

Brussels sprouts like broccoli and all other members of the cabbage family. But never follow Brussels sprouts in the same space that other members of this family have just occupied. They do well next to potatoes and Chinese cabbage. They are influenced by aromatic herbs and seem to be stimulated by close planting with sage, rosemary, hyssop, and thyme. They help repel the cabbage butterfly.

Cabbage

Cabbage and all other members of the cabbage family have undergone a rather specialized development. Cabbage itself, for instance, has developed a sensitive terminal bud. As a result, the cabbage relatives all seem a bit touchy and, under certain conditions, will deteriorate rapidly. You can follow an early cabbage crop with beets, kohlrabi, onions, and radishes. All members of this family grow well with marigolds.

Carrots

Carrots produce a root exudate that has a beneficial effect on peas. Carrots also grow well with chives, leaf lettuce, onions, red radishes, and tomatoes. In short, the carrot is an all-around plant in companionability. However, they don't like dill, fennel, or potatoes.

Cauliflower

Cauliflower, another member of the cabbage family, has most of the family's usual wants and needs. It is greatly influenced by aromatic herbs such as basil, borage, hyssop, sage, and thyme. Don't grow near strawberries.

Celery

Celery does well with cabbages and cauliflower because it repels the cabbage butterfly. It grows especially well with tomatoes.

Corn

Corn has interesting relationships with a lot of plants. It is stimulated by both peas and beans—probably because these two add nitrogen to the soil in usable form. Corn also has a beneficial effect on cucumbers, melons, squash, and other vine crops.

Cucumbers

Cucumbers are very adaptable in the garden. The plants grow well intermixed with corn or cabbage, and they like nearby companion plantings of such paired vegetables as lettuce and bush beans or lettuce and radishes. Raccoons dislike the odor of cucumbers. If you have a problem with these pests eating your corn, plant cucumbers between the plants. Cucumbers don't care much for the aromatic herbs.

Kale

Kale does well planted with its cabbage relative. It also benefits by being planted near aromatic herbs.

Lettuce

Lettuce seems to be a very chummy vegetable. It grows well in combination with beets and cabbage—that is, all three together. It aids onions and is aided by the presence of carrots and radishes. Also interplant it with French marigolds.

Melons

Cantaloupes like to be near corn. If you grow them up supports, they can benefit from marigolds planted underneath.

Onions

Onions and cabbage do well together. Onions like to grow with beets and seem to benefit when planted near lettuce, tomatoes, and summer savory. Apparently, they inhibit the growth of beans and peas. When planted around rose bushes, they increase the fragrance of the roses.

Peas

Peas are one of those great plants that seem to help almost everything. In particular, they fix nitrogen in the soil so that other plants can use it. They especially like beans, carrots, cucumbers, corn, radishes, and turnips. Their growth is retarded, however, by onions, garlic, fennel, and strawberries. Rotate the location of your peas every year.

Peppers

Peppers are relatives of tomatoes and eggplant and can be grown among them without any problems. Onions and carrots do well sown among pepper plants. Basil makes a good companion to peppers and adds flavor to sweet peppers.

Potatoes

Potatoes do especially well with peas and can be planted with beans, cabbage, corn, peas, and strawberries. They are especially helped by the nitrogen fixing ability of peas. Summer savory makes a good companion for potatoes, as do nasturtiums and marigolds. Surprisingly, they don't like cucumbers or tomatoes.

Radishes

Radishes and peas are mutually beneficial, and pole beans are aided by radishes. Nasturtiums give radishes a great flavor, and leaf lettuce makes them tender.

Spinach

Spinach helps to maintain soil microorganisms and soil moisture. It also produces an exudate that stimulates other vegetables, such as cabbage.

Squash and Pumpkins

Squash and pumpkins like to grow among corn plants. Winter squash and pumpkins provide a good ground cover for corn, holding the moisture in the soil. Good companions for all squash include beans, mint, and radishes. Nasturtiums protect summer squash (including zucchini) from aphids.

Tomatoes

Tomatoes and asparagus are mutually beneficial. Tomatoes also do well grown near cabbage, carrots, celery, onions, and peas. They help shade leaf lettuce in hot weather and benefit from its presence. They grow particularly well around basil and sage. When planted near members of the cabbage family, they help repel cabbage butterflies. They don't do well with potatoes.

Turnips and Rutabagas

Turnips and rutabagas are mutually helpful. And turnips are just generally helpful to a number of other vegetables including all members of the cabbage family.

Companion Herbs

Many herbs are quite pungent, and their scents can permeate the garden, especially if you occasionally crush a few of their leaves or stems to release the oils. Many old-time gardeners swear that herbs are cure-alls for everything that ails the garden—from bad vibes to crows to insects. If nothing else, with herbs you'll have the "smelliest" garden in town.

Basil

Sweet basil is generally beneficial to many vegetables. It enhances the flavor of summer savory and helps tomatoes grow larger. Basil is often planted near lettuce. It also repels white flies and aphids.

Borage

Borage is a great companion for tomatoes; the two plants seem to stimulate each other. Borage is especially good for strawberries. The one drawback is that it spreads rapidly in the garden.

Chervil

Chervil helps enhance the flavor of other plants. It is a good companion to carrots and radishes. It likes to be shaded by other plants.

Chives

Like most other herbs, chives seem generally good for the garden. They especially stimulate the growth of carrots and tomatoes.

Coriander

Coriander repels aphids when planted among other plants.

Coriander

Dill

Dill, in small quantities, has a beneficial effect. It is especially good with cabbages. When young, it helps carrots, corn, cucumber, and tomatoes. It repels carrot fly. Mature dill, however, retards carrots and tomatoes.

Garlic

As a member of the onion family, garlic has the same effects as onions.

Lemon Balm

Lemon balm can be a good companion for cucumbers and tomatoes.

Lemon Balm

Marjoram

Some people insist that sweet marjoram is absolutely indispensable in the vegetable garden because it stimulates almost everything.

Marjoram and peppers seem to stimulate each other. It also does well planted near sage.

Mint

Mint is generally beneficial to the garden and seems to repel many kinds of insects and pests. It helps repel aphids, cabbage butterflies, and white flies. Since one of its main benefits is to repel insects, plant it in pots and sink the pots in the ground to keep the roots contained.

Oregano

As a close relative of sweet marjoram, oregano is considered equally helpful in the garden. Oregano and peppers seem to stimulate each other. It also does well planted near sage.

Parsley

Parsley stimulates tomatoes and corn, especially when grown between the plants. Parsley and carrots encourage each other. It protects against carrot flies.

Rosemary

Rosemary and sage stimulate one another, and rosemary generally is beneficial to the garden. It is a good companion to beans, carrots, and cabbages. It repels bean beetles, cabbage butterflies, slugs, and snails. It is especially useful because it attracts bees in droves. Do not grow potatoes near rosemary.

Sage

Sage is especially helpful to cabbage, protecting it from some pests and making it more tender. Generally, sage is helpful to all plants.

Savory

Summer savory is beneficial to onions and to beans. It acts as a deterrent to many insect pests.

Tarragon

Some gardeners favor tarragon as much as they do sweet marjoram in insisting that it be planted in every vegetable garden. It is especially helpful to eggplants and peppers.

Thyme

Thyme seems generally beneficial and can be planted near egg-plant and cabbage. Many garden pests (cabbage root flies and white flies) are repelled by thyme.

Flowers

Geraniums

Besides providing wonderful scents in the garden, geraniums help repel white cabbage butterflies. Try them in the corner of a bed near members of the cabbage family.

Lupine

Lupine seems like a strange plant to put in a vegetable garden, but it does well with most vegetables and especially stimulates corn.

Marigolds

Every postage stamp garden needs a few marigolds. They are well known for controlling certain types of destructive nematodes, making marigolds a good companion for all root vegetables. They also help protect cabbage and potatoes. Marigolds also will help reduce the white fly population attracted to your tomatoes.

Nasturtiums

Nasturtiums act as a trap crop for slugs and snails and are effective in keeping these pests always from cabbage and lettuce. They also repel aphids, cucumber beetles, and white flies. Plant them near squash, tomatoes, and all members of the cabbage family.

Petunias

Petunias repel bean beetles, potato beetles, and squash beetles. They are a good companion to beans, potatoes, tomatoes, and all members of the cabbage family.

Sunflowers

Every postage stamp garden needs a couple of sunflowers. Two planted close to each other won't take up much space and will be spectacular when mature. They act as a host plant to several beneficial insects such as predatory wasps, which help keep garden pests under control. They also attract bees to the garden.

Making Companion Planting Work

Although plants do have an effect on other plants and all living things, our knowledge in this area is extremely limited and often tentative. Nevertheless, we have a lot of fun experimenting in our own garden, and we're sure you can too. Not everything that we've mentioned will necessarily work for you, but some things will. After all, vegetable gardening should be considered one of those fun hobbies that offer something unexpected around every cabbage.

CHAPTER SEVEN

The All-Inclusive Salad Garden

There is nothing like a big, bold, colorful salad to enhance meals. Salad lovers will want to grow varieties that include not only lettuce but also some unusual greens in colors ranging from green to magenta to chartreuse and in textures from smooth to curly. A gardener might want to plant radicchio, French dandelions, arugula, watercress, or curly endive among the various lettuces.

And what a choice of lettuces are available, with names like Lollo Rosa, La Brilliante, Flame, Red Fire, Green Ice, and Salad Bowl. Add all shapes and colors of radishes, onions, tomatoes, and even edible flowers to the greens, and you've made an introduction to a meal.

A salad lover's garden should also contain different colored sweet peppers, cucumbers, celery, cauliflower, broccoli, and endive. A salad garden can be anything as simple as a couple of types of lettuce growing in a container on a patio or as elaborate as a raised-bed garden devoted entirely to salads. See Figures 7-1 to 7-4 for sample postage stamp salad gardens.

There's a revolution going on today in the salad bowl. Salad lovers have so many greens at their fingertips that it's hard to know where to start. Prepackaged salad mixes are showing up at supermarkets all across the United States. They are beautiful and tempting but will never be as fresh as those from your own garden. Karen checks out the packages that look good to her and then duplicates the ingredients in our garden.

Don't be afraid to try different combinations of greens with lettuces. Mix in chicory, mustard, kale, Swiss chard, purslane, chervil (both a green and an herb), and even edible flowers such as bachelor's buttons, calendulas, pansies, or nasturtiums. Even a small garden will let you grow a number of different greens, making it easy to toss together a variety of colors, textures, and flavors that will spice up any salad. Most greens grow quickly and are ready to harvest in 6 to 12 weeks. The following section offers a quick tour of what you can grow in a salad garden.

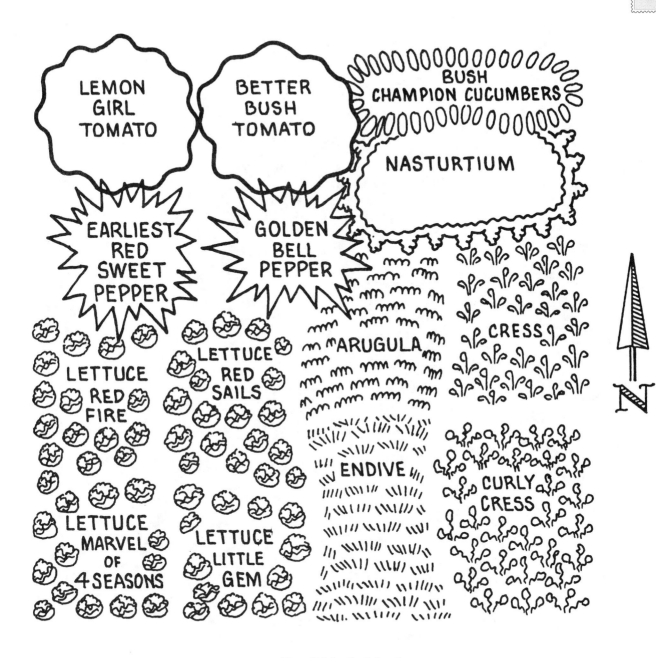

Figure 7-1. Small salad garden.

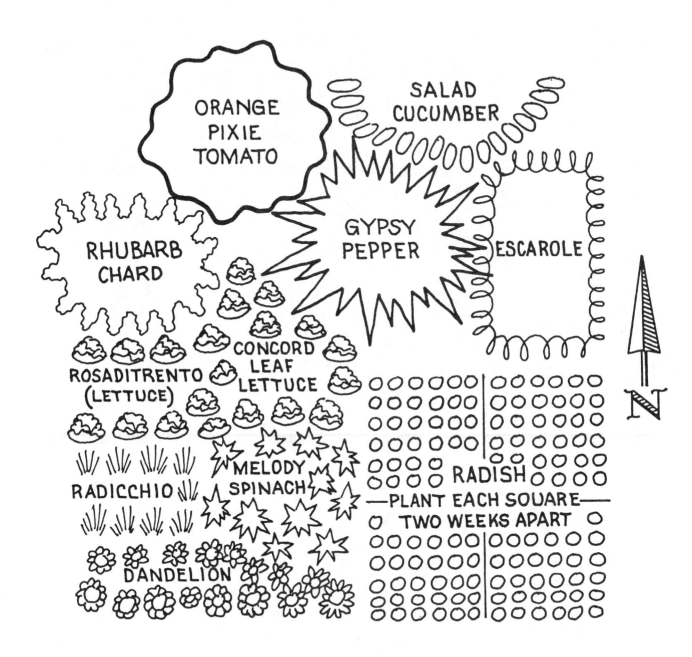

Figure 7-2. General salad garden.

Little Gem Romaine / Romaine Parris Island Cos	Little Gem Romaine / Romaine Parris Island Cos	Little Gem Romaine / Rouge D'Hiver Romaine	Little Gem Romaine / Rouge D'Hiver Romaine
Great Lakes Head Lettuce	Great Lakes Head Lettuce	Merveille Des Quatres Saisons Head Lettuce	Bibb Head Lettuce
Black Seeded Simpson Loose-Leaf Lettuce	Green Ice Loose-Leaf Lettuce	Salad Bowl Loose-Leaf Lettuce	Salad Bowl Red Loose Leaf
Lollo Rossa Loose-Leaf Lettuce / Oak Leaf Loose-Leaf Lettuce (Green)	Lollo Rossa Loose-Leaf Lettuce / Red Oak Leaf Lettuce	Red Sails Loose-Leaf Lettuce / Red Oak Leaf Lettuce	Red Sails Loose-Leaf Lettuce / Oak Leaf Loose-Leaf Lettuce (Green)

Figure 7-3. Lettuce bed. 4' x 4' bed.

Batavian Full Hearted Escarole	Tres Fine Maraichere Endive	Givlio (Radicchio)	Givlio (Radicchio)
Lettuce Red Sails	Majestic Red Lettuce Romaine	Jerico Romaine Lettuce	Buttercrunch Bibb Lettuce
Upland Cress	Garden Cress	Arugula	Tennis Ball Buttercrunch Lettuce
Montmagny Dandelion	Melody Spinach	Susan's Red Bibb Lettuce	Green Tea Lettuce

Figure 7-4. Small green bed. 4' x 4' bed.

Greens

Here are some salad green basics:

- Pick fresh crisp leaves.
- Wash them in a colander under slightly warm running water as soon as you pick them.
- Remove any wilted or bruised spots. Rinse them in cold water.
- Put the greens in a wire basket, and shake them to remove all water.
- Place the greens in a plastic bag along with a paper towel to remove the remaining moisture.

Greens that Thrive in Hot Weather

Many greens are cool-weather vegetables that struggle in hot summer weather. In our area, we can only grow them successfully in fall and spring. There are a few greens, however, that grow well in warm weather, so you can enjoy fresh salads all summer long.

AMARANTH	Tasty, tall, ornamental plant that grows 3 feet high. Plant the edible leaf varieties. Seed source: COO ORN SEE SEED
MALABAR SPINACH	A trailing vine that grows well up a trellis. The leaves taste much like spinach. Seed source: COO ORN SEE SEEO
ORACH	Also called Mountain Spinach. Comes in different colors. Tastes like spinach. Keep the end leaves pinched back. Seed source: COO ORN SEE SEED

Arugula

Sometimes called rocket, arugula has dark green leaves that are peppery pungent. We planted arugula several years ago and were surprised to find that it lasts the entire year, reseeds itself nicely, and spreads everywhere. For more zip, combine this with sweet or bitter greens such as mustard.

Seed source: GUR NIC RED

Arugula

Swiss Chard

Chard

Chard has huge leaves and crisp stems and is one of the easiest greens to grow. The stems have a celerylike taste and texture, and the leaves have a flavor that's stronger than spinach. The varieties that you can grow at home are sweeter than the ones you find in the market. Chard can be grown most of the year and has red or green, crumpled or smooth leaves.

ERBETTE	Smooth green leaves that make a great cut-and-come-again plant. Seed source: COO
FORDHOOK GIANT	Dark green, crumpled leaves have snow-white midribs. Seed source: ABU ALL BURP COM FIS GAR HIG JOH MEY ORN PON RED ROS SEE STO TER TWI VER WIL
LUCULLUS	Large, white midribs, light green crumpled leaves. Seed source: ABU ALL FAR GUR HEN JUN LED PAR SEE TIL VER WILL
RHUBARB CHARD	Crimson stalks with heavily crumpled green leaves. Seed source: ABU ALL BURP BURR COM DEG FAR FIS GAR JOH LED NIC ORG ORN PIN SEE SEED SHE STO TER TIL TWI VER WILL

Cress

All of the "cresses" listed here, although not in the same family, have the same peppery-sharp taste. All the cresses will add an extra sharp flavor to avocado salad, five-bean salad, or almost any other salad.

GARDEN CRESS	Finely curled parsleylike leaves. It's an annual, reaching maturity in about 35 days. Seed source: ABU ALL COM DEG FIS LEJ JOH JUN KIT NIC SEE SEED SHE STO TOM WIL
UPLAND CRESS	Not actually a cress but is similar to watercress. It has broad bright green leaves and dense growth. Grows in any type of soil. Seed source: ABU BURP COM DEG JLH NIC RIC SEE SOU TAY VER
WATERCRESS	This peppery-flavored green is a member of the nasturtium family and is often blended with lettuces for salads. Refrigerate watercress with its stems in a cup of water to keep it fresh. Watercress has small oval leaves and likes to grow near water or very moist soil. Seed source: RIC SOU

Dandelion

Dandelion

Dandelion is a bitter green. The leaves of the variety used in salads are elongated. They are not the dandelions growing in your lawn.

Montmagny: This is a thick-leaved, full-hearted dandelion. It can be used in a soup, salad, or stir-fry. Seed source: LEJ

Thick-Leaved: Has bitter broad leaves. Seed source: BURP STO

Endive

This particular plant can be confusing because it's classified as chicory, which includes radicchio, endive curled, and endive not curled, along with cutting chicory. Confusing!

Let's try to clarify some of the confusion here. All three can be used in salads calling for lettuce. Don't use endive in place of lettuce, but combine the two—Belgian endive, curly endive, escarole, frisee, and radicchio all have a sharp, jolting taste that adds a tongue-tingling sensation to any salad. They are definitely an acquired taste.

Cutting Chicory

SPADONA — Also called Dog's Tongue, has smooth leaves that should be cut when 4 to 6 inches tall. Seed source: COO

Endive (Not Curled)

BATAVIAN FULL HEARTED — Slightly crumpled, dark green leaves with a 12-inch spread. White rib and tender heart. Also called Escarole. Seed source: BOU GAR LED PIN STO TIL TWI

Endive (Curled)

Use it for its coarse frilly leaves and tart taste.

TRES FINE MARAICHERE — A French variety with green, frilly outer leaves. Crunchy white ribs. Seed source: GOU HIG SHE

Radicchio (Semiheading and Heading)

You can pick the outer leaves for the flavor and color.

GIULIO — Full-sized head, deep burgundy with white veins. Looks like a tiny red cabbage and is the type you'd find in

Radicchio

supermarkets. Bitter and beautiful in salads. Seed source: COO HIG JOH NIC ORN SHE

WITLOOF CHICORY   The forcing variety, with 4- to 6-inch-long white heads. Also known as Belgian Endive, this variety is found in supermarkets and mostly used as a stuffed appetizer. Seed source: COM HIG LED PIN RED SEE WILL

Kale

There are two kinds of kale: smooth leaved and curly. The curly kales have compact clusters of tightly curled leaves. The smooth-leaved type has coarse, but smooth leaves. Some varieties find their way into salads, either raw or slightly cooked.

DWARF BLUE   Leaves are finely curled and bluish green. A low compact,
  CURLED VATES   short-stemmed plant. Seed source: ABU BURP BUT COM DEG GAR GUR HEN JUN LED LIB MEY NIC ROS SEE SOU STO TIL TWI WIL

RUSSIAN RED   Wavy, red purple leaves. 2-foot-tall plant. Seed source: ABU BOU GAR JLH JOH NIC ORG ORN PIN SEED SHE SOU

Lettuce

We covered some lettuce varieties in the previous chapter, but there are so many good varieties that we'd like to give you even more choices to try. In our garden, we always have a spring and fall lettuce bed with many varieties to choose from. When spring turns to tomato planting season, we plant lettuce in this bed so that the tomatoes will provide shade and the lettuce will continue growing longer than it usually would. We also plant lettuce in clay pots, barrels, hanging baskets, or other creative containers for our patio, which is beneath a canopy of oak trees and provides a cool place for them to grow. Our patio is just steps from the kitchen and certainly qualifies as an IPS garden. One trick for summer lettuce is to water it heavily to avoid bitterness.

Here are some general tips for using lettuce:

- A pound of leaf lettuce or romaine produces 6 cups of torn pieces. A pound of endive produces about 4 cups.
- Greens last longer if you wash them as soon as you pick them.

- To keep greens perky, not wilted, wash, dry, and wrap them in a dish towel, and then refrigerate them until you're ready to make your salad.

- Clean tight heads of lettuce by tapping the firm end of the head against the counter, then twist the core out. Clean by rinsing with the core end up. Make sure water gets in between the leaves.

Head Lettuce

These varieties have large, firm heads that blanch in the center.

Head Lettuce

BURPEE'S ICEBERG	Light green, wavy leaves. Seed source: BURP
DEER TONGUE	A medium-sized butterhead type. Triangular, green leaves with rounded tips. Seed source: ABU GAR SHE
REINE DES GLACES	Also known as Ice Queen, has deeply cut, lacy, green leaves. Seed source: COO ORN SEE
SUSAN'S RED BIBB	Ruffled leaves have rose margins. Seed source: SOU

Romaine Lettuce

This lettuce is sometimes called cos, and has tall, loose leaves that form a head.

JERICHO	An Israeli variety with sword-shaped leaves. It is adapted to many climates. Seed source: SHE
MAJESTIC RED	Tall, green leaves overlaid with deep burgundy. This is a loose-leaf romaine. Seed source: TER WILL
PARRIS ISLAND COS	8- to 9-inch-tall head. Dark green leaves. Seed source: BURP COM GAR HEN JOH LIB MEY PIN POR RED SEE SEED SOU STO TIL VER WIL WILL

Loose-Leaf Lettuce

Loose leaf is a fast-growing lettuce. It's called the cut-and-come-again vegetable because the more leaves you remove, the faster it seems to grow.

CORCARDE	Trumpet-shaped head with lobed, dark green leaves with rusty red hues. This is an oak leaf type. Seed source: JOH SEED
GREEN ICE	Has savoyed, dark green leaves with fringed margins. Seed source: ALL BURP COM COO JUN LED ORN PAR PIN PON

RED FIRE	Savoyed and frilled, intensely red leaves. Seed source: GAR JOH LIB PIN STO VER
RED SAILS	Another prize, heavily ruffled, deep red bronze leaves. Seed source: ALL BOU BURR COM COO DEG GUR HEN JUN LIB MEY NIC ORN PAR PIN POR SOU STO TER TIL TWI VER WILL
ROSSA D'AMERIQUE	Italian cutting lettuce has pale green leaves tipped with sparkling rose red. Seed source: COO
ROSSA DI TRENTO	Another Italian cutting lettuce. Has savoyed green leaves with wine red margins. Seed source: COO

Mustard

Very few gardeners know how good mustard greens taste in salads. Tender young mustard leaves have a peppery nip and a mild, distinctive taste appreciated by almost all adventurous eaters. Substitute chopped mustard greens for half the lettuce in salads.

Three kinds of mustard greens are usually available: smooth leaf, curly leaf, and oriental. The curly leaved types are superior for salads. They seem to fluff up tossed salads, much like curly endive. We always grow oriental mustard in our spring and fall garden for a stir-fry. We also use the tender leaves in salads.

Curled Mustard

| SOUTHERN GIANT CURLED | Plant spreads 18 to 24 inches. Wide, crumpled bright green leaves. Seed source: BOU BURR DEG JUN LED MEY PAR POR ROS SEE SUN TIL TWI WIL |

Plain Mustard

| SAVANNAH | Smooth, thick, dark green leaves with narrow, cream-colored ribs. This is a large plant. Seed source: LED PAR TWI VER |

Oriental Mustard (Green Stalks)

| CHINESE TSI SHIM | Light green leaves and flowering stalks. Harvest when the flowers begin to open. Seed source: GAR SUN |
| MEI QUING CHOI | A vase-shaped plant with pale green stems and oval, green leaves. Seed source: BOU DEG JOH NIC ORN PAR PIN SHE STO TWI VER |

Chinese Cabbage

Oriental Mustard (White Stalks, Spoon-Shaped Leaves)

BOK CHOI — Thick, green leaves and broad, white stalks. Seed source: GUR HEN LIB NIC SEED STO SUN THE

MITSUBA — Plain, parsleylike leaves on long, slender white stems. Seed source: GLE VER

Bok Choi Sum (flowering stalks)

Sorrel

This is a relative newcomer as a garden green. It has narrow-shaped leaves with a crisp, yet tender, texture and a sharp lemon-like tang.

Seed source: BURP

Bok Choi

Spinach

Spinach is making a comeback as a major salad ingredient. You can fix a simple wilted spinach salad, or toss a salad with lettuce, spinach, and broccoli. Spinach is also used for a filling that goes into lasagna or quiche.

Sorrel

Savoyed

BLOOMSDALE LONG STANDING — Very crinkled, glossy, dark green leaves. Seed source ABU ALL BURP BURR BUT DEG FAR GAR GUR HEN HIG JLH JUN LED LIB MEY NIC PAR PIN PLA RED SEE SOU STO TIL VER WIL WILL

Spinach

Semisavoyed

MELODY — Has dark green leaves. Seed source: BURP FAR GOU HEN JUN LED MEY NIC PAR PIN POR STO TWI VER

Smooth-Leaved

NOBEL GIANT — Huge, thick, smooth, pointed green leaves with round tips. Seed source: BURR DEG HEN JLH SEE TIL

Spinach Substitutes

Use these just like you would spinach.

NEW ZEALAND SPINACH	Small, brittle, triangular-shaped green leaves. Plant spreads across the bed. Seed source: ALL BOU BURP BUT COM DEG FAR GAR GOU HEN JLH JUN LED LIB MEY NIC PIN POR RED ROS SEE SOU STO VER WILL
ORACH, GREEN	Will grow to 6 feet if not cut. Seed source: BOU PIN
ORACH, RED	Annual, red purple variety. Seed source: COO NIC PIN SEE
TAMPALA SPINACH	Tastes like an artichoke. Seed source: BURG POR SEE

Mesclun

Mesclun is a mixture of young salad greens grown in the same bed. This is the French approach to salad greens, and one that Americans are catching on to. They are usually cool-weather greens, sown to be harvested in spring or early fall. Plant four lettuce varieties, head and loose leaf in red and green. This creates color and texture. Then add arugula and radicchio for spice and a touch of bitterness. These will be tempered by the sweeter greens. Add mustards that range from mild to sharp. Remember that baby greens are naturally milder than the more mature ones. You can sprinkle in herbs such as chervil, chives, onion, and edible flowers—and this is your mesclun garden.

If you are mixing your own mesclun, just dump all the seeds in a bowl and stir. Then broadcast the seed as evenly as you can over a bed of loose, rich soil. Settle them with a rake, then water. When the greens are 4 to 6 inches high, snip them with scissors about an inch above the ground. Wash the greens, dry them, and then toss them into a salad bowl.

Tomatoes

Because there are literally thousands of varieties of vegetables to choose from, we try not to repeat from chapter to chapter, and tomatoes are no exception. Because tomatoes are an absolute for salads, we want to give you some varieties that will show off your salads or bring something special to them. Let your imagination go wild when it comes time to think about tomatoes.

Pink Tomatoes

| PINK GIRL | Indeterminate pink, 8-ounce, globe-shaped tomato. Seed source: GUR HEN LIB PAR PON TOM TOMA |

| TENNESSEE PEACH FUZZ | 2 inches in diameter, dark pink, unusual skin texture. Seed source: SEE |

Orange/Yellow/Gold Tomatoes

BRANDYWINE YELLOW	Indeterminate yellow version of the pink variety. Seed source: SEE TOM TOMA
GOLDEN BOY	Indeterminate plant. Large, deep yellow globe fruit. Seed source: COM LEJ PIN TOM TOMA VER WIL
LEMON BOY	Our favorite yellow tomato. Indeterminate plant. Bright lemon yellow, 8 to 10 ounces. Seed source: BURP DEG HEN JLH LIB NIC PAR POR STO TER TOM TOMA VER WILL

Small-Fruited Tomatoes

Cherry Grande VF	Determinate plant. 1½-inch red fruit. Seed source: STO TOM TOMA TWI
GARDENER'S DELIGHT	Indeterminate. Bite-sized, ½- to ¾-inch red tomatoes. Seed source: BOU BURP COO GAR PAR PIN SEE SEED THO TOM TOMA
ORANGE PIXIE	Determinate plant has orange, 1½-inch fruit. Seed source: TOM
PINK PEAR	Indeterminate plant. Tiny pink pear-shaped tomatoes. Seed source: TOM
RED CURRANT	Indeterminate plant with tiny red fruit. Spread a cloth beneath the plant, and shake to harvest. Seed source: COO DEG JLH JOH SEED TOM
RED PEAR	Indeterminate. Clusters of 1-inch red fruit. Seed source: BURG COO DEG GLE HEN JOH ORN SEE STO TOM
SUN GOLD	Indeterminate. Bite-sized, bright tangerine color. Seed source: JOH TER THO TOMA
SWEET 100	Our favorite small variety, it lasts an entire season with plenty to give away. Indeterminate plant with red, cherry-sized tomatoes that grow in clusters. Seed source: BURP COM COO GUR HEN LIB MEY ORN POR SHE STO THO TIL TOM TOMA TWI
YELLOW CURRANT	Indeterminate. Yellow currant-sized tomatoes. Seed source: COO GLE JOH NIC TOM TOMA
YELLOW PEAR	Indeterminate. Clusters of 1¼-by-2-inch yellow pear-shaped fruit. Seed source: ABU ALL BURP COO DEG GAR GLE GOU HEN HIG JOH MEY NIC ORN POR SEE SEED SHE SOU STO TOM TOMA WIL WILL

The Creative Salad Palette

Salads, of course, are a lot more than just pretty greens, and as already indicated, you can include almost any vegetable on your salad palette. Adding colored sweet peppers, cucumbers, tomatoes, and beans is a good start. Then include carrots, peas, corn, and a touch of herbs. You can also include fruit in any vegetable salad. Try adding melon balls and cucumbers, topped with a cucumber mint dressing. A crunchy chicken salad could be mixed with apple, spinach, and broccoli. Or try crab with wild rice, including celery, red pepper, and fresh snap or snow peas. You can add shrimp and prosciutto to dress up any salad, and if there are enough greens, color, and texture, the salad could be a main meal.

Want a tangy salad that makes your taste buds sit up and take notice? Try this one. Mix 2 cups of fresh basil leaves with about 8 cups of leaf lettuce. Combine with 3 tablespoons of vinegar and 2 teaspoons of olive oil.

Celeriac (celery root) doesn't exactly spring to mind when you say salad, but it can actually be the mainstay of a number of tasty salads, such as Waldorf salad. Celeriac is the exact opposite of celery. Celery is grown for its stalks and, sometimes, its leaves; celeriac is grown for its tuber, which has the crunchiness of celery with the texture of a turnip. Cook the tuber in boiling water until tender, cool, cut into cubes, and combine in your salad.

If you are looking for a different vegetable to add to your salad, try fennel. It comes in two forms: green and bronze. The seeds are used in baking; the leaves are used for flavor or for decoration in fish and egg dishes. To use in a salad, cut off and discard any woody stems. Cut off the feathery leaves, but save them. Mix both head and leaves with other ingredients, such as lettuce and onions. Fennel salad is good served hot or cold.

SWEET FENNEL	Smokey bronze leaves. Seed source: EOR PAR
SMOKEY FENNEL	Large fleshy variety, distinctive flavor. Seed source: ABU
FLORENCE FENNEL	Copper tinged foliage. Seed source: ABU COM NIC PIN RED SEE SHE SOU TAX

Finally, are you trying to find a gift for a good cook? Why not give a salad garden? A salad garden, for instance, might include a decorative pot, gloves, soil, and seed packages of salad greens such as arugula, butterhead lettuce, curly endive, escarole, and several varieties of loose-leaf lettuce.

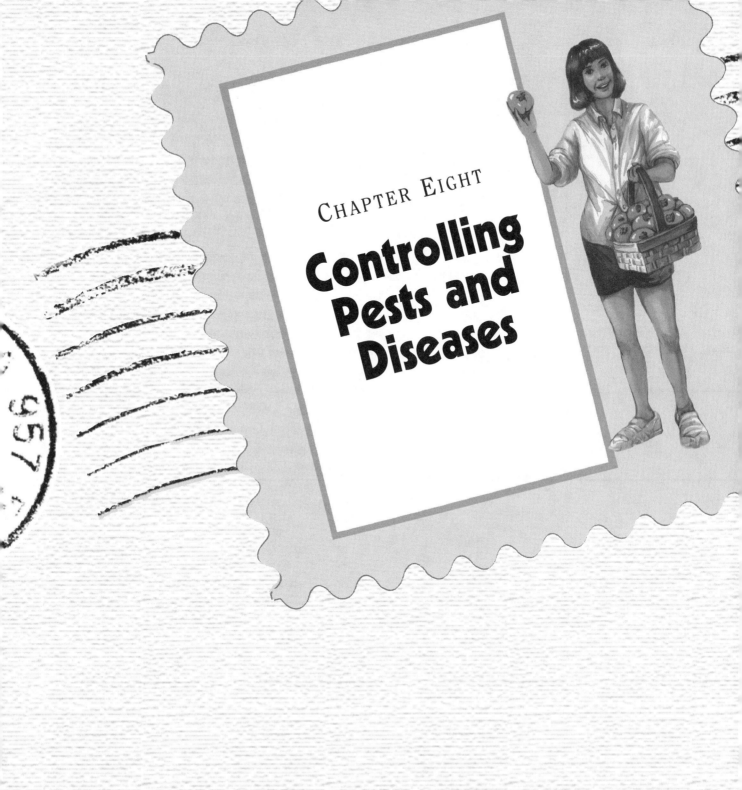

CHAPTER EIGHT

Controlling Pests and Diseases

What is it about bugs in the garden that causes a normally sane gardener to rush indoors, grab a spray can, and pour clouds of chemical spray all over a garden? This seems to be a form of insect insanity. Now, warfare may be justified if the garden is being overrun by hoards of insects, but I've seen gardeners do this when we couldn't find more than two bedraggled bugs in the whole garden.

That kind of vigilance is absolutely unnecessary. There are many factors determining whether or not a particular insect attacks your garden. Weather has a lot to do with it. Insects move from one place to another and are often influenced by temperatures and day lengths (which also affect vegetables, of course); any change can send them out of your garden and off in another direction.

Generally, we don't use chemical insecticides or fungicides in IPS gardens because they destroy the balance of nature. For one thing, they kill or scare off organisms and insects that help our garden as well as those that we want to get rid of. What we want to do is to keep our gardens vigorous and healthy by resorting to the simplest, safest, easiest methods possible. The IPS rule is this: Use whatever works, and don't hassle too much. There are a lot of ways to do that.

Being Mr. or Mrs. Clean

One gardener we know kept complaining bitterly that his garden was always overrun with insect pests, and indeed it was. Sometimes they almost wiped everything out. We had always felt sorry for the poor guy as he poured out his tale of woe, until one day we stopped by to see what the problem was. The minute we saw his garden we knew exactly what the problem was. The place was a mess: There were piles of brush everywhere, scattered scraps of lumber around the edges, and leaves and other organic material within a few feet of his growing vegetables. He had created great hiding places and breeding grounds for both insects and diseases. His garden didn't have a chance.

So, the first thing that you must do is keep your garden area clean. Get rid of all dead weeds, clean up piles of trash, move any lumber away from the edge of your garden, and don't let fruit, vegetables, or leaves lie on the surface. Simply haul the refuse away. Some organic materials can be put into your compost pile. (However, if you have diseased plants, don't throw them on the compost heap; burn them to keep them from spreading diseases.)

These rules of cleanliness are extremely elementary. Yet they are vitally important if you intend to garden without resorting to a full-scale chemical attack.

Getting Physical with Those Insects

All you really have to do with some insects is simply pluck them off with your fingers or spray them off with a water hose. These methods work well with slow-moving creatures. Insects with wings, of course, may just fly away and laugh at you from another plant—but not always, though. Thus, it's worth trying to eradicate them by knocking or hosing them. If insects do reappear in your garden, in the same or even greater numbers after you've tried simple methods, then you can haul out some bigger guns.

The Soap and Water Treatment

So you've tried cleanliness and physical therapy, and they don't work well enough. Well, don't give up yet. The next thing to try is soap and water. Although you can hardly use a chisel to pry scale insects like aphids off your plants, often soap and water will do the trick. Simply mix about 20 tablespoons of soap flakes (such as Ivory) in 6 gallons of water. Then put the mixture in a spray can or tank and go after your plants. (The diluted soap won't hurt your plants.) You'll be surprised how well this method works.

Or you can use Safer Insecticidal Soap (a commercial product). This popular product is derived from potassium salts and is totally biodegradable and environmentally safe. It is effective against aphids, earwigs, grasshoppers, leafhoppers, spider mites, scales, whiteflies, and others. It can be applied on the day of the harvest. You can also use it as a soil drench to control mealybugs.

Oil Products

Most oil products are effective as a smothering agent and a repellant. They control adult and egg stages for aphids, beetles, corn earworms, lace bugs, leafminers, mealybugs, and others. When mixed with Safer

Soap, its effect is enhanced. There are oil products on the market that don't contain petroleum.

Mother Nature's Insect Predators

We always feel that we've had the last laugh when we turn friendly insects loose in the garden, and they go around gobbling up the pests that have been destroying our beloved vegetables. There are some great predator insects just ready and waiting to go to work for you: lacewing flies (the larvae really go after aphids), ladybugs (they have a greedy appetite for aphids, thrips, tree lice, and the eggs and larvae of many other plant-destroying insects), praying mantises (the young eat aphids, flies, and other small insects; larger adults consume massive quantities of beetles, caterpillars, grasshoppers, and other damaging garden pests), and trichogramma wasps (they're especially effective on the larvae of the cabbage worm).

Predatory nematodes (*Steuberbena carpocaposae*) attack the pupal and larva stages of a number of insects in the ground: cutworms, army worms, June beetle grubs, onion maggots, cabbage root maggot, and others. They can be purchased through suppliers of beneficial insects and through many seed catalogs.

There are others. But these are the main beneficial insects used by home gardeners.

Mechanical Bugaboos

Some pests can be killed off or repelled easily using simple devices placed about in your garden. Some gardeners give up and don't bother to do anything to get rid of slugs and snails, for instance. But the solution is so simple that you'll hardly believe it. In researching the slug problem, a prominent scientific institution tried a number of very elaborate methods to eradicate snails and slugs. Finally, after many years of experimentation, they stumbled on an answer: Just put out shallow saucers of beer around the garden at night. Slugs and snails are attracted by the beer and drown in it. Or maybe you're having trouble with earwigs (they're the menacing-looking bugs with big pincers; you'll never forget them once you've seen one). Try rolling up a newspaper and putting it near the problem plants. Earwigs will hide inside the rolled-up newspaper in droves. Then you can simply burn them. Safer Insecticidal Soap and pyrethrin also works on earwigs.

Companion Plants

Here's our old friend from the last chapter: plants that exert a good influence on other plants (or animals). Some gardeners are enthusiastic about using particular plants or herbs to repel insects; other gardeners aren't so sure. The truth is that although scientific research has proven that some plants do repel pests (marigolds, for instance, repel or kill nematodes, a variety of parasitic worms that live in the soil), it has not verified the claims made for many other plants. Therefore, you will have to experiment yourself and see what works in your garden (see the last chapter for particulars).

Plant Sprays

Many gardeners believe not only that living plants repel insects but also that their leaves or petals can be liquified and turned into effective sprays that give your gardens strong protection. There are a couple of methods you can try. Choose plants with the most disagreeable odors, such as marigolds, chives, and garlic (just one garlic clove is enough, however).

In the first method, you put your cloves, petals, and leaves in a pot or pan, add enough water to cover the ingredients, bring the mixture to the boiling point, and then turn off the heat. Strain off the solid particles, dilute the remaining liquid with 4 to 5 parts of water, and stir for five to ten minutes. Now you're ready to spray.

In the second method, drop the clove, petals, and leaves into a blender. Put in enough water to cover, and turn on the blender. Blend until the contents seem fairly liquified. Strain off the solid particles (if any), add about 2 to 3 teaspoons of the remaining liquid to 1 quart of water, and use the diluted mixture in your sprayer.

The leaves of such companion plants as mint, rosemary, and radishes can similarly be turned into sprays and used against the specific pests that they're supposed to repel.

Or you can try hot pepper wax, a commercial product manufactured from capsaicin, an active ingredient in cayenne pepper that is a lethal stimulant for many soft-bodied insects. Combined with food-grade paraffin wax, it sticks to insects and to plant foliage, killing (within twenty-four hours) aphids, hoppers, leafminers, spider mites, scale, thrips, and whiteflies. This product is 100 percent natural. (Apply with a sprayer.)

Biological Sprays

Today there are spray preparations on the market that contain bacterial organisms that kill certain kinds of insects. One of them, Thuricide (containing *Bacillus thuringiensis*), paralyzes the digestive system of such leaf-chewing worms as caterpillars, cabbage loopers, and tomato hornworms without having any deleterious effect on birds, bees, pets, or humans. There are now a number of variations of Thuricide formulated for specific insects. You will find this preparation available at many nurseries and listed in many of the seed catalogs of companies cited in the appendix.

Grasshopper Bait infects grasshoppers with a predacious protozoa, *Nosema locustae.* The protozoa spread the disease among themselves by eating sick hoppers and by laying infected eggs. And Milky Spore disease attacks and kills Japanese beetle grubs in the soil.

Botanical Sprays

There are some extremely effective botanical sprays. Pyrethrum, a contact spray produced from the dried flowers of *Chrysanthemum cinerifolium*, is a knockdown insecticide. Also, it excites certain insects, flushing them from protected hiding places. It is effective against aphids, army worms, beetles (asparagus, blister, cucumber, Colorado potato, flea, Mexican bean), cabbage loopers, caterpillars, earwigs, fleas, flies, harlequin bugs, fruit flies, leafrollers, leafhoppers, thrips, whiteflies, and more. It can be applied up to the time of harvest.

Rotenone is derived from the *Derris* family of plants grown in the tropics. It is effective against a number of hard-to-kill insects, including cucumber beetle, harlequin bugs, squab bug, thrips, scales, mites, leafhoppers, flea beetles, Japanese beetles, and more. Rotenone is an insect stomach poison. You can buy pyrethrum and rotenone separately or mixed together.

In the table accompanying this chapter, there are suggestions on which deterrents will work best for you in attacking the pests in your garden.

Plant Diseases

Generally, IPS gardeners are organic gardeners and don't use chemical preparations to fight plant diseases, blight, and fungi. In an IPS garden we keep disease to a minimum without chemical help by resorting chiefly to two procedures: planting disease-resistant varieties of seeds and seedlings and destroying diseased plants whenever we find them in our garden.

Rooting out and burning diseased vegetation is part of the cleanliness that we mentioned earlier. A few of the most common diseases that you may encounter are mildew (appearing as a white or gray, powdery or downy coating on leaves and stems), rust (appearing first as whitish pustules or warts on the underside of leaves, then as powdery red or brown spores carried by the wind), blight and scab (both appearing as spreading yellow, brown, or red spots on leaves, especially shaded lower leaves), and wilt and root rot (both causing decayed roots and revealed by the wilting of foliage).

As for planting disease-resistant seeds and seedlings, currently there is much research under way to produce vegetable varieties that are resistant to major plant diseases. Each year something new reaches the market. For instance, there are cabbage strains resistant to virus yellows; cucumber strains resistant to anthracnose, downy mildew, mosaic, powdery mildew, and scab; cantaloupes resistant to fusarium and powdery mildew; and snapbeans resistant to mosaic, powdery mildew, and root rot. You can get these and other disease-resistant varieties from seed catalogs or seed racks; the catalog descriptions or package labels will state the diseases to which the varieties are resistant.

We don't recommend chemical preparations (such as captan and phaltan) to combat plant diseases. There are, however, organic products on the market that work well. Safer garden fungicide liquid (an all-natural sulfur fungicide) is used on vegetables. It controls most mites as well as powdery mildew, blackspot, scab, brown rot, brown canker, leaf spot, and more. Botanical fungicides (a neem oil derivative) are made from plants that have fungicidal properties. They are effective on the same diseases as the Safer fungicide. Most seeds purchased from seed companies have already been treated with fungicides. You can buy untreated seeds from some companies, but you must usually specify untreated seeds in your order.

So that gives you a rundown on what you can do to control insect pests and diseases without making your garden an armed camp. In most cases IPS gardens won't have these problems—not to any serious degree—because your vegetables will be healthy, fast-growing, and moderately disease resistant. If and when you do have trouble, however, it's best to try the easiest remedy first, moving on to the really big artillery, such as sprays, only when they're needed.

Animal Protection

In addition to certain insects and plant diseases, some species of animals can be a nuisance in the garden. These animals include gophers, rabbits, and birds.

Gophers can be driven out of your garden by using a device marketed under the name Klipty-Klop (available at many garden centers). It is essentially a small windmill that sets up a vibration in the ground that gophers can't tolerate.

Rabbits can be held off easily. Simply surround your small plot with a chicken wire fence.

Birds are a mixed blessing. They do feed on damaging insects, and thus many gardeners build birdhouses to attract birds into their gardens. On the other hand, some birds will eat tiny seedlings or such fruit as tomatoes, and you may have to drive them off if they get too pesky. One defense is to hang metal foil strips on strings extended two or three feet over your garden. An extreme measure would be to enclose your garden completely—sides and tops—with gauze or chicken wire held up by posts or a frame. Or you can spread floating row covers over the entire bed (available at any garden center). We use them especially for the cool season vegetables we grow in late fall.

TABLE 8-1. WHAT KIND OF CONTROL DO YOU USE FOR WHAT PEST?

VEGETABLE	SYMPTOM	PEST	REMEDY
ASPARAGUS	Shoots channeled; leaves eaten by larvae or beetles	Asparagus beetle	Pick off, hot pepper wax, pyrethrum, rotenone
BEANS	Colonies of black sucking insects on leaves	Aphids	Hose off with water, use soap solution, Safer Soap, mineral oil, hot pepper wax, sticky yellow traps, pyrethrum
	Circular holes eaten in leaves	Bean leaf beetles	Pick off, pyrethrum
	Small plants cut off at soil level at night	Cutworm	Put paper collar around lower stem of plant, extending into soil, beneficial nematodes
	Hopping, running insects that suck sap from leaves	Leafhoppers	Safer Soap, pyrethrum, rotenone
	Lower surface of leaves eaten between veins; skeletonized	Mexican bean beetles	Pick off, pyrethrum, rotenone
	Scaly nymphs on underside of leaves; white adults flutter about when disturbed	Whiteflies	Sticky traps, hose spray, mineral oil, hot pepper wax, pyrethrum
BEETS	Leaves eaten, leaving trail of silver slime	Snails and slugs	Put out saucers of beer
BROCCOLI	Colonies of small green insects on leaves	Aphids	Hose off with water, soap solution, Safer Soap, mineral oil, hot pepper wax, sticky yellow traps, pyrethrum
	Plants sickly; maggots attack underground parts of plant	Cabbage maggots	Wood ash around base of plant
	Holes in leaves eaten by larvae	Cabbage worms and loopers	Pick off, B.T. (*Bacillus thuringiensis*), pyrethrum
	Small plants cut off at soil level at night	Cutworms	Put paper collar around lower stem of plant, extending into soil, beneficial nematodes
BRUSSELS SPROUTS	Colonies of small insects on leaves	Aphids	Hose off with water, soap solution, Safer Soap, mineral oil, hot pepper wax, sticky yellow traps, pyrethrum
	Plants sickly; maggots attack underground parts of plant	Cabbage maggots	Wood ash around base of plant
	Holes eaten in leaves by larvae	Cabbage worm and loopers	Pick off, B.T. (*Bacillus thuringiensis*), pyrethrum
	Small plants cut off at soil level at night	Cutworms	Put paper collar around lower stem of plant, extending into soil, beneficial nematodes
CABBAGE	Colonies of small insects on leaves	Aphids	Hose off with water, soap solution, Safer Soap, mineral oil, hot pepper wax, sticky yellow traps, pyrethrum
	Plants sickly; maggots attack under-ground parts of plant	Cabbage maggots	Wood ash around base of plant
	Holes eaten in leaves by larvae	Cabbage worms and loopers	Pick off, B.T. (*Bacillus thuringiensis*), pyrethrum

CONTINUED

TABLE 8-1. WHAT KIND OF CONTROL DO YOU USE FOR WHAT PEST?

VEGETABLE	SYMPTOM	PEST	REMEDY
CABBAGE	Small plants cut off at soil level at night	Cutworms	Put paper collar around lower stem of plant, extending into soil, beneficial nematodes
CAULIFLOWER	Colonies of small green insects on leaves	Aphids	Hose off with water, soap solution, Safer Soap, mineral oil, hot pepper wax, sticky yellow traps, pyrethrum
	Plants sickly; maggots attack stems and underground parts of plant	Cabbage maggots	Wood ash around base of plant, beneficial nematodes
	Holes in leaves eaten by larvae	Cabbage worms and loopers	Pick off, B.T. (*Bacillus thuringiensis*), rotenone
CORN	Silks cut off at ear; kernels destroyed by fairly large larvae	Corn earworms	Pick off, mineral oil on tips, rotenone
	Ears and stalks tunneled by larvae	Corn borers	Pick off, pyrethrum
	Small plants cut off at soil level at night	Cutworms	Put paper collar around lower stem of plant, extending into soil, beneficial nematodes
CUCUMBER	Colonies of small insects on underside of leaves	Aphids	Hose off with water, soap solution, Safer Soap, mineral oil, hot pepper wax, yellow sticky traps, pyrethrum
	All parts eaten	Cucumber beetles	Pick off, pyrethrum, rotenone
	All parts of vines eaten	Pickleworm	Pick off, B.T. (*Bacillus thuringiensis*), pyrethrum
EGGPLANT	Plants defoliated (beetles are black striped, larvae brick red)	Colorado potato beetles	Pick off, mineral oil, pyrethrum, rotenone
	Colonies of small insects on underside of leaves	Aphids	Hose off with water, soap solution, Safer Soap, mineral oil, hot pepper wax, yellow sticky traps, pyrethrum
	Colonies on underside of leaves	Eggplant lace bugs	Hose off with water, rotenone
LETTUCE	Colonies of small insects on leaves	Aphids	Hose off with water, soap solution, Safer Soap, mineral oil, hot pepper wax, yellow sticky traps, pyrethrum
	Leaves eaten by pincer bugs	Earwigs	Trap in rolled-up newspapers, Safer Soap, pyrethrum
	Wedge-shaped insects found on leaves; tips of leaves turn brown	Leafhoppers	Safer Soap, hot pepper wax, pyrethrum, rotenone
	Leaves eaten, leaving trails of silver slime	Snails and slugs	Put out saucers of beer
KALE	Colonies of small insects on underside of leaves	Aphids	Hose off with water, soap solution, Safer Soap, mineral oil, hot pepper wax, yellow stick traps, pyrethrum
	Small pin-size holes chewed in leaves	Flea beetles	Pick off, sticky yellow traps, pyrethrum, rotenone
MELONS	Colonies of small insects on underside of leaves	Aphids	Hose off with water, soap solution, Safer Soap, mineral oil, hot pepper wax, yellow sticky traps, pyrethrum
	All parts of plant eaten	Cucumber beetles	Pick off, pyrethrum, rotenone

CONTINUED

TABLE 8-1. WHAT KIND OF CONTROL DO YOU USE FOR WHAT PEST?

VEGETABLE	SYMPTOM	PEST	REMEDY
MUSTARD GREENS	Colonies of small insects on leaves	Aphids	Hose off with water, soap solution, Safer Soap, mineral oil, hot pepper wax, yellow sticky traps, pyrethrum
	Leaves with holes eaten by larvae	Cabbage worms	Pick off, B.T. (*Bacillus thuringiensis*), rotenone
	Plants sickly; maggots attack root and stem underground	Root maggots	Wood ash around base of plant, beneficial nematodes
ONIONS	Older leaves wither; small yellow insects feed at base of leaves	Onion thrips	Pyrethrum, hot pepper wax, rotenone
	Plants sickly; maggots attack parts below ground	Onion maggots	Wood ash around base of plant
OKRA	Holes eaten in pods	Corn earworms	Pick off, mineral oil on tips
PEAS	Terminals deformed; colonies of small insects on leaves	Pea aphids	Hose off with water, soap solution, Safer Soap, mineral oil, hot pepper wax, yellow sticky traps, pyrethrum
	Beetles feed on blooms; larvae bore through pod and enter young peas	Pea weevils	Pick off, pyrethrum
PEPPERS	Colonies of small insects on leaves	Aphids	Hose off with water, soap solution, Safer Soap, mineral oil, hot pepper wax, yellow sticky traps, pyrethrum
	Plants defoliated by orange and yellow bodied beetles	Blister beetles	Pick off, pyrethrum, rotenone
	Small plants cut off at soil level at night	Cutworms	Put paper collar around lower stem of plant, extending into soil, beneficial nematodes
	Small pin-size holes chewed in leaves	Flea beetles	Pyrethrum, yellow sticky traps, rotenone
	Leaves and fruit eaten	Pepper weevils	Pick off, pyrethrum, rotenone
RADISHES	Plants sickly; maggots attack plants below ground	Root maggots	Wood ash around base of plant, beneficial nematodes
SPINACH	Colonies of small insects on leaves	Aphids	Hose off with water, soap solution, Safer Soap, mineral oil, hot pepper wax, yellow sticky traps, pyrethrum
	Larvae tunnel through leaves	Spinach leafminers	Pyrethrum, rotenone
SQUASH	Colonies of small insects underneath the leaves	Aphids	Hose off with water, soap solution, Safer Soap, mineral oil, hot pepper wax, yellow sticky straps, pyrethrum
	All parts eaten	Cucumber beetles	Pick off, pyrethrum, rotenone
	Plants wilted (brownish flat bug)	Squash bug	Pick off, pyrethrum, rotenone
	Sudden wilting of runners; holes in stem near base	Squash vine borer	Locate grub by "sawdust frass" around bored hole in stem, slit stem carefully with sharp knife and remove grub, mound earth over slit and along stem; pyrethrum

CONTINUED

TABLE 8-1. WHAT KIND OF CONTROL DO YOU USE FOR WHAT PEST?

VEGETABLE	SYMPTOM	PEST	REMEDY
SWISS CHARD	Colonies of small insects on leaves	Aphids	Hose off with water, soap solution, Safer Soap, mineral oil, hot pepper wax, yellow sticky traps, pyrethrum
TOMATOES	Colonies of small insects on leaves	Aphids	Hose off with water, soap solution, Safer Soap, mineral oil, hot pepper wax, yellow sticky traps, pyrethrum
	Small plants cut off at soil level	Cutworms	Put paper collar around lower stem of plant, extending into soil, beneficial nematodes
	Many shot-size holes in leaves	Flea beetles	Pyrethrum, beneficial nematodes, yellow sticky traps, rotenone
	Leaves eaten (large green worm with horn)	Tomato hornworm	Pick off, B.T. (*Bacillus thuringiensis*), pyrethrum
	Scalelike nymphs attached to underside of leaves	Whiteflies	Pyrethrum, hot pepper wax, mineral oil, yellow stick traps

CHAPTER NINE

Bringing Vegetables and Herbs to the Table

Surprisingly, how you harvest your garden makes a tremendous difference in both freshness and flavor. Corn, for instance, holds its sweetness for only 2 to 5 days and must be picked at exactly the right time. For flavor, beets must be picked when they are small. Lettuce is most flavorful when it's picked in early morning.

Many plants go through a chemical change that converts sugar to starch. The trick is to catch them when the sugar content (the flavor) is at its peak. The general rule is to pick them when they are completely mature and then cook them as soon as possible. This is what makes our garden-grown vegetables preferable to the supermarket vegetables; we can control when they are picked and how soon they are cooked.

Drying Vegetables

Vegetables can be dried without preservatives or salt on plastic stackable trays in an electric food dehydrator. Electric food dehydrators are available in many major retail outlets. Dehydrating removes the natural moisture from food by slowly drying it out, preventing the growth of bacteria. Dried foods are low in calories and high in nutrients. Dehydrated vegetables are great to take along on camping trips. Put them in hot water with a few of your dried herbs and presto, you have vegetable soup.

Now let's look at the individual vegetables and herbs.

Vegetables

Artichokes

Cut the individual flowers before they start to open. The smaller, more immature artichokes are the most tender. Cut artichokes darken in color once they are exposed to the air. To slow the discoloration, drop them in water fortified with 2 or 3 tablespoons of lemon juice.

To prepare whole artichokes, slice about $1/2$ inch off the tops and remove the main cluster of thorny bracts (leaves). If you want artichokes to sit upright when served, trim the stems flat with the bottoms of the bracts before cooking. Select a pan large enough to hold whole artichokes, fill the pan halfway with water, and add 1 teaspoon of salt. Cover the pan and bring to a boil. Simmer until the bottoms pierce easily.

Asparagus

Choose firm, brittle, 6- to 20-inch-tall spears that are bright green almost their entire length and have tightly closed tips. Break them off at ground level. To store, wrap the ends in a damp paper towel and refrigerate. Asparagus can be boiled, microwaved, steamed, or stir-fried.

Beans (Pole/Bush)

Green beans are ready for harvesting about 2 weeks after they bloom. Pick when the slender, crisp pods are nearly full size but the seeds are still small. Pull the pods from the plants gently to avoid uprooting bush beans or pulling vines away from their supports. Discard beans that have large seeds or swollen or limp pods. Keep plants well picked to ensure a continuous harvest and an increased yield.

Bean pods that become lumpy are no longer prime snap beans. You can let them dry and use them as dry beans. When shelled out, these are called *shelly beans*, and they are delicious.

Harvest lima bean pods when they swell yet remain green and show 3 to 4 beans per pod.

Beans (Dry/Shelling)

Pick fresh beans when the seeds are fully formed and plump, but still soft. Or permit them to dry fully on the vine and harvest them when 90 percent of the leaves have yellowed and/or fallen off and the pods are dry. Dry beans fully. Shell pods individually. Store in airtight containers.

You can reduce the cooking time for dry beans by soaking them overnight. To cook, rinse the beans, cover them with fresh water in a pan, and bring the water to a boil. Take the pan off the stove, and let it stand about 3 hours. Drain. Then use the beans in your favorite recipes.

Beets

Harvest firm, smooth-skinned beets when they are 1 to 2 inches in diameter. Pick those beets with deep green leaves. For a pickled beet treat, cook and slice 2 cups of beets. Put in glass bowl. In a saucepan combine 1 cup water, 1 cup rice wine vinegar, $\frac{1}{2}$ cup sugar, and $1\frac{1}{2}$

tablespoon chopped ginger. Heat until sugar is dissolved. Pour over beets. Refrigerate several hours or several days.

Broccoli

Pick broccoli while the central heads are still dark green and firm. Cut the central head on a 45-degree angle while the bud tips are still firm. After that, side shoots will develop in clusters. Some cooks use the broccoli stems extensively in all sorts of recipes. The trick is to peel the stems so they will be as tender as the flower buds.

Broccoli will keep in the refrigerator for 5 to 7 days. It must be chilled quickly. During storage it will lose Vitamin C and its stems will become tough. You can preserve broccoli by freezing it. Separate the head into bite-sized pieces, and cut the stems into 1-inch pieces. Cook the broccoli pieces in boiling water for three minutes, then plunge them into cold water for three minutes. Drain and store in plastic freezer bags. You can store frozen broccoli for up to 1 year.

Brussels Sprouts

High quality sprouts should be firm and well formed. Begin picking at the bottom. Break off a leaf below the sprout, and then remove the sprout. The upper sprouts will continue to mature as the lower ones are picked. Small, young, bright green sprouts taste best. High quality fresh sprouts will store for approximately 3 to 4 weeks at 32°F. Steamed sprouts are delicious with a mustard glaze. You can also marinate them in oil and vinegar and add them to a salad.

Cabbages

Choose firm heads that have good color. To keep the early types from bursting, harvest them promptly. Late-maturing cabbages will hold much longer. When cutting the heads from the stems, leave 2 or 3 of the wrapper leaves (outside leaves) to protect against bruising. Overmature heads are subject to splitting, especially if they are exposed to moisture fluctuations. Late-storage types will keep up to 6 months at 32°F. Early types will store 1 to 2 months. You can cook cabbage with caraway seed.

Carrots

You can use the young carrots, thinned from the carrot bed, in soups and stews. Mature carrots should be pulled when they are bright orange. This is the peak time for flavor and texture. Young carrots often haven't stored enough sugar in their roots to give them good flavor. You can leave fall carrots in the ground until you need them. Protect them, in areas where the ground freezes, with a 4-inch layer of mulch. Nutrients are stored near the skin. To preserve the nutrients, scrub carrots under running cold water with a vegetable brush, instead of peeling.

Serve carrots raw with a dip. Cooked carrots also have a wonderful flavor when topped with melted herb butter. Carrots make delicious cakes and appetizers.

Cauliflower

For peak flavor, cut the cauliflower heads from the stalk when they are compact and creamy white. They are overmature when the flower buds begin to open. If left in the garden past their prime, cauliflower heads will have a mealy texture when cooked. Serve raw cauliflower with a dip. Steam and add an herb sauce.

Celeriac (Celery Root)

Celery root is knobby and hairy, covering creamy white flesh. Pull the plants when the roots are small to medium and the tops are bright green. To prepare celeriac for cooking, scrub it with a vegetable brush. Peel the thick outer skin with a knife. Cut them into strips or cubes. To keep the peeled celeriac flesh white, submerge it in a quart of water fortified with 3 to 4 tablespoons of lemon juice.

Celery

The stalks should be crisp and ridged, with bright green leaves. Pick individual stalks as needed. The unopened flower and the tender stalks below them are particularly delicious. In mild-winter areas, many celery varieties will stand in the garden until spring, allowing light picking for soups and salads. Celery stalks stuffed with cheese make a delicious appetizer. Add raw sliced or diced celery to any dish.

Collards

Collards are hardy and usually survive to 10°F. Collards could be called a green with a bite, although they are milder than mustard greens. Start picking the tender, deep green leaves about 2 months after planting. Avoid leaves with thick, coarse veins. Discard tough stems or center ribs. Cut or tear into bite-sized pieces. Add to soups or stews, or cook with ham hocks.

Sweet Corn

Most varieties of sweet corn are ready to eat $2\frac{1}{2}$ to 3 weeks after pollination. The hotter the weather, the quicker the corn will mature.

When corn is at its prime, the kernels will be soft and full of milk, making it very succulent. As the ear matures, the water content decreases, the sugar turns to starch, and the kernels become tough and doughy. Tough kernels indicate overmaturity.

To determine when the ears are ready, look for brown, dry silks and a round, blunt tip to the cob. If the husk fits tight to the cob, the corn is ready. If the ear is loose or soft, allow the kernels to fill out for another day or two. As a final test for sweet corn, pull back the husks of one ear and pop one of the kernels with your thumbnail. If the juice is clear, wait another day. If it is milky, the ear is ready to pick. Note that both SH2 and SE types are mature when the kernel juice is clear.

Remove the ear with a sharp downward pull, and a quick twisting wrist action. Longtime gardeners will tell you, "Don't pick the corn until the water is boiling." This isn't always practical. To retain the most flavor, store the corn in the refrigerator. You can also can or freeze corn. To freeze, blanch corn for 8 to 10 minutes and chill thoroughly in cold water. Freeze in containers or plastic freezer bags.

Popcorn

If popcorn is too dry or too wet, it won't pop properly. Let the ears dry on the stalks, and pick them when the stalks and husks are completely brown and the kernels are hard. If you can't dent the kernels with your fingernail, the popcorn is ready.

Cut small holes in a paper grocery bag, and place four or five ears inside. Hang the bag to dry for two to three weeks. When the kernels press off the cob easily, they're ready to pop.

Give popcorn a different flavor by mixing it with various spices and seasonings.

Cucumbers

Pick them when they are firm and dark green after they are about 3 to 4 inches long. The seeds get larger and harder as the fruits approach full size. Put yellowing cucumbers in the compost. Lemon cucumbers should be picked when they are 2 to 3 inches in diameter and have pale yellow skin. Keep them picked, and they will keep producing. Cut them into spears and serve with a dip. Use in salads or as a cold soup. Here's a recipe for cold cucumber soup:

3 medium cucumbers, peeled and sliced
3 cups chicken broth
$1/4$ cup chopped onion
$1/2$ teaspoon salt
1 cup half and half
$1/3$ cup sour cream
2 tablespoons lemon juice
$1/4$ cup chopped fresh parsley
$1/2$ cup cucumber slices

Combine the first four ingredients in a pan, cover, and simmer for 20 minutes. Cool. In a blender, blend until smooth. Stir in half and half, sour cream, and lemon juice. Garnish with parsley and cucumber slices.

Eggplant

Select firm, heavy fruit with taut, glossy, deeply colored skin. Purple selections should be glossy and deeply colored. White selections should be pure white, not yellowish or colored. Dull fruit is overripe and contains hard seeds.

When some eggplants are picked while small, the plants are encouraged to produce abundantly. To prepare, rinse and dry. Cut off and discard the stem. Spoon sautéed eggplant into pocket bread with other ingredients. You can also create a taste treat by sandwiching mozzarella cheese between thin slices of eggplant, then breading and frying them. For a delicious sandwich, place fried eggplant slices along with lettuce and tomato between toasted bread.

Garlic

When you can see the cloves forming in a cut open bulb, stop watering. Wait until the leaves are mostly dry, or the tops lie down in mid- to late summer, then dig up the bulbs with a garden fork. The heads should be closed with tight skins. To store, tie the plants in small bunches, and hang them in a cool, dark, well-ventilated location. Braiding is a great way to show off your garlic (Figures 9-1a-c).

Mince or cut the cloves into small pieces. Use as a basic ingredient in garlic butter. You can also rub uncooked cloves over a roast, or rub a raw clove inside a salad bowl before adding the salad.

To create mild-flavored garlic for cooking, roast it. The tempered bulb can be made into a pulp to impart a subtle flavor to any dish.

Figure 9-1a. Braiding garlic: Start with 3 garlic plants and wrap the stem of the center garlic around the cross stems of the other two bulbs.

Figure 9-1b. Add another bulb each time you pull an outer stem into the center.

Figure 9-1c. Stop when you have added 25–40 garlic plants. Pull the stems tight as the braid dries. To finish, wrap ends of briad with string.

Horseradish

Horseradish roots should be firm. To store, wrap in a damp paper or cloth towel. Place in a plastic bag and refrigerate. Scrub, peel, and grate or cut into cubes. Horseradish will add bite to any food. Here's a recipe for fresh horseradish:

1 medium horseradish root
1 cup white vinegar

1 teaspoon salt
$^1/_2$ teaspoon sugar

Blend in a food processor. You can temper the heat by mixing in a grated potato.

Kale

Kale has beautiful, curly leaves. Begin picking individual leaves in late October to November. Look for fresh, tender leaves; avoid leaves with a thick, heavy midrib. The unopened flowers taste like the sweetest broccoli. You can boil or microwave kale. Season with an herb butter and serve.

Kohlrabi

Pick kohlrabi when the bulbs are less than 2 inches in diameter. The smaller the bulb, the more delicate the texture and flavor. Cut off the leaves and use as a seasoning for soups. You can slice and serve kohlrabi with a dip as an appetizer. The bulbs can be hollowed out and stuffed with pork and bread crumbs.

Leeks

Dig out with a spading fork any time the leeks are 1 inch in diameter or larger. Leeks will overwinter in the ground in many areas. Harvest them before they can develop seedlings the following spring. Select those with crisp, fresh-looking, green tops. Small to medium-sized leeks (under $1^1/_2$ inches) are the most tender.

Cut off the leaf tops while still in the garden, and strip the tough outer skin from the bulb end. Spray with a hose to wash off the dirt. Put the tops and skin in the compost. Cook leeks until tender, and serve warm or chilled. You can top leeks with crumbled bacon and grated lemon peel.

Leeks

Lettuce

Lettuce remains in prime eating condition for only about 3 weeks. Plant lettuce in succession so that you may enjoy fresh garden salads as much of the season as possible. Rinse greens under warm tap water to reduce bitterness. Select iceberg lettuce with fresh outer leaves. The head should give a little when squeezed. Leaf lettuce should look crisp. Put any discolored leaves in the compost. Cut out the core of iceberg lettuce. For most salads, tear leaf lettuce into bite-sized pieces. Place loose-leaf lettuce in a plastic bag, and store it in the refrigerator.

Melons

There are many types of melons. Cantaloupes are ready to eat when the stems pull off easily, usually with only a slight touch. When ripe, the rind begins to look like a corky net and turns from green to yellow or tan. The stem cracks all the way around. If cantaloupes are picked early, the fruit won't mature off the vine.

When ripe, crenshaws are medium yellow all over. The blossom end should give when pressed. When fully ripe, the green honeydew has a cream-colored rind and a fruity or honey smell. Orange honeydew rind turns from white to light salmon pink.

Juan Canary melons are ripe when the rind has turned bright yellow all over. Persian melons also have a fruity smell when ripe. The background color of the sweetest melon turns from gray green to bronze.

Judge the ripeness of the green and gold Santa Claus melon by the color of the stripes on the shell. The brighter the yellow, the riper and more flavorful the melon will be. Sharlyn melons are ripe when the background color turns from green to completely orange. Sharlyns get overripe quickly.

Season melon wedges with lemon or lime juice. You can also grill Persian melons. Here's a recipe for sweet pickled cantaloupe:

4 large firm cantaloupes
½ cup salt
2 quarts water
2 tablespoons whole allspice
1 tablespoon whole cloves
4 cinnamon sticks
5 cups sugar
2 cups white vinegar
2 cups water

Peel and seed cantaloupes and cut into bite-sized pieces. Dissolve salt in water. Add cantaloupe and let stand 2 hours. Drain and set aside. Tie spices in a cheesecloth bag. Combine spices and remaining ingredients in a large Dutch oven and bring to a boil. Cook 5 minutes. Add cantaloupe, return to a boil and cook 3 to 5 minutes. Remove from heat, cover, and let stand 8 hours. Remove the spice bag, and bring the syrup to a boil. Pack cantaloupe in hot, sterilized pint jars. Cover with boiling syrup, leaving $1/2$ inch of headspace from top of jar. Remove air bubbles; wipe jar rims. Cover at once with metal lids, and screw on bands. Process in boiling water bath for 15 minutes. Yield: 4 pints.

Mustard Greens

Regular mustard greens have a strong bite. Oriental mustard greens are milder. Pick fresh, tender green leaves, or fresh, tender plants. Shred mustard greens, and boil or microwave. Season with herb butter. Here's a recipe for mustard greens and salt pork, a staple of the Old South:

5 pounds fresh mustard greens
$1/2$ pound salt pork
6 to 8 cups of water
2 teaspoons bacon drippings
Green onions

Tear mustard greens into bite-sized pieces. Cut salt pork into 2-inch pieces. Combine salt pork and water in a large Dutch oven. Bring to a boil, cover, reduce heat, and simmer 30 minutes. Add mustard greens and bacon drippings. Simmer another 10 minutes. Serve with green onions.

Okra

Select small to medium pods that are deep green and firm. Trim stems and rinse, using a vegetable brush to remove the thin layer of fuzz on the stem. Cut with a sharp knife; the pods don't break or pull off easily. If you keep the pods whole, the mucilaginous juices will remain inside. Cook until tender but crisp. Slices of okra are used to thicken soups and stews. Top whole cooked okra with chives and lemon butter.

Okra is a staple vegetable in the South, and no one fries okra better than southerners. To fry okra, pick about 20 small okra pods. Soak them in buttermilk, and then roll them in flour or cornmeal. Deep-fry the okra until crisp. Yum!

Onions

When the tops begin to dry out and fall over, wait about one week to dig up the bulbs. Spread the bulbs out in the sun to cure them for a week or so to toughen the skins. Store dried onions in well-ventilated containers or in clean panty hose, tying a knot between each onion.

There are two ways to tone down the onion taste and still keep the crisp texture:

1. Immerse thin slices in ice water for about 30 minutes. They will retain some of the tanginess and remain crisp.
2. Squeeze the slices in water to break up the cells. The water will wash away some of the tanginess.

You can bake onions for a mild flavor or boil them to release the sweetness. Other choices include deep-frying slices and rings, slicing and cooking slowly, or chopping and sautéeing. You can also microwave onions. Add them to salads, soups, stews, or casseroles. There is nothing like a fresh, sliced raw onion on a hamburger.

Create a borscht by fortifying red onion soup with shredded beets. Add cream to white onion soup, and top with nutmeg and grated white cheese. Lace yellow onion soup with sherry and flavor with coriander, then top with Parmesan cheese. Here are some more tips about onions:

- Onions chopped by hand have a milder flavor than those that are chopped in a food processor. The reason is that more onion cells are bruised in a food processor, releasing compounds associated with flavor, aroma, and bitterness.
- A short cooking time over high heat releases more of these compounds; longer cooking over lower heat reduces the strong taste and brings out the natural sweetness. Too high a temperature for too long a time results in bitterness.
- Soaking in water leaches out the natural color of red onions.
- Soaking in vinegar turns a red onion a bright pink.
- Soaking in a solution of baking soda turns a red onion yellow green.

Parsnips

Harvest in late fall after the first frost. The flavor is improved by a couple of good frosts. Dig the roots anytime from October throughout the winter, as needed. Protect from freezing in the soil with a thick straw mulch. Pull the small to medium roots. Large roots have a woody core. Add diced parsnips to soups and stews, or bake until tender. You can even use parsnips in a stir-fry.

Peas

Raw sugar snap peas make great nibbling. Snap peas are sweetest picked just before the pods fill out. Break off the ends of the snap pea, pull any strings free, and rinse well. You can serve them on a snack tray or combine them with your favorite dip. Both sugar snap and snow peas cook quickly and turn bright green. For regular peas, remove the peas from the pod, rinse, and cook.

If peas overmature, don't throw them away. Instead, treat them like beans, and add them to soups and stews. Lightly cooked peas can be added to salads.

Pea greens—the tender stems, leaves, and shoots of pea plants—have become a gourmet treat in many fine restaurants. Pop them into salads or use in stir-fries.

Peppers, Sweet

Expect 5 to 10 large bell peppers per plant. For a sweeter flavor, let your peppers ripen to maturity. It usually takes from 20 to 30 days for peppers to turn from green to red or yellow or to other colors. Cut peppers from the plants with a knife.

Bell peppers can be sliced or frozen in halves with no more than a wash to remove garden soil. You don't need to blanch peppers before freezing them. Slice all colors of peppers, and put them into a freezer bag for later use in stir-fries or spaghetti.

Peppers are great for stuffing or used as containers to show off other vegetables. Golden Bell peppers make wonderful containers for individual soufflés.

Peppers, Hot (Chilies)

Expect 20 to 50 chili peppers per plant. Pick bright, glossy peppers. Chili peppers vary from mild to hot. Anaheim and Pasilla are mild and a little bitter. In general, the smaller varieties pack the most heat. When preparing hot chili peppers, wear rubber gloves, and keep your hands away from your face. The volatile oils can cause severe burning.

Potatoes

Seventy-five days after planting, a few potatoes can be removed around the edge of each plant without threatening the main harvest. These "new potatoes" are deliciously sweet because the sugar content hasn't yet converted to starch. Use them immediately. Some cooks boil them and wrap them in bacon or sauté the little potatoes in butter.

Wait to harvest the main crop until the tops of the plants die down. Then use a pitchfork to break the small roots connecting the potatoes. Leave them for a week or two so that the skins will harden, but don't let them sit in direct sunlight. Store potatoes in a relatively dry location and at the lowest temperature possible without freezing.

Scrub the potatoes with a vegetable brush and then peel them. To keep potatoes from discoloring, cover them with cold water before cooking. Potatoes are a great choice for microwave cooking.

Pumpkins

Choose the smaller pumpkins for eating. Pumpkin seeds baked in butter and garlic salt make a delicious snack. Cut a smaller pumpkin (2 to 3 pounds) in half and bake it at 325°F until it's tender. Peel the pumpkin pieces, and puree them in a food processor. Use the mashed pumpkin to make breads and pies.

If you scoop out the little pumpkins, you can fill them with soup and use them as individual soup bowls. Here's a recipe for seasoned pumpkin seeds:

3/4 cup of pumpkin seeds
1 tablespoon margarine
1/4 teaspoon garlic salt
1/2 teaspoon Worcestershire sauce
1/4 teaspoon seasoned salt

Remove membranes from seeds; rinse and pat seeds dry. Place seeds in a pie plate, add remaining ingredients, and toss to coat all sides. Microwave at High for 8 minutes. Stir at 2-minute intervals.

Radishes

Make multiple sowings for a steady supply of radishes throughout the season. Look for bright green tops and well-formed roots. In some countries, radishes are added to soups. The green leafy tops are edible. Try mixing some, along with the radish, in salads. You can also let a few plants go to seed, and then pick the seed pods while they are immature. The pods are a crunchy addition to salads.

Oriental radishes take a little longer to mature and are a lot hotter than the regular variety.

Rhubarb

Cut the firm, crisp stalks as desired. Wash and cut the stalks into 1- or 2-inch pieces. Cook uncovered in enough water to cover the rhubarb. Sweeten with sugar to taste. Cooked rhubarb can be used in pies or served with whipped cream.

Rutabaga

Thin rutabaga in July for tasty roots by October and November. Rutabaga tastes best after a couple of good frosts. They almost always have yellow to orange skin and flesh. Peel and dice. Add to soups and stews. They can also be added to stir-fries.

Salsify

Harvest the roots in the fall. They can also be lifted and stored in damp sand for use throughout the winter, or left in the ground. Salsify has white flesh. *Scozonera* is a black-skinned relative of salsify. To keep the peeled roots white, place the roots in lemon water (3 tablespoons of lemon juice to 1 quart of water). Fry salsify, and cover it with freshly grated cheese, or use the sharp-tasting leaves in salads.

Shallots

Dry shallots in a warm dry spot, or braid the tops and hang them out to dry. They are completely cured when the foliage loses its green color and the bulbs are papery.

Shallots

Spinach

Pick only fresh, green leaves. Tear into bite-sized pieces. Raw spinach can be served with a vinaigrette or mixed with other greens. It is also used in soufflés, soups, stews, lasagna, and many other dishes. In mild-winter areas, you can grow spinach all year round.

Squash, Summer

Never plant too many summer squash, or you'll find yourself knocking on doors trying to give it away. A couple of plants go a long way. There are many types of summer squash. All have a mild, delicate flavor. Pick when the fruit is small to medium and firm with smooth skin. Never let a zucchini grow too large, or it will only be good as a club. Check plants every few days once they start to bloom.

Summer squash can be eaten raw, grilled, added to salads, or cooked in soups and stews.

Squash, Winter

Cut the vine about 1 inch from the fruit when the vine starts to dry. Allow the fruit to air cure for 7 to 10 days. To help prevent rot during storage, wipe the fruit with a solution composed of 1 teaspoon of bleach to 1 quart of water. Store at 45° to 60°F. The best squash have a hard, thick shell and feel heavy for their size.

Winter squash can be used in many different dishes, including pies, soups, stews, or baked casseroles.

Sweet potatoes

When we grew these, we were delighted with the results. The taste was sweet and delicious. You can also root the tops in jars of water placed under your sink or in another dark spot.

Sweet potatoes can be boiled, baked, or added to other dishes. Sliced thin, they can be fried or baked in the oven as potato chips.

Swiss Chard

Cut individual stalks that have fresh, glossy leaves and heavy white or red stems. The stems have the crunch of celery and, some say, the taste of celery. Treat the leaves as you would spinach. Separate the leaves from the stems; slice the stems to use in salads. Add chard to soups, stir-fries, or lasagnas, or as a side dish steamed with a little butter.

Tomatoes

Pick smooth, well-formed tomatoes that are heavy for their size. There is nothing like the taste of a vine-ripened tomato. The larger tomatoes are great stuffed. Scoop out the pulp and leave the shells intact. Cut scalloped edges around the tomato, and add crab and avocado, turkey and dill, or a variety of cooked vegetables.

You can also ripen green tomatoes at the end of the season by wrapping individual tomatoes in newspaper and placing them in a cardboard box, or by storing them on a drying rack in a cool basement. Tomatoes ripen at different rates.

Turnips

Pick turnips when they are young and tender. The tastiest roots are 1½ to 2 inches in diameter. The larger they are, the tougher they will be. Turnips are good sliced raw or added to soups and stews. Turnips can be peeled, boiled, and mashed like potatoes for a tasty side dish. The turnip tops (called greens) can be harvested at any size.

Watermelon

A watermelon is ready to harvest when the fruit is uniform in shape and the stem end slips off easily. If there are small blotchy spots around the stem end, it means the melon is very sweet. When ripe, the skin on the bottom of the melon turns from white to yellow. And the thump test? Hold the melon in one hand and thump it; if you feel a vibration in the hand holding the melon, it's a full, solid melon.

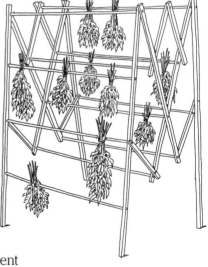

Figure 9-2. Drying herbs.

Herbs

Herbs brighten up the simplest meal or provide the finishing touch to fine cuisine. The bold flavors of herbs can replace salt or fat in some recipes and can permeate cooked dishes to add an extra dimension.

When snipped frequently, herbs respond with renewed vigor. Any excess should be dried or frozen (Figure 9-2). To enhance a dinner meal, place a bouquet of fresh herbs in the middle of the table. The aroma will fill the entire room.

Tie together sprigs of oregano, rosemary, and sage, and use them like a pastry brush to apply marinade for barbecuing.

Dried herbs can be made into herbal wreaths. Pick an assortment of herbs, such as dark green mints, Italian parsley, purple opal basil, variegated sage, and other basils. Dry the herbs, and gather them into bundles of 5 to 7 stems, cut about 5 inches long. Using glue or pins, attach the bundles to a straw base from a craft store. Alternate any contrasting colors. Overlap the leaves to cover the stems, working from the inner edge to the outer edge. You can also add dried flowers if you like.

Herbs can be added to vinegars and sugars. To make a white wine herb vinegar, fill a glass jar with fresh herb sprigs. Use rosemary, thyme, or basil by themselves, or combine several herbs, such as lemon thyme, marjoram, and oregano. Fill the jar with white wine, secure the lid, and let it stand at room temperature for several weeks. Strain the mixture through cheesecloth. Use the vinegar as desired.

You can also buy a fancy vinegar jar, add a fresh sprig of your favorite herb, and fill the jar with the strained vinegar. Add a bow, and give the jar as a delightful gift.

Seed sources for many herbs are included in the previous text or listed here.

Anise

Harvest the seeds about one month after the flowers bloom, when they turn gray brown, by clipping them into a paper bag. Use the fresh leaves to spice up a green salad, or in soups, stews, and sauces. Seed source: ABU ALL COM DEG GOU GUR HEN JUN LED LEJ MEY NIC PIN POR RIC SOU STO TAY TER TIL VER WIL WILL

Balm, Lemon

Harvest the leaves anytime during the season. You can cut the plant back to within 2 to 4 inches of the ground, and it will regrow the following year. You can dry the leaves for use during the winter. The aroma of lemon balm becomes faint when it's dried. Use the fresh heart-shaped leaves in teas, salads, soups, and stews. Bees love this plant. Seed source: BOU BURP COM DAB GOU GUR HEN HIG JOH JUN LEJ NIC ORN PAR PIN POR RED RIC SHE SEE SOU STO TAY VER WILL

Basil

Gather basil leaves before they bloom or when blooming begins. Pinch the top third of the basil plant regularly. Dry the leaves in a paper grocery bag with holes cut in the sides for ventilation. Hang the bag if possible. This drying process takes about 2 weeks. Store the leaves in an airtight container away from direct sunlight. Basil may also be preserved by freezing the leaves and stems, or by pureeing the leaves and freezing them. Try chopping fresh basil and adding it to spaghetti sauce. It adds a wonderful flavor to chicken, fish, pasta dishes, and vegetables.

Bergamot (Bee Balm)

Bergamot has citrus-scented leaves and flowers. Both can be used in salads or teas. Lemon Bergamot leaves were used by Hopi Indians to flavor wild game. Seed source: NIC RIC VER

Borage

Clip leaves before the buds flower. Use the blossoms to decorate beverages, and use fresh chopped leaves in salads and summer drinks. Seed source: ALL ABU BOU BURP BURR COM COO DEG GAR GOU HIG JLH JOH JUN LEJ LED LIB MEY NIC PAR PIN POR RED RIC SEE SOU STO TAY TER TWI VER WILL

Burnet Salad

This herb has nutty, cucumber-flavored leaves that are used in dressings, salads, casseroles, vinegars, cream cheeses, and soups. Seed source: BOU COM DEG GOU NIC PAR RED RIC SEE SOU TAY VER

Chervil

Pick leaves just before buds break. Green tender leaves may be cut and dried. To harvest, clip whole plants before they flower, and hang them upside down in a shady location. Chervil has a mild licorice or tarragonlike flavor and can be used in every dish in which parsley is used. Seed source: ABU ALL BOU COM DEG GAR JLH LED NIC PIN POR SEE SHE STO TAY TER TIL

Chervil

Chives

Chives are an essential culinary herb. Clip the leaves with scissors. Use the leaves fresh or frozen. Chives lose their flavor quickly and don't dry well, but they can be chopped and frozen in a plastic bag. Make up an herb seasoning for omelettes, creamy sauces, and salads by mixing chopped parsley, chives, marjoram, and thyme.

Garlic Chives

Cilantro/Coriander

Harvest plants when they are 6 inches high by clipping the leaves. You can dry the leaves in a paper bag and store them in an airtight container. Use fresh or dried, and add the seeds to many dishes. If you let the plant go to seed, gather the seeds as they ripen in mid-summer.

Dill

Pick fresh leaves as soon as the flowers begin to open. Harvest leaves early in the day before the plant begins to set its flower buds. Snip the leaves close to the stem. Cover seed stalks with a plastic bag, close the bag loosely, and collect the seeds as they ripen. Some cooks grind the dill seeds into a powder. You can also freeze the stems and snip off the leaves as you need them. Dill has a robust flavor that adds life to potatoes, eggs, cream cheese, dips, pickles, and carrots. It also gives an aromatic flavor to salmon, salads, soups, and stews. When you use fresh dill, add it near the end of cooking so that it retains its sharp flavor. Seed source: ABU ALL BOU BURP COM FAR GUR HEN HIG LED MEY NIC ORG PAR PIN POR RED RIC SEE SOU STO TAY WIL

Fennel

Pick the stems just before the flower blooms. Pick the leaves when the flowers start to bloom and as soon as they are large enough. You can chop and freeze them in plastic bags. They add a slightly licorice flavor to salads. The seeds are ready to harvest when they are hard and turn from green to brown. Pick them before they get scattered, and finish drying them indoors. They add a unique taste to baked breads, cakes, and cookies. They also brighten up fish, meat, cheese, and vegetable dishes.

Hyssop

Hyssop is a decorative plant with slightly bitter leaves. The leaves are used in salads, game meat, soups, and stews. Pick before they flower. Seed source: ABU BOU COM DAB DEG GAR GOU LEJ NIC ORN PIN RIC SEE SEED SOU TAY TER WILL

Lovage

Lovage resembles a giant celery plant; even the flavor resembles celery. Lovage is used in tea, meat, fish, and vegetable dishes. Pick before they flower. Seed source: ABU BOU COM DEG GAR GOU HEN JOH LEJ NIC PAR PIN SEED SOU TAY TER VER WILL

Marjoram, Sweet

Trim off the ball-shaped flower clusters before they bloom, or remove sprigs as needed. Marjoram adds flavor to chicken, cheese, and vegetables.

Mint

The more frequently you cut the sprigs, the better mint will grow. Fresh mint is best, and young leaves are more flavorful than older ones. Many cooks use mint as a garnish or in jellies. There are many kinds of mint, and each complements a beverage, cottage cheese, potatoes, or vegetables. Choose your flavor! You can freeze or dry mint.

Oregano

You can start harvesting sprigs of oregano when the plants are 6 inches high. Use fresh leaves as needed. Leaves may also be preserved by drying; just hang them in bunches. Cretan, Greek, and Syrian varieties have the strongest flavors. Sicilian and Italian types are milder. The leaves add an aromatic, if somewhat minty, flavor to tomato dishes.

Parsley

Pick mature leaves from first-year plants. Harvest leaves from second-year plants before the flowers bloom. You can dry by hanging the whole plant in a shady, well-ventilated area. Crumble when dry, and store in airtight containers. It has an even better flavor if you chop it up and freeze it. Toss chopped parsley into salads, soups, casseroles, and vegetables. Parsley has a strong flavor that can enhance almost any food. It is famous as a garnish.

Perilla (Shiso)

This herb is highly prized for Oriental dishes. Green Perilla (Aoshiso) is the preferred variety for sushi. Purple Perilla (Akahisho) is preferred for pickling. Red Perilla (Red Shiso) leaves are used in salads and soups and as a garnish for fish. Pick in all seasons. Seed source: GOU JOH NIC ORN SEE SEED SOU SUN THE VER

Rosemary

Pick after the morning dew has dried but before the sun can leach out the essential oils that keep herbs fresh and flavorful. Rosemary is the star of many Mediterranean-style dishes. Use fresh or dried. Dry by hanging or placing in a paper bag that has holes cut around the sides. Drying takes about two weeks.

Sage

Sage leaves can be used fresh or dried. Pick leaves as soon as they are large enough to handle, and dry them on a tray. Then store them away from light. There are many varieties that flavor meats, dressings, and sauces. Most sages can be grown in pots inside or out. Pinch back to keep bushy.

Summer Savory

Summer savory is preferred most for culinary use. Gather leaves from prebloom until bloom. Lemon savory has an intense lemon scent. Seed source: ABU ALL BOU BURP BURR COM DEG GAR GOU JOH JUN LEJ LIB MEY NIC ORG ORN PAR RIC SEE SEED SHE SOU TAY TER TIL TWI VER WIL

Tarragon

The leaves are most flavorful when picked prebloom or just before blooming begins. Preserve tarragon by drying. French tarragon makes a good green sauce and is the true tarragon, but it doesn't propagate by seeds. The anise-flavored leaves of Mexican tarragon (also called sweet mace) are narrow, glossy, green, and serrated. They are used extensively in Mexican dishes.

Use tarragon in mayonnaise, butter, white wine vinegar, and vegetables.

Thyme

Harvest heavily just before the bloom, and pinch off sprigs as needed up to 6 weeks before the first fall frost. Clip the tops of plants when in full bloom. Orange balsam thyme has an orange flavor and is well suited to fruit salads. Other varieties have the scent and flavor of nutmeg, caraway, and lemon. Thyme is excellent in soups, sauces, and breads. Seed source: DAB RIC.

CHAPTER TEN

Watering the Garden

Watering your intensive postage stamp garden, like doing everything else recommended in this book, should be simple and easy. In fact, it is simple and easy, but it is also absolutely crucial to the success of your garden. The truth is that water—or the lack of it—can sometimes create tremendous garden problems. A gardening friend of ours, for instance, spent hours on end spading his plot, staking out the sections, and planting the various vegetables.

When thereafter it came time to water, however, he couldn't seem to find the time. As a result, some of his cabbages cracked, and his other vegetables just didn't turn out right. He, of course, blamed his failure on bad luck, but actually his entire problem was poor watering.

Without enough water, bean pods produce only a few seeds and the rest of the pods shrivel, beets become stringy, radishes get pithy, cucumbers stop growing well, and more. Once started, vegetables must grow rapidly, without interruptions or slowdowns. Stop growth by checking the water supply, and you really set your vegetables back. Agronomists tell us that when a plant isn't getting enough water, it's under "water stress." And although this may be useful for flowers, since water stress can induce blooming, it nearly always sets vegetables back. Once you do this, they never seem to recover.

How Much to Water and When

You've heard that old saying, "Damned if you do, and damned if you don't." Well, watering is like that in a vegetable garden. It's absolutely essential, but it can also create problems. Water itself is a nutrient used directly by the plants, and it also dissolves and carries other nutrients to the roots. That's the good part. The roots of plants also need air just like we do. Oxygen must reach the roots, and carbon dioxide must be given off by the roots to return to the air. Most soil has enough air space for this exchange to take place. If you eliminate the oxygen by filling all the soil space continually with water, however, root growth stops, and if this condition continues long enough, the plant dies. That's the bad part.

An ideal soil for plant growth contains 50 percent solid matter and 50 percent pore space (that's what our IPS soil has). About half this pore space should be occupied by water, and that's the object of your watering program.

The general rule for watering IPS gardens is this: Water thoroughly, regularly, and infrequently. When you soak the soil thoroughly, you add water until it reaches "field capacity"—that is, roughly all the water that the air spaces of the soil can hold. And you want to keep your garden between this condition and the point at which moisture is so scare that plant roots can no longer take water from the soil.

Whenever you water your IPS beds, you must water them thoroughly to a depth of about 3 feet. The length of time that it takes to water this deep will depend on the type of soil under the bed, but it will usually take at least an hour or two. A good rule is to simply water until you can easily sink a stick about 3 feet deep. If there are a lot of rocks below your IPS subsoil, you may not be able to do this; then just estimate. After thoroughly watering your beds, don't water again until the soil has almost dried out to a depth of 10 inches. Just take a trowel and check. If the soil is almost dry to this depth, water deeply again—and then don't water until the moisture has receded to 10 inches again.

At some times of the year, for example, when it's cool or rainy, this interval between waterings may extend two weeks or more, but when it's hot and dry, you may have to water every two to six days. Thus, it generally doesn't matter one bit whether or not it rains. You simply don't water until your 10-inch trowel test shows that watering is necessary. By letting the soil almost dry out this way, you give it a chance to take in a good supply of air as the water supply is removed.

After a few years of vegetable gardening, you'll have acquired enough experience to sense whenever watering is necessary and how much to water. You'll have adjusted to the special needs of your climate and seasonal rainfall.

Which Way to Water

Some gardeners insist that the only way to water an IPS garden is with a hose lying on the ground. Others simply set up a sprinkler in the middle of their bed and turn it on when it's time to water.

What should you do? We personally feel that you should do whatever is easiest (using either a hose or a sprinkler), as long as you water thoroughly until the soil reaches field capacity. Then don't water again until the soil is almost dried out.

In our own case, we originally set up a sprinkler in the garden and turn it on at regular intervals. This is easy and simple. There's no doubt that cool-season root crops take well to this method. But overhead watering like this can damage hot-weather crops like squash and tomatoes (tomatoes will crack). You can prevent tomato cracking and other problems by watering overhead until the plants start to produce fruit, and then use a ground hose after that.

As a rule, you should water in the morning during the spring and fall (that is, in cool weather) and in the evening during the summer heat. (If you live in an area where the humidity is high—like along the coast or in a region with lots of fog—overhead sprinkling can encourage mildew. Generally, you can overcome this by watering in the morning so that the plants are dry by evening). We currently use an automatic drip system in our beds.

If you find that the leaves of your vegetables wilt somewhat during the hot summer, don't panic. Actually, some plants deliberately let their leaves droop in order to prevent the hot sun from drawing moisture from their exposed flat surfaces. A squash vine, for instance, that looks quite wilted in the afternoon will snap back next morning crisp and fresh.

Besides watering the garden with a hose or a sprinkler, some gardeners really Rube Goldberg it and wind up with all sorts of innovations. For deep-rooted plants like tomatoes, for instance, you can push a piece of 2-inch hollow pipe 6 to 12 inches into the soil and then send water down the pipe to those deep roots. Or you can lay out two or three pieces of perforated plastic pipe or hose just under the vegetable leaves in your garden. When you're ready to water, just attach a hose and allow the water to trickle out.

Drip systems, however, currently provide the best way to water postage stamp gardens. A drip-watering system supplies water to plants at ground level through emitters. It uses a $\frac{1}{2}$-inch polyethylene hose that runs throughout the garden or an ooze hose and a $\frac{1}{2}$-inch perforated plastic line that delivers water along its length.

The controls consist of a shutoff valve (manual or electric), a filter to catch sand and foreign material, and a pressure regulator that keeps your drip system from getting too much pressure. We also use an automatic time clock that turns the system off and on at the same time each day. Our clock can be set to run several layouts at the same time.

This takes the guesswork out of when to water and allows us to leave for several days at a time, confident that the garden will be watered while we are gone.

For widely spaced plants like squash, eggplant, and tomatoes you will want at least one 1-gallon-per-minute emitter at each plant. For root and leaf crops that are close together, use an ooze hose or a perforated plastic hose that will run water across the entire space.

You can buy drip kits and all the necessary supplies, such as rolls of plastic tubing and automatic timers, at any garden supply store. Or purchase them through some of the seed catalogs listed in the Appendix.

Figure 10-1. A do-it-yourself drip watering system can serve most home landscape needs and will use 40 to 60 percent less water than conventional methods. A drip system can be connected to a faucet, as shown here, or to a valve on an automatic underground sprinkler system.

In sum, that's the watering system for our IPS beds. Water deeply, and then don't water again until the soil is almost dry. Do this and your garden will work its heart out growing big healthy, tender vegetables for your dinner table; it also could produce so much extra that you'll wind up having to beg the neighbors to take the surplus off your hands. If this happens, you can pat yourself on the back: It means you mastered the techniques of growing lots of vegetables in a very small space and are well on your way to becoming a wise and enlightened harvester of the fruits of nature.

Now Break Out the Seed Catalogs

Okay, so now you know how to grow intensive postage stamp gardens and produce all you can eat in a very small space. We do hope that as you garden from here on out, you'll try as many of the suggested garden combinations as possible.

Maybe, for instance, you might try one of the standard vegetable gardens the first year, all compact and by itself; then the next year you might grow corn in 4-by-4-foot boxes, root crops in a special garden, and other vegetables in other special gardens.

Or maybe you'd like to try several kinds of gardens all at once— flower bed gardens with vegetables, boxes, and ground gardens in various shapes, while at the same time trying to coax out more and more vegetables. That's really part of the fun and excitement of IPS gardening—the continual opportunities for experimentation.

The best thing about IPS gardening, of course, is that it's simple, easy, and in balance with nature, making the soil better and more productive each and every season. And if in the beginning you started out with a brown thumb, like we did, somewhere along the way you're bound to discover that it isn't brown at all any more but has turned to a very satisfying green.

Appendices
and
Glossary

Appendix A

How to Compost

For the amateur gardener, the word *composting* is often terrifying. It should not be. A compost pile is simply any collected mixture of vegetation, manure, or other organic materials that is allowed to decay and is then used for fertilizing and soil conditioning. It can be simply an unconfined heap, or it can be an enclosed bin or other container. It usually takes time to make one because it takes time to collect the material and also time for the material to "ripen," but anyone can compost successfully.

TABLE A-1. COMPOST TROUBLESHOOTING		
SYMPTOMS	PROBLEM	SOLUTION
The compost has a bad odor	Not enough air	Turn it
The center of the pile is dry	Not enough water	Moisten materials while turning the pile
The compost is damp and warm in the middle but nowhere else	Too small	Collect more material and mix the old ingredients into a new pile
The heap is damp and sweet-smelling but still will not heat up	Lack of nitrogen	Mix in a nitrogen source such as fresh grass clippings, fresh manure, blood meal, or ammonium sulfate

Before learning some specific methods of building compost, you should be aware of certain principles governing "traditional" composting. You should know that good old-fashioned composting depends primarily on particle size, on the amount of nitrogen available, on the heat produced, on the moisture of the pile, and on whether or not the pile is turned over periodically. Here are some guidelines:

1. The smaller the particle size, generally the faster the decomposition, because bacteria can then attack more surface area faster. Thus, if the leaves, stems, and other materials are shredded into small pieces before being added to the compost pile, they'll decay quicker and be ready sooner.

2. The bacteria in the pile need nitrogen. If there is too much organic material (carbon) in proportion to the available nitrogen, the bacteria will not work as fast, and the decomposition will go slowly. The evidence of this will be poor heat production in the compost pile. Generally, you can correct this deficiency by adding nitrogen in the form of fresh manure or blood meal here and there throughout the pile.

3. A compost pile must heat up for good bacterial action to occur. The degree of heat depends on the size of the pile. If the pile isn't high enough, it will lose heat and bacterial action will slow down. Too high a pile is also bad because it will then be compressed too much, shutting off the air supply to the bacteria.

4. Every pile also needs moisture for decomposition to take place. A moisture content of about 40 to 60 percent is about right; more than this can cut down on the oxygen available to the bacteria. You can keep your pile at about the right moisture content by making sure that it remains about as wet as a squeezed-out wet sponge. Just put your hand in the pile and feel. (Watch out, however, for it can be really hot—about 130° to 160°F.) If it doesn't seem moist enough, just add water with a hose until it has the right consistency.

5. A compost pile also needs turning. Using a manure fork or a shovel, turn it so that the top and side materials become the center. This allows air penetration and also brings raw matter to the center where more action is taking place.

When finished or "ripe," the materials placed in the compost pile will have been converted into a crumbly brown substance with the fragrance of good earth. It's then ready to use. (The volume of organic materials, by the way, will have decreased considerably. As decomposition proceeds, most piles shrink to about half their original size; a 5-foot pile, for instance, will end up hardly more than 2½ feet high. One

TURNED
PERIODICALLY
↓
MOISTURE
↓
HEAT
↓
PARTICLE
SIZE
↓
NITROGEN
↓

cubic foot of ripe compost is usually enough to make up 4 square feet of an IPS garden.)

We're now going to show you how to make compost piles with almost no effort. We'll also show you some more complicated ways to make compost. Remember, though, that we're dedicated to doing things easy. After all, mother nature doesn't care. Just provide her with the right conditions (no matter how quickly or easily you created them), and she'll work hard for you.

Using a Garbage Can

You can produce an entirely acceptable compost in a garbage can, placed either outdoors or in a corner of your garage. The method isn't governed by all the principles just outlined, and it doesn't have all the refinements of some of those bulky piles out in the garden, but it works, and that's what counts. Now here's how you do it:

1. Buy a galvanized garbage can (a 20- or 30-gallon size), and line it with a plastic bag.
2. Inside, on the bottom of the liner, put a 2-inch layer of soil or peat moss.
3. Add randomly almost any kind of waste kitchen materials—scraps from the table, vegetable and fruit leftovers, orange peels, coffee grounds, tea leaves, egg shells, and so on. Although you can also add garden wastes such as grass clippings and leaves, you should use mostly garbage, because you want a moist, gooey, rotting mixture for quick results.
4. Always keep the lid on the garbage can between additions of new material. You want to keep air out.
5. When the can is full, put it out in the hot sun and let it stand covered and untouched for about three weeks. The heat will cook it, and it will then be ready for use.

Some people object to this method, complaining that the compost smells excessively. It does. Unlike most other kinds of composting, this one uses anaerobic bacteria (the kind that don't need air). You don't have to expose the odor, however. Just close off the plastic liner with a wire twist, and keep the lid on the can.

Household Garbage

Soil

Using a Plastic Bag

This method is essentially identical to the one just given, except that no garbage can is used:

1. Buy a dark-colored plastic bag, the kind used to line 20- or 30-gallon garbage cans.
2. Inside, put a 2-inch layer of soil or peat moss.
3. Add randomly any kind of waste kitchen materials (as noted before) and maybe, occasionally, garden wastes.
4. When full, set the bag out in full sunlight for about three weeks. The compost will then be ready to use.

Using Another Garbage Can

Here is a longer but more customary method of composting (using a garbage can, though, makes it somewhat unusual):

1. Buy a galvanized garbage can (a 20- or 30-gallon size), and punch several small holes in the bottom. Put the can up on a few bricks, and place a pan underneath to catch any liquid that might drain out from the moisture contained in the decaying garbage that you will be adding.
2. Inside, on the bottom of the can, put a 3-inch layer of soil or peat moss.
3. If you like, buy some red worms—the fishing kind—and add them to the soil at the bottom.
4. Add 2 to 3 inches of kitchen garbage, then a 2-inch layer of grass clippings and leaves, another layer of kitchen garbage, a layer of grass clippings and leaves, and so on until the can is full.
5. Put the lid on the can. The compost will be ready in about three or four months. If you start the can in the fall, the compost will be ready to add to your garden by spring. (You don't need to worry about the moisture content of this kind of pile, nor does it need to be turned.)

Using a Barrel

If you have a space problem in your yard or if you simply want to confine your compost pile to a small space, here's a good method:

1. Buy or find a large barrel—the 50- to 55-gallon kind. It can be wooden, or it can be one of those big steel oil drums. Cut the bottom and the top out, and set the barrel anywhere you wish on exposed soil. Make sure that you fashion some kind of tight-fitting lid for the top.
2. Put in a 6-inch layer of kitchen wastes, then a 2-inch layer of garden soil, and then a 2-inch layer of leaves, grass clippings, and other garden wastes. Repeat the layering as materials become available. You might also want to add red fishing worms to speed up the process.
3. When the barrel is full, lift it off the pile, and start a new pile right next to it. The contents of the first pile will more or less stand alone without the support of the barrel.
4. Water and turn the compost as necessary. It will be ready for your garden in about four to six months.

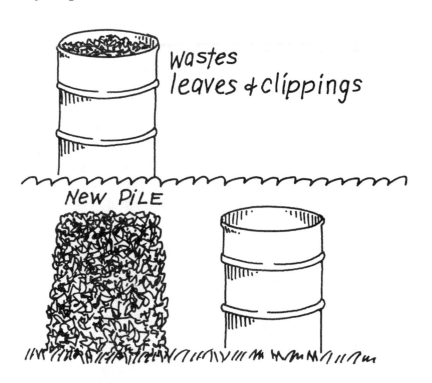

Big Conventional Pile

Some gardeners aren't happy unless they're building a big messy compost pile out in the backyard. For these types, here's a method that will keep them happy for almost a quarter of the year:

1. Clear off a 5- or 6-foot-square ground area.
2. On top of the cleared area, put down a 6-inch layer of fairly coarse material—twigs, brush, a few corn stalks, sunflower stalks, and so on. This provides ventilation underneath the pile.
3. Start building the main body of the heap in layers. Put down a 6-inch layer of vegetation materials—grass clippings, leaves, weeds, vegetable remains, organic garbage, and so on. On top of this greenery, add a 2-inch layer of fresh manure. (You can also add a thin layer of limestone to improve bacterial action and hasten the decomposition.)
4. For every two or three layers of vegetation (and manure), add a 1-inch layer of soil. This soil contains bacteria that will help break down the organic material. Now wet down the pile until it is just moist, not saturated.
5. Repeat this procedure until the pile reaches a height of about 5 feet.
6. When finished, add a thin covering of soil to the pile to help seal in the moisture. You must, however, also keep air flowing throughout the pile in order to keep the bacterial action high. Thus, take a stick or thin pole and punch vertical holes into the top of the pile, reaching all the way to the bottom. Make the holes about 2 or 3 feet apart.
7. Always keep the moisture content of the pile at 40 to 60 percent—about the consistency, as I've said, of a squeezed-out wet sponge. Check the moisture by feeling inside the pile with your hand, and then add water whenever necessary. Watering may be required every four or five days in hot weather.
8. Except for watering, let the pile sit undisturbed for two to three weeks. Then turn it, putting the material from the top and sides into the middle. Turn it again at three-week intervals. When the inside materials turn brownish and crumble on touch, you can

be sure that the compost is ready for your garden. This usually takes three-and-a-half to four months.

The University of California Quick Method

In 1954 the University of California's Organic Experimental Farm developed a composting method that's great for impatient types because the compost is ready in just fourteen days. The decomposition is speeded up by shredding the materials and mixing them all together so that the bacteria have many surfaces to work on at once. Here's how it works:

1. Mix together one part fresh manure and two parts other compost ingredients (leaves, grass clippings, cut-up corn stalks, table scraps, and so on). You can obtain fresh manure from a local riding stable or from a nursery. It must be fresh, not processed, manure, however.
2. Using a rotary lawnmower, shred everything completely. (You have to catch everything in a bag, naturally.) Simply put down a small pile of materials, and run the lawnmower over it. Then put down another pile, and repeat the process. Better yet, use a power shredder, but, in any case, the materials must be shredded into very small particles for this method to work well.
3. Mix everything together, and form the mixture into a 4-foot high, 4-by-6-foot heap.

Now, here's what to expect:

4. By the second or third day, the middle of the pile should have begun to heat up to about 130° to 160°F. If it hasn't, add more manure.
5. Turn the heap on the fourth day. Make sure that it's warm and moist. Simply put your hand inside, but be careful because it can be quite hot. If it doesn't feel moist to the touch, about like a squeezed-out wet sponge, add some water.
6. Turn the heap again on the seventh day.
7. Turn it once more on the tenth day. The heap should now have started to cool off, for it's almost ready.
8. It should be ready on the fourteenth day. It won't look like fine humus, but the materials will have broken down into a dark,

rich, fairly crumbly substance. You can let it rot further if you wish, or you can use it in your garden right away.

Composting in a Bin

Many gardeners like to put their compost in bins. There's no doubt that it's easier and neater to work with that way. After all, who likes a big, messy pile in the middle of the backyard—or even a little messy pile for that matter.

You can make a good compost bin with a few boards. Twelve pieces of board—each 12 inches wide, 1 inch thick, and 30 inches long—will work fine. Just take four of the boards and nail them together to make a frame or bottomless box. Using the remaining boards, make two more frames. You then set one frame on the ground and stack the other two on top of it to make a large bin. Now all you do is chop up your waste materials with a lawnmower and throw them in. You then proceed, using the composting method that suits you—either the Big, Conventional Pile or the University of California Quick Method.

You can steadily multiply these bins or piles easily by simply taking off the top frame after the compost has sunk below its level. Place the frame on the ground beside the other two, and start to fill it with new materials for compost. As the compost in the first bin subsides some more, you take the second frame off and put it on your new bin. When finished, your original bottom frame goes on top of your new bin, forming a three-frame compost bin again.

A compost bin actually can be made from almost anything. Just make it about 3 feet high and about $2\frac{1}{2}$ feet square. A neighbor or ours nailed four window screens together with a screen over the top to keep out flies. There are lots of other materials you can use: concrete blocks, stones, a simple picket fence with slats, chicken wire, and more. Let your imagination soar, and see what you can come up with.

Commercial Compost Bins

If you like, you can also buy a ready-made compost kit that includes a bin, instructions, and sometimes compost-maker tablets ("starters"). You can get one from many nurseries or by mail from many seed companies listed in Appendix B.

Commercial firms also manufacture a variety of compost bins that work well. Most are made from recycled plastic and range from 10 cubic feet to 27 cubic feet or so. If you are especially concerned about neatness, try one of these. They range in price from about $50 to $100. You will find them available in some of the seed catalogs.

Appendix B

Seed Catalog Sources

Code

ABU Abundant Life Seed Foundation
P.O. Box 722
Port Townsend, WA 98368
Order: 206/385-7192
Office: 206/385-7455

ALL Allen, Sterling & Lothrop
191 U.S. Route One
Falmouth, ME 04105
Order: 207/781-4142

BOU Bountiful Gardens
18001 Shafer Ranch Road
Willits, CA 95490
Order: 707/459-6410

BURG Burgess Seed and Plant Company
905 Four Seasons Road
Bloomington, IL 61701
Order: 309/663-9551

BURP W. Atlee Burpee & Company
300 Park Avenue
Warminster, PA 18974
Order: 800/888-1447

BURR D.V. Burrell Seed Growers Company
Rocky Ford, CO 81067
Order: 719/254-3318

Code

BUT Butterbrooke Farm
78 Barry Road
Oxford, CT 06478-1529
Order: 208/888-2000

COM Comstock, Ferre & Company
P.O. Box 125
Wethersfield, CT 06109
Order: 203/529-6255

COO The Cook's Garden
P.O. Box 535
Londonderry, VT 05148
Order: 802/824-3400

DEG DeGiorgi Seed Company
6011 N Street
Omaha, NE 68117-1634
Order: 800/858-2580

FAR Farmer Seed and Nursery
1706 Morrissey Drive
Bloomington, IL 61704
Order: 507/334-1623

FIS Fisher's Seeds
P.O. Box 236
Belgrade, MT 59714
Order: 406/388-6052

Code

GAR   Garden City Seeds
1324 Red Crow Road
Victor, MT 59875-9713
Order: 406/961-4837

GLE   Glecker's Seedmen
Metamora, OH 43540

GOU   The Gourmet Gardener
8650 College Boulevard
Overland Park, KS 66210
Order: 913/345-0490

GUR   Gurney's Seed & Nursery Company
110 Capital Street
Yankton, SD 57079
Order: 605/665-1930

HEN   Henry Field's Seed & Nursery
415 North Burnett
Shenandoah, IA 51602
Order: 605/665-9391

HIG   High Altitude Gardens
P.O. Box 1048
Hailey, ID 83333
Order: 208/788-4363

HOR   Horticultural Enterprises
P.O. Box 810082
Dallas, TX 75381-0082

JLH   J.L. Hudson, Seedman
P.O. Box 1058
Redwood City, CA 94064

Code

JOH   Johnny's Selected Seeds
Foss Hill Road
Albion, ME 04910-9731
Order: 207/437-4301

JUN   J.W. Jung Seed Company
Randolph, WI 53957
Order: 414/326-3123

LED   Oral Ledden & Sons
P.O. Box 7
Sewell, NJ 08080-0007
Order: 609/468-1000

LEJ   Le Jardin du Gourmet
P.O. Box 75
St. Johnsbury Center, VT 05863
Order: 800/659-1446

LIB   Liberty Seed Company
P.O. Box 806
New Philadelphia, OH 44663
Order: 216/364-1611

MEY   The Meyer Seed Company
600 S. Caroline Street
Baltimore, MD 21231
Order: 410/256-8128

NIC   Nichols Garden Nursery
1190 North Pacific Highway
Albany, OR 97321-4598
Order: 503/928-9280

Code

ORG Organic Seeds
1130 Tetherow Road
Williams, OR 97544
Order: 503/846-7173

ORN Ornamental Edibles
3622 Weedin Court
San Jose, CA 95132
Order: 408/946-SEED

PAR Park Seed
Cokesbury Road
Greenwood, SC 29648-0046

PIN Pinetree Garden Seeds
P.O. Box 300
New Gloucester, ME 04260
Order: 207/926-3400

PLA Plants of the Southwest
Route 6, P.O. Box 11A
Santa Fe, NM 87501
Order: 505/471-2212

PON Pony Creek Nursery
P.O. Box 16
Tilleda, WI 54978
Order: 715/787-3889

POR Porter & Son, Seedsmen
P.O. Box 104
Stephenville, TX 76401-0104

RED The Redwood City Seed Company
P.O. Box 361
Redwood City, CA 94064
Order: 415/325-SEED

Code

ROS Roswell Seed Company
P.O. Box 725
Roswell, NM 88202
Order: 505/662-7701

SEE Seeds Blum
Idaho City Stage
Boise, ID 83706

SEED Seeds of Change
P.O. Box 15700
Santa Fe, NM 87506-5700

SHE Shepherd's Garden Seeds
6116 Highway 9
Felton, CA 95018
Order: 408/335-6910

SOU Southern Exposure Seed Exchange
P.O. Box 170
Earlysville, VA 22936
Order: 804/973-4703

STO Stokes
P.O. Box 548
Buffalo, NY 14240-0548
Order: 716/695-6980

SUN Sunrise Enterprises
P.O. Box 330058
West Hartford, CT 06133-0058

TER Territorial Seed Company
20 Palmer Avenue
Cottage Grove, OR 97424
Order: 508/942-9547

Code

THE   The Good Earth Seed Company
P.O. Box 5644
Redwood City, CA 94063

THO   Thompson & Morgan Inc.
P.O. Box 1308
Jackson, NJ 08527-0308
Order: 800/274-7333

TIL   Tillinghast Seed Company
P.O. Box 738
La Conner, WA 98257
Order: 206/466-3329

TOM   The Tomato Seed Company Etc.
P.O. Box 1400
Tryon, NC 28782

TOMA   Tomato Growers Supply Company
P.O. Box 2237
Fort Myers, FL 33902
Order: 813/768-1119

TWI   Otis S. Twilley Seed Company, Inc.
P.O. Box 65
Trevose, PA 19053
Order: 800/622-7333

VER   Vermont Bean Seed Company
P.O. Box 250
Fair Haven, VT 05743
Order: 802/273-3400

Code

WIL   Willhite Seed Company
Poolville, TX 76487
Order: 800/828-1840

WILL   William Dam Seeds
P.O. Box 8400
Dundas, Ontario
Canada L9H 6M1

Herb Sources

DAB   Dabney Herbs
P.O. Box 22061
Louisville, KY 40252
Order: 502/893-5198

RIC   Richters
Goodwood, Ontario
Canada L0C 1A0
Order: 905/640-6677

TAY   Taylor's Herb Garden
1535 Lone Oak Road
Vista, CA 92084
Order: 619/727-3485

Glossary

acid soil. *See* **pH**.

alkaline soil. *See* **pH**.

annual. Plant that completes its life cycle in one growing season.

Bacillus thuringiensis. *See* **thuricide**.

blanch. (1) To immerse (a vegetable) briefly in boiling water to stop enzyme action and thereby retard further flavor loss and toughening. (2) To bleach (a growing vegetable) by excluding light, as by drawing leaves over a cauliflower head to keep the buds white.

blood meal. Dried animal blood used for fertilizer. Its nitrogen content ranges from 9 to 15 percent.

bolting. Going to seed, especially prematurely. Some cool weather plants, such as head lettuce, if exposed to high temperatures (70° to 80°F), will not form heads but will undergo premature seeding and be useless as vegetables. Young cabbage will bolt at low temperatures (50° 55°F).

bonemeal. Finely ground steamed animal bone used for fertilizer. It contains from 20 to 25 percent phosphoric acid and 1 to 2 percent nitrogen.

breathing, soil. *See* **soil aeration**.

catch cropping. Planting quick-maturing vegetables in a plot where slow-maturing main crops have just been harvested. It may

be done between plantings of main crops, or it may be done toward the end of a season, to utilize the last bit of frost-free time.

clay. Soil composed of fine particles that tend to compact; it is plastic when wet but hard when dry. It takes water slowly, holds it tightly, drains slowly, and generally restricts water and air circulation.

companion plants. Plants that influence each other, either beneficially or detrimentally. The influence may be chemical (odors or other exudates may have an effect), luminescent (a tall sun plant may protect a shade-loving low plant), and so forth.

compost. Mixture of loose vegetation, manure, or other once-living wastes that is left to decay through bacterial action and that is used for fertilizing and soil conditioning. Ripe compost is compost that has completed its decomposition and is ready for use.

cottonseed meal. Ground cottonseeds used for fertilizer. It contains from 6 to 9 percent nitrogen, 2 to 3 percent phosphorus, and 2 percent potassium.

crop rotation. Growing different crops in a plot or field in successive years, usually in a regular sequence. Its purpose is to balance the drain on soil nutrients and to inhibit the growth of certain plant diseases. For nutrient preservation, for instance, heavy-feeding plants may be succeeded one year by plants that restore fertility to the soil; the following year light feeders may be planted, and the next year heavy feeders may be planted again to begin the cycle anew.

crop stretching. Any mode of vegetable planting that efficiently extends the use of a plot of ground. It may involve intercropping, succession cropping, or catch cropping, or it may involve the use of trellises, poles, or other devices to train plants in the air to save ground space.

crown. Section of a plant at which stem and root merge.

cutting. Section of a stem or root that is cut off and planted in a rooting medium (such as vermiculite or soil) so that it will sprout roots and develop into a plant that is similar in every respect to the parent plant. Nurseries sell powdered "rooting hormone," which encourages root growth for this purpose (directions for use are given on the package).

dormant. Passing through a seasonal period of no active growth. Most perennials and other plants go dormant during the winter.

fish emulsion. Liquid mixture containing discarded soluble fish parts, used as fertilizer. It contains usually 5 to 10 percent nitrogen and lesser amounts of phosphorus and potassium.

flat. Shallow box in which seeds are planted to produce seedlings, generally indoors.

frass. Sawdustlike refuse left behind by boring worms or insects. The term less commonly denotes the excrement left by insects.

frond. Leaf of a fern or palm; also, any fern-like leaf.

germination. Sprouting of a new plant from seed.

granite dust. Finely ground granite, used as a fertilizer. It contains about 8 percent potassium and a number of trace elements.

greensand. Sea deposit containing silicates of iron, potassium, and other elements, usually mixed with clay or sand. It contains 6 to 8 percent potassium and is used for fertilizer.

gypsum. Mineral containing the soil nutrients calcium and sulfur and often used as a soil conditioner.

hardening off. Getting an indoor-grown seedling used to outdoor weather by exposing it gradually to the outdoors.

hardpan. Compacted clayey layer of soil that is impenetrable by roots and moisture. If near the surface, it can be spaded up and mixed with compost, manure, and other elements to make it more open, fertile, and hospitable to plants.

heavy feeder. Any vegetable that absorbs large amounts of soil nutrients in the process of growth. Heavy feeders include cabbage, cauliflower, corn, cucumbers, leafy vegetables, rhubarb, and tomatoes.

hot cap. Small waxed-paper cone that is set over an individual young plant to protect it from springtime cold. It is commercially made; one brand is called Hotkap.

humus. Black or brown decayed plant and animal matter that forms the organic part of soil.

intercropping. Also called interplanting. Planting quick-maturing and slow-maturing vegetables close together and then harvesting the quick-maturing ones before the slow-maturing ones have become big enough to overshadow or crowd them. Quick-maturing lettuce, for instance, can be seeded between beans.

leaching. Dissolving nutrients or salts out of soil or fertilizer by the action of water percolating downward.

legume. Plant or fruit of a plant that bears edible pods, such as beans and peas. Legumes restore fertility to a soil by taking nitrogen compounds from the air and making them available in the soil.

light feeder. Any vegetable that requires small or moderate amounts of nutrients in the process of growth. Root crops are light feeders.

loam. Soil containing a fertile and well-textured mixture of clay, sand, and humus.

manure. Livestock dung used as fertilizer. Fresh manure consists of recent excretions that have not decayed; it is generally unsuitable for direct application to soil in which plants are growing, but it is used in composting. Processed or rotted manure is decayed manure that is suitable for direct application as fertilizer.

microclimate. Sometimes called mini-climate. (1) Climate from the surface of the soil to the top foliage of a plant; plants set close together overarch their leaves, creating trapped air beneath with moderate temperatures and less air flow. (2) Uniform climate of a local site or geographical region.

mulch. Protective covering placed over the soil between plants. It may be peat moss, sawdust, compost, paper, opaque plastic sheeting, and so on. Its purpose is to reduce evaporation, maintain even soil temperature, reduce erosion, and inhibit the sprouting of weeds.

nematode. Microscopic parasitic worm that infects plants and animals (phylum *Nematoda*).

nitrogen. One of three most important plant nutrients, the others being phosphorus and potassium. It is particularly essential in the production of leaves and stems. An excess of nitrogen can produce abundant foliage and few flowers and fruit.

nutrient. Any of the sixteen elements that, in usable form, are absorbed by plants as nourishment. Plants obtain carbon, hydrogen, and oxygen from water and air, and the other elements from the soil. The main soil elements are nitrogen, phosphorus, and potassium; the trace elements are boron, calcium, chlorine, copper, iron, manganese, magnesium, molybdenum, sulfur, and zinc.

organic. Deriving from living organisms, either plants or animals. In gardening, it denotes fertilizers or sprays of plant or animal origin, as opposed to those employing synthetic chemicals.

peat. Prehistoric plant remains that have decayed under airless conditions beneath standing water, such as in a bog. Peat moss, the most common form, is the remains of sphagnum moss. Its nutrient content is low—less than 1 percent nitrogen and less than 0.1 percent phosphorus and potassium; it is also highly acid. Added to the soil, it makes soil finer and more water-absorbent but will also increase its acidity.

peat pellet. Small net-enclosed peat wafer that rises to six or seven times its original size with the addition of water. When expanded, it takes seeds, which develop into seedlings. Pellet and seedling together can be sown in the garden.

peat pot. Tiny molded container made of peat, usually containing its own soil or planting medium. Seeds are planted in the pot, and seedling and pot together are transplanted to the soil outdoors. Pot shapes vary from cubes to truncated cones or pyramids.

perennial. Plant that continues living over a number of years. It may die down to the roots at the end of each season but shoots up afresh every year. In areas of mild winters, the foliage may remain all year.

pH. Index of the acidity or alkalinity of a soil. Technically, it refers to the relative concentration of hydrogen ions in the soil. The index ranges from 0 for extreme acidity, to 7 for neutral, to 14 for extreme alkalinity. (The extremes, however, are rarely reached. A pH of 4.0 would be considered strongly acid; 9.0, strongly alkaline.) Soils in areas of heavy rainfall tend to be acid; those in areas of light rainfall tend to be alkaline. Adding peat moss, sawdust, or rotted bark to the soil increases acidity; adding lime increases alkalinity. Vegetables do best in a slightly acid soil, with a pH of 6.5 to 7.0; a safe range is 6.0 to 7.5.

phosphorus. One of the three most important plant nutrients, the others being nitrogen and potassium. It is especially associated with the production of seeds and fruits and with the development of good roots.

pinching. Snipping off or shortening (shoots or buds) in order to produce a certain plant shape or to increase or decrease blooms or fruits. The snipping is done with finger and thumb. Pinching the terminus of the main stem forces greater side branching. Pinching off the side shoots, conversely, stimulates more growth in the main stem, as well as in other remaining side stems.

pollination. Sexual reproduction in plants. Pollen, the fine dust produced by the male stamen of a flower, joins with the ovule of the female pistil of a flower, and the result is a seed to produce the next generation.

potash. Any potassium or potassium compound used for fertilizer. The potash in wood ash is potassium carbonate.

potassium. One of the three most important plant nutrients, the others being nitrogen and phosphorus. Its special value is to promote the general vigor of a plant and to increase its resistance to disease and cold. It also promotes sturdy roots.

pyrethrum. Insecticide made from the dried powdered flowers of certain plants of the Chrysanthemum genus. It is especially effective against aphids, leaf hoppers, caterpillars, thrips, and leafminers.

rock phosphate. Finely ground rock powder containing calcium phosphate. It contains up to 30 percent phosphoric acid. Superphosphate is rock phosphate that has been specially treated to yield phosphorus in various grades—16, 20, or 45 percent. It also contains the nutrients calcium and sulfur.

rotenone. Insecticide derived from the roots (and sometimes the stems) of certain New World tropical shrubs and vines of the genera *Derris* and *Lonchocarpus*. It is especially effective against beetles, caterpillars, leafminers, thrips, aphids, and leaf hoppers.

ryania. Insecticide made from the ground stems of a tropical South American shrub, *Patrisia pyrifera*. It is used especially against the corn borer.

sand. Tiny, water-worn particles of silicon and other rocks, each usually less than 2 millimeters in diameter. The granules allow free movement of air and water—so free, however, that water flows out readily and leaches out nutrients quickly.

seedling. Very young plant, especially one grown from seed.

set. (1) Small bulb, tuber, or root, or a section of a bulb, tuber, or root that is planted. (2) As a verb, often with *out*, to fix (a plant) in the soil, as in *to set out seedlings*.

sewerage sludge. Sediment produced by sewage treatment processes and used as fertilizer. It contains about 5 percent nitrogen and 3 to 6 percent phosphorus and is usually sold under the trade name Milorganite.

soil aeration. Flow of oxygen and carbon dioxide within the soil, between the ground surface and plant roots and soil microorganisms. Plant roots absorb oxygen and release carbon dioxide (as opposed to plant leaves, which absorb carbon dioxide and release oxygen). Oxygen is also necessary to soil bacteria and fungi to decompose organic matter and produce humus.

subsoil. Bed of earthy soil immediately beneath the topsoil. The size of the soil particles may be larger than that of topsoil, sometimes approaching gravel size.

succession planting. Planting a new crop as soon as the first one is harvested. This harvesting and replanting in the same spot may occur more than once in a season, and it may involve the planting of the same vegetable or of different vegetables.

superphosphate. *See* **rock phosphate**.

thinning. Pulling up young plants from a group so that the ones that are left in the soil have more room to develop properly.

thuricide. Insecticide containing bacteria (*Bacillus thuringiensis*) that infect and kill several kinds of worms and caterpillars, without being toxic to plants or other animals.

topsoil. Surface layer of soil, containing fine rock particles and decayed or decaying organic matter. Its thickness varies from 1 to 2 inches to several feet, depending on the geographic region and past treatment of the soil.

vegetable classification. Categorization of vegetables on the basis of the part of the plant that is used for food. Major root vegetables are beets, carrots, radishes, turnips, and rutabagas. A common stem vegetable is asparagus. Major tuber vegetables are potatoes and yams. Major leaf and leafstalk vegetables are Brussels sprouts, cabbage, celery, endive, kale, lettuce, mustard greens, rhubarb, spinach, and Swiss chard. Major bulb vegetables are onions and garlic. The chief immature flowering vegetables are broccoli and cauliflower. Major vegetables that come as fruits (the seed-bearing parts) are beans, corn, cucumbers, eggplant, melons, okra, peas, peppers, squash, and tomatoes.

vermiculite. Artificial planting medium consisting of inflated mica. It is highly water absorbent and lightweight and is used mainly for growing seeds or plant cuttings. It can also be used to increase the water absorbency of soils.

wood ash. Burnt residue of wood, used as fertilizer. Its nutrient content varies greatly. Hardwood ash can contain as much as 10 percent potassium; soft-wood, as little as 2 percent. Exposure to rain can also leach out the nutrients. Wood ash runs high in lime (alkaline) content—sometimes as much as 40 percent lime.

Index

A

Acid soil, 36
Alkaline soil, 36
Amaranth, 159
Animal manures, 37–38
Animal protection, 176
Anise, drying, 198
Arugula, 159
Asparagus, 72–74
    as companion vegetable, 144
    drying, 183
    pest and disease control for, 177
Autumn sage, 6

B

Barrel, composting in, 214
Basil, 136
    as companion herb, 149
    drying, 198–199
Beans, 74–78
    bush, 10, 75–76
    as companion vegetable, 145
    drying, 183
    lima, 77–78
    pest and disease control for, 177
    pole, 76–77
Bee balm, 5
    drying, 199
Bees, Orchard Mason, 6
Beets, 71, 78–80
    baby gourmet, 29
    as companion vegetable, 145
    drying, 183–184
    pest and disease control for, 177
Bergamot, drying, 199
Bins, commercial compost, 217–218
Biological sprays, 174
Birds, repelling, 176
Blanching, 72
Blight, 175
Blood meal, 37, 39
Blue boy, 5
Blue daze, 6
Bok Choi, 165

Bonemeal, 37, 39
Borage, 10
    as companion herb, 149
    drying, 199
Botanical sprays, 174–175
Boxed gardens, 23–24
Broccoli, 80–82
    as companion vegetable, 145
    drying, 184
    pest and disease control for, 177
Brussels sprouts, 82–84
    as companion vegetable, 145
    drying, 184
    pest and disease control for, 177
Burnet salad, drying, 199
Bush beans, 10, 75–76
Butter beans, 74
Butterflies, plants that attract, 5
Butterfly bush, 5–6

C

Cabbage, 23, 71, 84–86
    baby, 29–30
    as companion vegetable, 145–146
    drying, 184
    pest and disease control for,
        177–178
Calcium, 37
    deficiency of, 51
Calendula, 5
California, University of, quick
    composting method, 216–217
Cantaloupes, 106–108
Caraway theme, 141
Carrots, 71, 86–89
    baby, 30
    as companion vegetable, 146
    drying, 185
Casabamelons, 109
Catalogs, seed, 6–7, 208, 219–222
Catch cropping, 67
Catmint, 6
Cauliflower, 89–91
    baby, 30

    as companion vegetable, 146
    drying, 185
    pest and disease control for, 178
Celeriac, 168
    drying, 185
Celery, 10, 168
    as companion vegetable, 146
    drying, 185
Chemical fertilizers, 41
Chervil
    as companion herb, 149
    drying, 199
Chinese tsi shim, 164
Chives, 10, 136
    as companion herb, 149
    drying, 199
Cilantro, drying, 200
Clay, 35
Collards, drying, 186
Columbine, 6
Companion herbs, 148–151
Companion plants, 173
Companion vegetables, 144–152
Composting, 37, 210–218
Compost pile, 215–216
Containers
    gardening in, 24–32
    soil mixes for, 27
    starting seeds indoors in, 63–65
Cool season plants, 54–55
Copper deficiency, 51
Coral bells, 6
Coreopsis, 5
Coriander
    as companion herb, 149
    drying, 200
Corn, 23, 91–96
    baby, 30
    as companion vegetable, 146
    drying, 186
    pest and disease control for, 178
Cornflower, 5
Cosmos, 5–6
Cottonseed meal, 39

Cress, 160
Crops
   catch cropping, 67
   intercropping, 66
   rotation of, 50
   succession planting, 66–67
Cucumbers, 10, 23, 96–99
   baby, 30–31
   as companion vegetable, 146
   drying, 187
   pest and disease control for, 178

D
Dandelion, 161
Dill, 137
   as companion herb, 149
   drying, 200
Disease control, 170–180
Drip systems, 206

E
Earthworms, 40–41
Edible flowers, 4–5
Eggplant, 10, 99–101
   baby, 31
   drying, 187–188
   pest and disease control for, 178
Endive, 106, 161–162
Expert method of preparing soil, 47–49

F
Fennel, drying, 200
Fertilizers, chemical, 41
Fish emulsion, 37, 40
Fishworms, 41
Flats, 65
Flowers, 10, 23
   companion, 151–152
   edible, 4–5
Freezing vegetables, 72
French thyme, 141
Frost map, planting with, 57
Fruits, midget, 29–32
Fuchsia, 6

G
Garbage can, composting in, 212–213

Garden fork, 44
Gardens
   air space above, 9
   attracting bugs to your, 6
   cost of, 7–8
   deciding on plants for, 3–6
   designing, 8–9
   flower, 23
   plans for, 10–22
   putting, on paper, 9–10
   rules for locating, 2
   salad, 153–168
   time needed for, 7
   watering, 203–208
Garden trowel, 44
Garlic, 10, 137
   as companion herb, 149
   drying, 188
General hand method of preparing soil, 46–47
Geraniums, 151
Gilia, 6
Golden thyme, 141
Gophers, repelling, 176
Granite dust, 40
Green beans, 74
Green peppers, 118
Greens, 159–167
   for hot weather, 159–167
   mustard, 110–111, 164–165, 179, 191
Greensand, 40

H
Herbs, 9–10, 26, 136–141
   companion, 148–151
   drying, 197–202
Hoe, 44
Honeydew, 108–109
Honeysuckle, 6
Horseradish, drying, 188–189
Hot peppers, 119
Hot weather, greens that thrive in, 159–167
Hummingbirds, plants that attract, 5–6
Humus, 35–36
Hyssop, drying, 200

I
Insects
   attracting, to your garden, 6
   repellents for, 171–175
Intercropping, 66
Iron, 37
   deficiency of, 51

K
Kale, 101–102, 162
   as companion vegetable, 146
   drying, 189
   pest and disease control for, 178
Kohlrabi, drying, 189

L
Lady in red, 5
Lavender, 6
Leeks, drying, 189
Lemon balm
   as companion herb, 149
   drying, 198
Lemon queen, 6
Lemon thyme, 141
Lettuce, 103–106, 162–164
   baby, 31
   bibb, 104
   as companion vegetable, 147
   drying, 189–190
   head, 23, 104, 163
   leaf, 23
   loose-leaf, 104–105, 163–164
   pest and disease control for, 178
   romaine, 105, 163
Lima beans, 74, 77–78
Liquid seaweed, 40
Loam, 35–36
Lovage, drying, 200–201
Lupine, 151

M
Magnesium, 37
   deficiency of, 51
Malabar spinach, 159
Manganese, 37
   deficiency of, 51
Manure, 37
Manure fork, 44

Manures, animal, 37–38
Marigolds, 5, 9–10, 151
Marjoram, 137
    as companion herb, 149–150
    sweet, drying, 201
Mei quing choi, 164
Melons, 10, 23, 106–110
    baby, 31
    as companion vegetable, 147
    drying, 190–191
    pest and disease control for, 178
Mesclun, 166
Metal foil pans, 63–64
Miksuba, 165
Mildew, 175
Milorganite, 39
Mint, 137–138
    as companion herb, 150
    drying, 201
Mock orange, 5
Modified French Intensive method
    of preparing soil, 44–46
Moisture, putting, into soil, 49
Molybdenum deficiency, 51
Monkey flower, 6
Moon cycles, planting by, 58–59
Morning glory, 5
Mountain spinach, 159
Muskmelons, 106
Mustard greens, 110–111, 164–165
    drying, 191
    pest and disease control for, 179

N
Nasturtiums, 4–6, 151
New Zealand spinach, 124–125, 166
Nicotonia, 6
Nitrogen, 36, 39–40
    deficiency of, 51

O
Oil products, 171–172
Okra, 111–112
    drying, 191
    pest and disease control for, 179
Onions, 112–115
    Bermuda, 114
    bulb, 114

as companion vegetable, 147
    drying, 192
    green, 10, 114
    pest and disease control for, 179
Orach, 159
Orchard Mason bees, 6
Oregano, 138
    as companion herb, 150
    drying, 201
Oriental mustard, 164–165

P
Paper pulp pots, 27
Parsley, 138
    as companion herb, 150
    drying, 201
Parsnips, drying, 193
Patio, planting on, 26–27
Peas, 10, 115–117
    as companion vegetable, 147
    drying, 193
    pest and disease control for, 179
Peat pots, 64
Peppers, 10, 23, 117–120
    as companion vegetable, 147
    hot, 119
        drying, 194
    pest and disease control for, 179
    sweet, 118–119
        drying, 193
Perilla (Shiso), drying, 201
Persian melons, 109
Pest control, 170–180
Petunias, 151
pH of soil, 36
Phosphorus, 37, 39–40
    deficiency of, 51
Plants
    attracting butterflies with, 5
    attracting hummingbirds with,
        5–6
    deciding on, 3–6
    diseases of, 175–176
    spacing of, 10, 60
    sprays for, 173–174
    time table for planting, 54–67
Plastic bag, composting in, 213
Pole beans, 76–77

Popcorn, drying, 186–187
Potash deficiency, 51
Potassium, 37, 39–40
    deficiency of, 51
Potatoes
    as companion vegetable, 147
    drying, 194
Predatory nematodes, 172
Pumpkins
    baby, 31
    as companion vegetable, 148
    drying, 194–195

R
Rabbits, repelling, 176
Radicchio, 161–162
Radishes, 10, 120–122
    as companion vegetable, 148
    drying, 195
    pest and disease control for, 179
Red peppers, 118–119
Red rocket, 5
Refeeding, 49–50
Rhubarb, 122–123
    drying, 195
Rocket, 159
Rock phosphate, 39
Root diffusates, 144
Root rot, 175
Root vegetables, 8, 26
Rosemary, 138–139
    as companion herb, 150
    drying, 202
Rototillers, 44
Rust, 175
Rutabagas, 71, 134–136
    as companion vegetable, 148
    drying, 195

S
Sage, 6, 139
    as companion herb, 150
    drying, 202
Salad garden, 153–168
Salsify, drying, 195
Sand, 35
Savannah mustard, 164
Savory, 140

as companion herb, 150
drying, 202
Scab, 175
Seed catalogs, 6–7, 208
   sources of, 219–222
Seedlings
   buying, and transplanting, 62–63,
      65–66
   planting, in containers, 28
Seeds
   planting, in containers, 28
   shopping by catalog, 6–7, 208,
      219–222
   sowing directly, 61–62
   starting indoors in containers,
      63–65
Self-watering pots, 29
Sensation white, 5
Shallots, drying, 195
Silver thyme, 6
Silvia coccinea, 5
Snap beans, 74
Snapdragon, 5
Soap and water treatment, 171
Soil, 34–41, 204
   acid, 36
   alkaline, 36
   condition of, 34
   container, 27
   and crop rotation, 50
   nutrient deficiencies in, 51
   nutrients in, 36–37
   pH of, 36
   preparing, 44–51
      expert method of, 47–49
      general hand method of,
         46–47
      modified French Intensive
         method of, 44–46
   putting moisture into, 49
   refeeding, 49–50
   structure of, 35–36
Sorrel, 165
Spinach, 123–125
   as companion vegetable, 148
   drying, 196
   pest and disease control for, 179
   as salad ingredient, 165–166

Spirea, 5
Sprouts, 26
Squash, 10, 71, 125–127
   as companion vegetable, 148
   drying, 196
   pest and disease control for, 179
   summer, 125–126
   winter, 10, 125–127
Starter kits, 65
Storage of vegetables, 71
String beans, 74
Succession plantings, 10, 66–67
Sulfur, 37
   deficiency of, 51
Summer savory, 140
   drying, 202
Summer squash, 125–127
Sunflowers, 151–152
Superphosphate, 39
Sweet basil, 149
Sweet potatoes, drying, 196
Swiss chard, 23, 128–129, 160
   drying, 196
   pest and disease control for, 180

T
Tarragon, 140
   as companion herb, 150
   drying, 202
Thyme, 141
   as companion herb, 151
   drying, 202
Tomatoes, 10, 26, 32, 129–134
   as companion vegetable, 148
   drying, 197
   pest and disease control for, 180
   for salads, 166–167
Trailing rosemary, 6
Transplants, 62–63
   hardening, 65
Turnips, 71, 134–136
   as companion vegetable, 148
   drying, 197

V
Vegetables, 10, 70
   companion, 144–152
   drying, 182–197

freezing, 72
harvesting, 70–71
home storage, 71
midget, 29–32
root, 8, 26
starting, 61–66
Verbena, 5–6
Vines, 10, 23

W
Warm season plants, 54–55
Watering techniques, 28–29, 203–208
Watermelons, 106, 109
   drying, 197
Wax beans, 74
Whiskey barrel halves, 26
Wilt, 175
Windowsill and window box
   gardens, 25–26
Winter savory, 140
Winter squash, 10, 125–127
Wood ash, 37, 39–40
Wooden boxes, 26–27

Z
Zinc, 37
   deficiency of, 51
Zinnia, 5
Zucchini, 126–127
   baby, 32